The European Union and the Return of the Nation State

Antonina Bakardjieva Engelbrekt
Karin Leijon • Anna Michalski
Lars Oxelheim
Editors

The European Union and the Return of the Nation State

Interdisciplinary European Studies

palgrave
macmillan

Editors
Antonina Bakardjieva Engelbrekt
Faculty of Law
Stockholm University
Stockholm, Sweden

Karin Leijon
Department of Government
Uppsala University
Uppsala, Sweden

Anna Michalski
Department of Government
Uppsala University
Uppsala, Sweden

Lars Oxelheim
University of Agder
Kristiansand, Norway

Research Institute of Industrial Economics (IFN)
Stockholm, Sweden

ISBN 978-3-030-35004-8 ISBN 978-3-030-35005-5 (eBook)
https://doi.org/10.1007/978-3-030-35005-5

Cover illustration: Borislav Bajkic/Shutterstock.com

This Palgrave Macmillan imprint is published by the registered company Springer Nature Switzerland AG.
The registered company address is: Gewerbestrasse 11, 6330 Cham, Switzerland

Contents

Notes on Contributors

Fredrik N. G. Andersson is Associate Professor at the Department of Economics at Lund School of Economics and Management. His research interests include economic policy and long-term economic change.

Antonina Bakardjieva Engelbrekt is Professor of European Law at the Faculty of Law of Stockholm University. She is the chair of the Swedish Network for European Legal Studies (SNELS) and she has been Torsten och Ragnar Söderberg Professor of Legal Science (2015–2018). Her research interests include processes of Europeanisation and globalisation and their influence on national law and institutions.

Torbjörn Bergman is Professor of Political Science at the Department of Political Science, Umeå University. His research interests include coalition politics and issues of delegation and accountability in parliamentary democracy and the European Union.

Magnus Blomgren is Associate Professor of Political Science at the Department of Political Science, Umeå University. His main research interest is political parties, especially within multi-level systems such as the European Union.

Niklas Bremberg is Associate Professor at the Department of Political Science, Stockholm University, and a senior research fellow at the Swedish Institute of International Affairs. His research interests include EU foreign and security policy, European diplomatic practices, regional secession and European integration, and international cooperation on climate-related security risks.

Cécile Brokelind is Professor of Business Law at the Department of Business Law at Lund University and programme director of the Master of European and International Tax Law (MEIT). Her research interests include EU tax law, international tax law and taxation.

Rikard Forslid is Professor of Economics at the Department of Economics, Stockholm University. His research interests include the effects of economic integration on firm location and on environmental emissions.

Magnus Henrekson is Professor of Economics and CEO of the Research Institute of Industrial Economics (IFN) in Stockholm, Sweden. His main research interest is entrepreneurship economics.

Karin Leijon holds a PhD in Political Science and is a researcher at the Department of Government, Uppsala University. She is a coordinator for the Swedish Network for European Studies in Political Science (SNES). Her research interests include judicial politics, European legal integration, and public administration.

Anna Michalski is Associate Professor of Political Science at the Department of Government, Uppsala University, and Associate Research Fellow at the Swedish Institute of International Affairs. She is Chair for the Swedish Network for European Studies in Political Science (SNES). Her research interests include European foreign policy, EU-China relations, strategic partnerships, and socialisation in international organisations.

Andreas Moberg is Associate Professor of International Law at the Department of Law, School of Business Economics and Law at the University of Gothenburg. His research interests include matters of constitutional EU law, with a particular focus on the Court of Justice of the EU.

Sten Nyberg is Professor of Economics at the Department of Economics at Stockholm University. His research interests include industrial organisation, political economy, and social norms.

Özge Öner holds a PhD in Economics and is Lecturer in Spatial Economics at the Department of Land Economy and Fellow in Economics and Land Economy at the Sidney Sussex College at Cambridge University. She is also a research fellow at the Research Institute of Industrial

Economics (IFN) in Stockholm. Her research interests include migration, labour mobility, micro-geography of segregation, and the geography of entrepreneurship.

Lars Oxelheim is Professor of International Business and Finance at the University of Agder and affiliated with the Research Institute of Industrial Economics (IFN). He is the founder of the Swedish Network for European Studies in Economics and Business (SNEE). His research interests include economic and financial integration, corporate governance, and risk management.

Jane Reichel is Professor in Administrative Law at the Faculty of Law, Stockholm University. Her research interests include global and European administrative law and its implication on Swedish law.

Tino Sanandaji holds a PhD in Public Policy from the University of Chicago and is a researcher at the Institute for Economic and Business History Research. His research interests include public economics, entrepreneurship, and historical economics.

Malin Stegmann McCallion is Reader in Political Science at Karlstad University, Sweden. Her research interests include Europeanisation, multi-level governance, paradiplomacy, regionalisation processes, and awkwardness in the European integration process.

List of Figures

List of Tables

CHAPTER 1

The EU, the Nation-State, and the Perennial Challenge to European Integration

Antonina Bakardjieva Engelbrekt, Karin Leijon, Anna Michalski, and Lars Oxelheim

Introduction

Ever since the first steps towards European integration were taken in the early 1950s, the relationship between the nation-state and the European Union (EU) has been a crucial issue. Throughout the years and in various ways, this relationship has defined the form and scope of European integration. In particular, the movement towards deeper integration has followed two distinct and partly contrary lines of development: increased supranationalism, in the form of greater powers for the Union; and

A. Bakardjieva Engelbrekt
Faculty of Law, Stockholm University, Stockholm, Sweden
e-mail: antonina.bakardjieva@juridicum.su.se

K. Leijon • A. Michalski (✉)
Department of Government, Uppsala University, Uppsala, Sweden
e-mail: karin.leijon@statsvet.uu.se; anna.michalski@statsvet.uu.se

L. Oxelheim
University of Agder, Kristiansand, Norway

Research Institute of Industrial Economics (IFN), Stockholm, Sweden
e-mail: lars.oxelheim@ifn.se

A. Bakardjieva Engelbrekt et al. (eds.), *The European Union and the Return of the Nation State*,
https://doi.org/10.1007/978-3-030-35005-5_1

intensified intergovernmentalism, in the form of greater reliance on common decisions by member states governments. In fact, the EU has embraced both types of integration since its inception. This can be seen in its treaties, in its common institutions, and in the formulation of its actual policies. However, this essentially natural and balancing relationship has recently been challenged by individual member states acting in their self-interest; and the foundations of European cooperation have been called more loudly into question. This raises two issues: First, if indeed we are witnessing the return of the nation-state, in what form is this occurring? Second, is the come-back of the nation-state a lasting phenomenon with which the EU must deal for a long time to come, or is it rather a transitory trend?

In this book, we reflect on the relationship between the Union and its member states. Our main reason for asking whether the nation-state is returning lies in the increasingly egoistic behaviour of the member states in several policy areas, which can be best understood in light of the recent crises that have struck the EU. Tendencies towards economic nationalism, whereby countries seek to protect jobs within their own borders, are growing stronger in the wake of the economic crisis. Moreover, countries such as Hungary and Poland are refusing to implement commonly agreed decisions in the area of migration policy, on the grounds that they violate their sovereignty. Britain's decision to leave the Union (Brexit) was preceded by a long debate about whether the Union undermines the autonomy of its member states in crucial policy areas.

Across Europe, the view of the nation-state as a safeguard against external threats and a guarantor of national economic interests seems to be resurfacing, despite its close historical association with war and suffering on the European continent. New divisions have clearly arisen between the EU's institutions and the member states, and between different groups amongst the latter. These divisions reflect the sovereign-debt crisis, the refugee and migration crises, the growth of populist currents around Europe, and the challenge raised by the Hungarian and Polish governments to the fundamental values of the Union. Populist parties have come to power in Hungary, Italy, and Poland, and they now form a prominent feature of the political landscape in virtually every member state. Victor Orbán and Matteo Salvini, Hungarian prime minister and the former Italian deputy prime minister and interior minister, respectively, have expressed an interest in forming a political alliance at the European level to protect the borders of the member states and to act as a counterweight to the liberal EU establishment. Both leaders and their parties did exceptionally well in the European parliament election in May 2019. Furthermore, traditional political parties—in the UK, for instance—contain highly Eurosceptic factions which have influenced the policies of incumbent governments while new Eurosceptic parties have surfaced in several member states (Blombäck 2019).

New populist winds have clearly filled the sails of existing Eurosceptic groupings, and the policies and powers of the Union are being called into question. However, there is also an opposite trend. Internal and external challenges—amongst them Brexit, aggressive Russian policies, and the assault by US President Donald Trump on international organizations and the liberal world order—have helped bring the member states of the Union closer together. Despite everything, the member states have been able to agree on political solutions and initiatives that were previously thought impossible. During the Brexit negotiations thus far, for example, cohesion amongst the 27 governments represented in the European Council has been exemplary. We are thus faced with a paradox: on the one hand, the EU's fundamental values and objectives are being called into question by prominent political currents and a group of member states; on the other, integration is being deepened in a number of policy areas. Now is a good time, then, to re-examine the complex relationship between the Union and the nation-state—here in its capacity as EU member state—with an eye to discerning the contours of the next step of European integration.

Origins and Significance of the Nation-State

Viewed historically, the nation-state is a relatively modern state form. Its origins are usually thought to lie in the treaties which established the Peace of Westphalia in 1648. These gave legitimacy to smaller political units and reduced the power of multinational empires and the Catholic Church. There is a tight link between the nation-state and the principle of state sovereignty, which has both an external and an internal dimension. The external dimension relates to the state's territorial inviolability, its independence, and its capacity to conclude international agreements; while the internal dimension involves mandatory powers in connection with the administration of justice, the enactment of laws, and the possession of a legitimate monopoly on force (Tilly 1990; Weber 1978). There is also the view of the state as inseparable from the nation (the latter being understood here as a majority population with a common national identity). Nation-states base their legitimacy, then, on their control over a defined territory, their autonomy from outside powers, their recognition by the same, and their support from a (relatively) homogeneous population (Giddens 1985; Greenfeld 1992). They thus differ from vassal states that lack sovereignty, as well as from empires that contain numerous nations and ethnicities (Eisenstadt 1965; Held 1992).

The legitimacy of the nation-state in Europe was in the first half of the twentieth century undermined by the appeal of authoritarian regimes to nationalism, and by territorial claims made in the name of an area's 'rightful' people. Nationalist and chauvinist movements in Germany and Italy contributed to the outbreak of the Second World War. Elite and popular support for such ideas lay behind the First World War too, when most of the warring parties were lingering empires. We must understand the roots of European integration in this light. The original movement for integration was animated by a strong desire to circumscribe nationalism, which had been the driving force in the ruinous and self-destructive struggle between the countries of Europe, and which had made lasting forms of cooperation impossible. This was the motivation behind early efforts to create a political union in Europe—a union which, some of its advocates maintained, ought even to take the form of a European federation (Burgess 2002; Delzell 1960).

The Nation-State and European Integration

The relationship between the nation-state and European integration has always been ambiguous. Early efforts at integration were inspired by the sense that selfish states had to be checked, in order to prevent them from pursuing their national interests at the expense of others. The basic idea behind the European Coal and Steel Community was to prevent further wars in Europe (Dinan 2010, 2014). Yet it is the member states, as sovereign states, which have concluded the Union's treaties: thus they are 'masters of the treaties'. This is revealed with particular clarity when fundamental power relations within the Union are undergoing change, as in the case of negotiations over treaties or over enlargement. The member states act then as sovereign states, whether they appoint a special negotiator to represent them or not. In other areas, by contrast, the Union has exclusive powers. The member states have relinquished their national sovereignty in respect to monetary policy, fisheries, competition rules, trade policy, and the customs union. In these areas, they have authorized the Union to act independently in their stead.

There are several other aspects as well to consider in connection with the double-edged nature of the EU's institutions in regard to supranationalism and intergovernmentalism. The European Commission, the European Parliament, the European Central Bank, and the Court of Justice of the European Union are all supranational in character. They have their own autonomous existence, with powers and prerogatives endowed by the treaties. Then we have the European Council and the Council of the European Union (or Council of Ministers). These represent the member states, which negotiate amongst themselves until a decision is taken. Yet the latter two bodies are also Union institutions in their own right, in which capacity they represent the member states as a collectivity. They also often act together in relation to the other institutions in the decision-making process. Finally, the double-edged quality of EU institutions in connection with supranationalism and intergovernmentalism is most clearly seen in the roles which the Parliament and the Council of Ministers play in the Union's legislative process—wherein the Council pursues a ***unified*** line vis-à-vis the Parliament.

We mentioned the Union's five exclusive powers above. In the vast majority of the EU's policy areas, however, decision-making competence is shared between the Union and the member states. There are also a number of areas where the Union has only a supporting function, and common binding rules cannot be established. Another interesting aspect of the double-edged nature of the Union is that both intergovernmental and supranational decision-making can be found within one and the same policy area. This is evident in the case of the Economic and Monetary Union (EMU), where fiscal policy is conducted on an intergovernmental basis and monetary policy on a supranational one—something that has caused major problems in the eurozone and which is regarded as a real system failure. In addition, the states in the eurozone have resorted to intergovernmental solutions outside the framework of the treaties in order to meet the major challenges entailed by the sovereign-debt crisis. An example hereof was the creation of the European Stability Mechanism (ESM) in 2012 (Joerges and Glinski 2017). When it comes to asylum and migration policy, moreover, a mixture of intergovernmentalism and supranationalism prevails—which can reduce the Union's capacity for effective action and make its policy in the area less transparent. Finally, it is important to pay due attention to EU law, which constitutes an independent legal order located somewhere between national law and international law. The importance of the autonomous standing of EU law for the Union's consolidation as a political system marked by the rule of law cannot be overstated (Cappelletti et al. 1986).

What does this brief review of the Union's intergovernmental and supranational features tell us about the EU? One thing is plain: European integration has not developed in a straightforward way. In certain periods it has proceeded rapidly; at other times it has stalled. The integration process is furthermore incremental, and it differs between policy areas. It has gone furthest in regard to the single market. Progress has been much slower, on the other hand, in respect of migration policy and foreign and security policy, even though the Union faces major problems in these areas for which citizens expect a common solution. Clearly, the development of the EU has not followed the template of a classic state, with clearly delineated powers in a constitutional order. This can be seen as a sign that the Union is evolving towards a confederation rather than a federation.

According to the conventional view, the nation-state—in the form of the EU member state—has succeeded in keeping the core of its sovereignty against any excessive intrusion on the part of the Union. The rejection of the Constitutional Treaty in the Dutch and French referenda of 2005 would seem to indicate as much. According to some scholars, however, the relationship of the member states to European integration is much more complex. In *The European Rescue of the Nation-State* (1992), for example, the political scientist Andrew Milward depicts the relationship between the nation-state and European integration as less conflictual than previously supposed. Instead, he avers, it should be seen as a fruitful and mutually supportive one. In particular, the single market has enabled member states to get around domestic stumbling blocks which had previously prevented them from carrying out necessary economic reforms. Another interesting perspective is offered by Christopher Bickerton in *European integration: From nation-states to member states* (2012). In this book, Bickerton claims that the governments of the member states—in particular the heads of state or government in the European Council—exercise a form of collective leadership within the Union. This is particularly evident in areas where the intergovernmental logic prevails, such as foreign and security policy, and in the handling of the many crises the Union has undergone during the 2010s. Particularly relevant to the theme of this book is Bickerton's contention that we must dispense with the simple notion of a conflict between the nation-state and supranationalism if we are to understand what is going on in the EU. In the distinctive system that now prevails, Bickerton claims, the member states frame and implement policy in a fundamentally different way than they did earlier. We must continue, accordingly, to explore the relationship between supranationalism and intergovernmentalism from a variety of perspectives.

Alternative Perspectives on Power and Sovereignty Within the EU

As European integration has deepened, it has taken a variety of forms. In order to better understand its shifting dimensions, we can employ the various perspectives of earlier researchers to advantage. We shall briefly discuss some of the most influential ones here. An early but still relevant perspective, functionalism, was presented in the 1950s and 1960s by the political scientist Ernst Haas (1958, 1964). It is often referred to as neofunctionalism. In this view, the development of the Union can be explained in terms of 'spillover' effects, whereby integration spreads from one policy area to another. An example of such spillover can be seen in how, due to the establishment of a customs union and the introduction of common rules on exports and imports, trade across borders increased—whereupon transnational actors, such as corporations, began to demand common rules in adjoining policy areas as well. The result was a common trade policy and broader and deeper supranational cooperation thereby. In the same way, according to neofunctionalism, national officials who take part in the Union's policy processes change their behaviour and help to deepen integration. Due to their repeated interactions with each other and with EU representatives in Brussels, such officials adopt a new outlook—with a shift in loyalty from the nation to a new political centre at the level of Europe.

The logic behind neofunctionalism seems perfectly reasonable when we consider the deepening of the single market, where common rules within a given sector made cooperation possible and desirable in other policy areas too. However, the functionalist approach runs up against difficulties in explaining why integration in areas such as migration, internal security, and foreign and security policy has been slow and beset with sharp contradictions. As for national officials, they have not permanently shifted their loyalties to the European plane (Beyers 2005). They have rather developed an embedded dual loyalty: they retain their national identity and are prepared to defend national interests in the EU's institutions, while at the same time embracing common European standards and interests to a degree. Nor have developments since the turn of the millennium pointed to any diminution in the importance of the member states. On the contrary, the standing of the European Council within the EU—and its role in finding solutions to the crises which the Union has experienced—has been and remains absolutely central (Puetter 2012). Instead we see the emergence of a collective executive, with the governments of the member states at the helm—an executive in relation to which the Union's institutions sometimes act independently, sometimes as a support.

Another approach to understanding the Union, which has become prominent in the last twenty years, is that put forward by empirically oriented scholars like Helen Wallace (2014), Giandomenico Majone (1996), Claudio Radaelli (2003), and Jonathan Zeitlin (2005). This approach focuses on governance within the Union's policy processes. These take different forms depending on the degree of integration which has taken place in a given policy area. Thus, the formal powers of the Union within different policy areas give rise to a variety of forms for cooperation and decision-making. The instruments used to implement policy decisions, and the actual outcomes as well, can also be explained in terms of the forms of governance characteristic of a given policy area.

To help make this reasoning more concrete, we can take the EMU as an example. Monetary policy lies within the exclusive authority of the Union for the countries that use the euro. These countries have relinquished the power to regulate the price of their currency. Responsibility lies instead with the European Central Bank, which follows the guidelines set out in the treaties. Power over other aspects of economic policy, on the other hand, remains in all essentials with the member states, although they have undertaken to comply with the rules for sound state finances set out in the Stability and Growth Pact. Furthermore, it follows from membership of the eurozone that countries should strive to improve their economic competitiveness, in order if possible to even out the excessive differences between them. To this end the Lisbon Strategy was launched in 2000, followed in 2010 by its successor, Europe 2020. Both Europe 2020 and the Stability and Growth Pact are characterized in all essentials by governance through the exchange of experience, a form of governance commonly known—inasmuch as it is conducted on a (more or less) voluntary basis—as the 'open method of coordination' (Verdun and Zeitlin 2018).

In the context of the EMU, we must not forget to mention regulation of the financial market. Although the regulation of financial markets lies close to the functioning of the EMU, it actually forms part of one of the single market's four freedoms—that for capital—and so figures amongst the Union's shared powers. As cooperation within the single market has deepened, the EU has enacted a large number of laws regulating the financial market. These laws have been established through the ordinary legislative procedure, whereby the Commission draws up a proposal, and the Council and the Parliament consider it. The law finally adopted often takes the form of a framework directive, which is then incorporated into national regulations governing the financial market and its actors.

To complete the picture of the Union's various forms of governance, it is important to discuss an area where member states have been very reluctant to relinquish sovereignty to the Union: foreign and security policy, and defence (Wong and Hill 2011). This policy area is special in the sense that member states have remained responsible for their policies and actions, but have nevertheless engaged in an increasingly extensive cooperation on various issues in international affairs. Because the formal competence for foreign and security policy remains with the member states, the Union coordinates national policies with the aim of establishing common positions, joint missions, and collective stances on a number of international issues along with developing a shared international identity, including norms and principles of international engagement.

Although Europeans and a variety of international actors have long held that foreign and security policy is an obvious candidate for becoming a Union policy, member states have jealously guarded their national prerogatives in this field. However, cooperation in foreign and security policy has grown more extensive as a consequence of the deepening of European integration and the challenges posed by globalization and an increasingly tense international climate (Keukeleire and Delreux 2014). The Lisbon Treaty strengthened the powers of the Union's High Representative and created the European External Action Service (EEAS) in order to increase the visibility of the EU abroad and make its external policies more efficient. A decade later, these reforms have started to bear fruit in the sense that the EU is now recognized as a foreign policy actor by most states and organizations. The Union has a diplomatic network of some 140 diplomatic representations around the world which is far more extensive than most EU member states, bar the UK, Germany, and France, and has the responsibility for a number of missions in Africa, Eastern Europe, and Asia.

Due to its economic clout, the EU has negotiated a number of association and free trade agreements with third countries and is a major player in the process of setting international standards of production in a number of sectors (Hill et al. 2017). It has been steadfast in its support for a rules-based international system, important not least given the rise of new powers more inclined towards a power-based international system and the recent negation of the rules-based principle by the Trump administration (Fägersten 2019). Notwithstanding this progress, the EU is still far from developing a European strategic culture which would form the necessary foundation of an effective foreign and security policy (Meyer 2006). The rising dissent among member states about the extent and orientation of European integration has a clear impact on the shaping of foreign and security policy given that member states need to reach consensus on common stances, not least in the area of human rights. The EU is expected to take a progressive position in international organs, such as the United Nations Human Rights Council. However, lately the Union has been unable to agree on statements condemning human rights abuses due to the refusal of certain member states to support common policies in this area (Michalski and Danielson 2019). The increasing dissent among member states in the preparatory bodies of the Common Foreign and Security Policy does not bode well for the EU as an international actor.

Integration Through Law

The relationship between the nation-state and the Union has also been discussed in connection with the process of legal integration (Cappelletti et al. 1986). The EU is a community of law, wherein national law is subordinate in almost all areas to EU law. The Court of Justice of the European Union (CJEU) is the institution ultimately responsible for interpreting EU laws and for resolving legal disputes (between the Commission and the member states, for example). It is often noted in the literature that the Court has been able to push integration forward above all during periods of political division between the member states. An example hereof can be seen in the well-known rulings of the 1960s, in which the Court laid down basic principles for the EU's legal system. The Court established that Union law has direct effect and enjoys primacy over national law. These principles have been crucial for the progress of European integration during periods when the member states have been reluctant to delegate decision-making power to the EU (Alter 2001; Weiler 1991).

Scholars are divided in how they see the role of the Court in relation to the tension between the Union and the member states. According to the neofunctionalist view, the CJEU is a strong supranational court with a clear agenda: to deepen integration (Stone Sweet 2004; Burley and Mattli 1993). The member states may have found this supranationalism to be excessive and wished to limit the power of the Court, but such a change has essentially been impossible: amending the treaties in this area requires unanimity. A competing approach here, however, depicts the role of the Court quite differently. According to this view, intergovernmentalism, the CJEU has been a tool for serving the interests of the major member states (Garrett 1995; Moravcsik 1998). Irrespective of which approach best captures its behaviour, it is clear that many actors—in the UK not least—have been critical of the Court, painting it as a threat to national sovereignty. The core of this criticism is that the Court, through far-reaching interpretation of the EU's acts and treaties, has engaged in legal activism (Scharpf 2009). The result has been deeper integration and increased supranationalism, with consequent limits on the member states' room to manoeuvre.

Dieter Grimm (2015) and Fritz Scharpf (2009), legal scholar and political scientist, respectively, have argued too that the Court pays insufficient heed to national legal and political traditions when deciding issues which the member states consider to belong to the (national) political arena. In the long term, they believe, such behaviour threatens to undermine the entire legitimacy of the Union, by making it difficult for the political leaders of the member states to justify the Court's rulings to their citizens. With Britain's decision to leave the Union, this fear may be said in part to have come true. While the research points to several reasons why the British voted in 2016 to leave the Union, public debate in the UK has long been dominated by the view that the EU, with the CJEU at the forefront, violates the autonomy of the member states in key political areas. In an interview with the *Financial Times* in 2016, for instance, former Brexit Secretary Dominic Raab criticized the supranational court sharply: 'They undermine the basic principle for our democracy—that the British people can hold to account those who write our laws.'

The CJEU's greatest achievement has been to persuade the member states' own courts to apply EU law loyally at the national level. In this way, the EU's treaties have avoided the fate of many international agreements—of not being complied with at the domestic level. Instead, the courts have jointly ensured that EU law has become an integral part of 28 different national legal systems. Neofunctionalists, amongst others, often cite the acceptance of EU law by national courts in support of the proposition that the EU's legal system has basically assumed the character of a national legal system (Alter 2001).

However, even if the courts of the member states largely comply with the rulings of the CJEU, some national courts have displayed a degree of opposition to the latter's interpretations of EU law—something which neofunctionalists have found hard to explain. The highest courts of several member states have shown openly that they do not wholly accept the principle that EU law enjoys primacy over all national law. The German Constitutional Court, for example, has indicated on a number of occasions (Solange I and II, Brunner) that there is a limit to how much decision-making power can be transferred to the Union. The German constitution is still the ultimate guarantor of the values of liberal democracy. The highest court of Denmark has also defied the CJEU—in the Ajos case from 2016, when it refused to override a Danish law that violated EU law. The Danish court considered that, amongst other things, it lacked support in the country's constitution for overriding the national provision. Overruling the law in question would mean going against the express will of the Danish parliament. Legal analysts claim the Danish court thereby undermined one of the most important principles enunciated by the CJEU—that national law is subordinate to EU law (Madsen et al. 2017).

The Return of the Nation-State?

Are we really witnessing the return of the nation-state in Europe? If so, what will that mean for European integration? Will it undermine the EU's ability to meet the challenges it faces from within and without? Or is the return of the nation-state in fact a necessity for restoring stability, the vigour of national democracy, and effective action by the member states?

These questions are complex and they will occupy many a researcher and politician in the future. We cannot supply definitive answers in this book. Yet we think it important, at a time when political currents and actors are openly opposing Union policy and questioning the foundations of European cooperation, that we again focus attention on the driving forces affecting the relationship between the member states and the Union. European integration is obviously affected when certain member states openly and demonstratively thwart common policy, and refuse to implement political decisions which the EU has adopted. At the same time, the Union must assess in a clear-sighted manner the import of the fact that the member states hold differing views, and that they vary in their economic and to some extent political capacity to adjust to the Union's policies and its political and administrative processes. The Union has grown ever larger and more diverse with the years. It must somehow strike a balance between standardization and respect for difference, between divergent norms and notions, and between national and European powers.

The allocation of power, we know, is not a zero-sum game. When the Union is able to act more effectively, the capacity of the member states to meet challenges is strengthened as well. At the same time, the member states have no wish to see far-reaching integration in all policy areas, and opinions are divided on how EU policy should be framed. Some member states have stressed the need for the Union to strengthen its capacities, in order to meet the tough challenges it faces; others oppose any increase in its political powers. Still others doubt such a strengthening is possible. Yet it is clear that, in the wake of Britain's decision to leave the Union, the EU has taken some important steps to strengthen its capacity to act in connection with trade policy, security and defence policy, the social dimension, and the Economic and Monetary Union. In many areas, the EU is one of the few remaining international actors to defend the multilateral rules-based world order against illiberal and destructive forces. The words of Angela Merkel and Emmanuel Macron, German chancellor and French president, respectively, are of interest in the context. In the Meseberg Declaration of June 2018, the two leaders proclaimed that:

> France and Germany are strongly committed to not only preserve the achievements of the European Union but also to further strengthen their cooperation within the European Union, with the constant preoccupation to ensure both the unity of its member states and its efficiency. The European Union will live up to its values and be a strong voice for the protection of human rights and a force to defend, reform, and strengthen multilateralism.

Signs of the Return of the Nation-State

In the nine chapters of this volume, our contributors analyse the relationship between the Union and the nation-state. They shed light on what the possible return of the nation-state means for political, economic, and legal integration within the EU. How can democracy at the European and national levels be strengthened? What are the ways forward for the integration process? Can a division of the euro into several currencies strengthen both the common currency and the Union in the long run? What can explain the paradigm shift from liberalization of the single market to stricter regulation of EU tax law? How should the EU respond when a member state repeatedly violates the fundamental values of the Union? Can demands for an independent Catalan or Scottish state be reconciled with the goal of a united Europe? Should the Union have a common refugee policy, or is it better if the member states decide matters on their own in that area? Where EU law is concerned, is it the Union or the member states which ultimately guarantee fundamental rights when sanctions against individuals are in question? How are we to understand the negotiations over Brexit, and how might the Union dissuade other member states from leaving? These are some of the issues addressed in this book.

What kind of political system should the EU have? Torbjörn Bergman and Magnus Blomgren note that debate over the proper relationship between the member states and the EU's institutions runs like a red thread through the history of the Union. But instead of just recounting the positions in this classical debate—between those who say the emphasis should be on intergovernmental principles, and those who argue that the Union should have a significant element of supranationalism—the authors analyse current debates within four major policy areas: migration, the economy, the social pillar, and security and defence policy. As becomes clear from their examination of the member states' positions on these issues, the debate has little to do with any choice between the two poles of supranationalism and intergovernmentalism. Instead, national political elites seek solutions to various problems on a pragmatic basis. The leaders of the member states take an incremental approach: in their negotiations with each other, they are largely agreed on the need for action but uncertain about the shape it ought to take. Reforms are therefore implemented gradually and evaluated successively, and harmonization is often done on a voluntary basis.

As Bergman and Blomgren see it, this raises a number of normative questions around democracy in the EU. Intergovernmentalism and supranationalism have one important point in common: they both offer clear chains for citizen influence over political institutions. By contrast, the third approach, incrementalism, makes things more complex from a democratic point of view. The authors contend that, since this third account is the most realistic depiction of how the EU actually works, and since the 'hybrid' of supranationalism and intergovernmentalism will likely prove lasting, we should devote much greater attention to the question of which democratic principles ought to prevail within the complex multi-level system. The democratic system characterizes many European states, with its singular chain of delegation and accountability, accords but little with the incremental process of integration seen in the EU. What is needed instead, the authors aver, is an arrangement based on a Madisonian separation of powers, wherein different institutions check and balance one another, preventing an excessive concentration of power thereby. The great challenge, according to Bergman and Blomgren, is to combine a system where the majority will expressed in general elections is operative, with another in which the distribution of powers between the Union and the member states is clear. To date there has been no constructive discussion on what can and should be done to form such a legitimate European political order, in which democratic arrangements within the member states feature as well. The EU hybrid will only function democratically, as the two authors see it, if politicians and citizens can see the link between the national and European levels. This means we must be able to discuss the political issues decided at each level at the same time. National democracy cannot be understood unless we take into account its connection with the EU, and vice versa.

Are democratic values under threat in the EU? To answer this question, Andreas Moberg analyses how the EU, through the Commission, has dealt with the judicial reform introduced by the Polish government in the autumn of 2015, and with the challenge to the Union's values which this reform has entailed. The reform in brief provides, amongst other things, for the mandatory retirement of judges on the country's Constitution Tribunal. Said reform represents, in Moberg's view, a return of the nation-state, because Poland is persisting with its lustration. This despite the fact that more and more voices, both within the Union and amongst international organizations, are calling upon the Polish government to rescind the reform, as a threat to judicial independence and the rule of law. The chapter begins with a description of the tension between supranationalism and intergovernmentalism within the EU. Then, on the basis of this background, Moberg reviews and analyses Article 7 TEU, which provides for suspending the rights of a member state—especially its voting rights in the Council of Ministers—if it violates the fundamental values of the Union.

Having placed the rule of law in its historical context, thereby shedding light on how it has come to be a fundamental value of the Union, Moberg reviews the 'EU framework to strengthen the rule of law', adopted in 2014. The case of the Polish judicial reform is the first and hitherto only time this framework has been used, affording us a first opportunity to analyse its strengths and weaknesses. What conclusions, Moberg asks, can be drawn from the Polish case, in light of the tension between supranational and intergovernmental decision-making which is inherent in Article 7 TEU? His analysis of this question forms the basis for a number of policy recommendations on how the EU can handle the situation when a member state questions the fundamental values of the Union. To begin with, Moberg argues, the Commission should refrain from using the EU framework mentioned above. The traditional mechanisms for dealing with treaty breaches—with the greater role for the CJEU that they afford—are to be preferred. It would also be desirable for the Commission and the Council to achieve better cooperation on issues pertaining to protection of the Union's fundamental values.

What should be the response to the complex challenge of migration and asylum into Europe? Magnus Henrekson, Tino Sanandaji, and Özge Öner argue that differences in the number of refugees arriving in the different member states in 2019 are so great and systematic that it makes no sense to speak of a common refugee policy in the Union. The agreements concluded on a common refugee policy leave, in their view, wide latitude to the individual member states, enabling them to regulate refugee immigration and yet to comply with their international commitments. It is the member states themselves, the authors point out, which are responsible for border controls, for the assessment of applications for asylum, and for regulations that determine what financial support and welfare services refugees are entitled to. In other words, the commitments made by the member states at EU level are largely voluntary; refugee policy is mainly a national affair.

The refugee crisis of 2015, the authors argue, revealed two things about the Union and the nation-state: the inherent weakness of the former as a federal project, and the continued importance of the latter. The Union failed, namely, to manage the increase in the number of asylum-seekers within the framework of a common policy. Several member states introduced border controls, citing the provisions of the Schengen Agreement which allow them to do so in case of a serious threat to public order and internal security. Amongst the countries that did so was Sweden, which had taken in by far the most refugees per capita during the 2010s.

Given the great variation in the number of refugees received by each member state, the question is whether the Union should keep trying to elaborate and enforce a common policy in this area. As the authors see it, the fact that the refugee question gives rise to such tension between the member states ought to tell us that the Union is not an optimal region for the conduct of a common refugee policy. The resistance has a real basis, and it must be heeded if the whole project of European integration is not to be endangered by the imposition of measures from above. Refugee policy ought therefore, in the view of the authors, to be formulated mainly at the national level—and in cooperation with local and regional authorities, which are responsible for the practical implementation of measures for integration in the form of training, job-matching, and the like. Yet the EU can play an important role, the authors note. It can provide assistance to countries afflicted by wars or natural disasters; it can conclude agreements on refugees with third countries; it can carry out rescue operations in the Mediterranean; it can guard the external borders of the Union. In sum, the authors conclude, the nation-state remains the most suitable unit for regulating the refugee flow, for processing applications for asylum, and for maintaining border controls. This ensures that the actions undertaken are in line with national opinion.

How will Brexit affect the prospects for European cohesion? To address this complex question, Rikard Forslid and Sten Nyberg begin by reviewing the evolution of the Union in relation to economic and political forces which promote international integration and national autonomy respectively. The EU emerged in competition with the European Free Trade Association (EFTA); and despite the fact that the former body incorporates a degree of supranationalism—of which many of the former EFTA countries were sceptical—the benefits of a large integrated market ultimately exceeded the costs.

In view of the strong gravitational force exerted by a large market, Forslid and Nyberg ask whether the Union can grow in size indefinitely. At least one thing, however, clearly pushes in the opposite direction: the increased heterogeneity that expansion brings. Under such conditions, the disjunction between uniform policies and local preferences grows progressively worse. The interaction between these forces, which the authors analyse with the help of earlier research on the optimal conditions for state formation, affects the prospects for European cohesion and conditions the risk that a member state will seek to withdraw from the Union. The authors then discuss what can happen if a country actually leaves the

Union, based on the Brexit negotiations and the central points at issue therein—trade and migration. Forslid and Nyberg highlight the incentive of the parties to position themselves politically and rhetorically, and they stress the impact of the structure of the negotiating process on the prospects for achieving less harmful outcomes. On the basis of both their own analysis and the results of previous research, the authors conclude that British voters opted for Brexit because large numbers amongst them, like their counterparts in other countries, see themselves as having lost out from globalization and from the market integration entailed by the EU's single market. The authors then consider how trade theory can help us to understand Brexit, and how citizens' attitudes towards the Union have developed in different countries. While British scepticism of the Union is of long standing, Forslid and Nyberg see no corresponding pattern in other countries. The risk of more 'exits' has diminished in light of the Brexit negotiations, which have clearly shown that even so large a country as the UK has difficulty attaining an economically advantageous agreement on exit. In the chapter's conclusion, the authors offer some recommendations on how exit negotiations can be conducted in order to reduce the risk of unfavourable outcomes. In view of the EU's increased heterogeneity, they stress, it is very important that the Union show sensitivity to legitimate criticism and that it clarify the advantages of membership besides. Adjusted in this way, EU policies can reduce the risk that other member states will choose to leave.

How can the issue of national versus European-wide taxation be tackled? Cécile Brokelind provides an intriguing perspective on this by analysing EU efforts to counteract the erosion of member states' corporate tax bases. This phenomenon drew particular attention in connection with the disclosure that multinational corporations, such as Apple, had basically escaped taxation through favourable deals with the Irish tax authorities. In light of the opportunities which an increasingly globalized world economy affords multinational corporations to reduce their tax liability by exploiting differences between the tax systems of different countries, Brokelind examines how the EU has tried to handle the problem. Despite the difficulty of reaching an agreement—due to differing views amongst the member states about the need to regulate tax competition—the Union was able in 1997 to establish a code of conduct for minimizing such competition. Thanks to digitization, however, tax competition has intensified in recent years at a global level. Digitization and globalization have made it harder for countries to tax corporations, since it is often the case that the latter no longer meet conditions for being taxable on the territory where they conduct their sales.

Against this background, Brokelind reviews how the preferences of the member states have changed on the issue of which state should have the power to tax international companies. Initially, the EU followed the model prescribed by the Organization for Economic Cooperation and Development (OECD)—that the state where a company's main office is registered has the right to tax said company. But the Union's view on the matter has changed. The feeling now is that the right to tax should lie with the state where a company conducts its sales. In recent years, accordingly, the Union has adopted a number of laws embodying this protectionist approach. Furthermore, Brokelind explains, multinational corporations like Apple have been able to exploit differences between the tax systems of member states in order to maximize their profits. The author shows too how the Commission has used EU rules on state aid to limit this kind of tax competition, with the drain on the revenues of member states it entails. Brokelind then presents the thesis that the member states, through the EU, have managed to defend their interests in protecting their own corporate tax revenues under the pretext of securing financing for welfare. However, the measures adopted by the EU to prevent tax competition may be viewed as contrary to the Union's basic principles of competition and free movement. Brokelind sees this as a sign that the return of the nation-state is affecting the political and economic development of the Union, inasmuch as the EU is helping to strengthen the sovereignty of its member states. In view of this trend, Brokelind recommends that the Union and its member states agree on a common tax policy for cross-border transactions—such as the proposed directive on a common consolidated corporate tax base—in order to prevent individual member states from trying to safeguard their sovereignty through protectionist measures.

How to deal with the euro's current problems and uncertain future prospects? To Fredrik N. G. Andersson, the challenge for the euro is not that the nation-state has returned, but rather that it never disappeared. If the benefits of a common currency are to exceed its costs, the participating countries must join in a political union with common rules, in amongst other areas taxes, welfare, and labour markets. The states of the eurozone, however, have not wished to part with their power over economic policy. Andersson shows that, in many areas, the participating states have acted in accordance with their national interest instead of the common good, giving rise to economic divergence. This divergence in turn has exacerbated political conflict between the member states, and made European cooperation as a whole more difficult. Andersson also explores the ideas for reform presented by the Commission, which are aimed at strengthening the euro. He takes a critical view of these proposals, seeing them both as backward-looking and as insufficient to restore economic balance in the eurozone.

On the basis of this analysis, Andersson then asks whether the euro should be split into two or more currencies. In practice, after all, the participating countries have proved unwilling to do what it takes—establishing a political union—to secure the euro's future. Given that, the most reasonable course would be for one or more of the states in question to leave the common currency. A scenario of this kind could help reduce the social and economic pressures which have built up in the eurozone, and which now—in the year 2019—are undermining the prospects for European cooperation. Splitting the euro is not easy, however, and it may prove terribly expensive in the short term. Nevertheless, Andersson argues, the long-term advantages of so doing will likely be greater than the short-term costs. Andersson concludes by recommending that the Union and its member states prepare a friendly divorce, in which the short-term costs of splitting the euro are minimized by carrying out the divorce in as controlled a manner as possible. In this way, less euro may mean more Europe down the line.

Are citizens' rights being compromised as the EU's legal order deepens? Jane Reichel takes up one of the most widely debated issues in European constitutional law: how to guarantee fundamental rights and the rule of law within the scope of application of Union law. In a democratic constitutional state, public power is exercised in accordance with the rule of law. This means, according to Reichel, that the exercise of public power is constrained and held accountable through principles of legality and legal certainty, as well as constitutional guarantees for the protection of fundamental rights. What are the implications hereof for EU law? As we saw earlier, EU law lodges a claim to direct effect and to primacy over national law. This makes it necessary to elaborate rules and protections under EU law which set limits on how penalties can be applied in individual cases. The idea is that, the more interventionist the measures that can be taken under EU law, the more urgent is the need to put clear and unambiguous limits on their application. The overarching question Reichel addresses in her chapter is this: who is it—the Union or the member states—that ultimately guarantees the rule of law and the protection of fundamental rights when sanctions against individuals are decided within the ambit of EU law? As we have seen, the rule of law is now being openly challenged in certain member states, such as Hungary. Can the member states rely, in times such as these, on the EU to guarantee that decisions which may subject individuals to sanctions are made on a secure basis?

Reichel begins by noting that, during the 2010s, more and more rules have been adopted under EU law which makes it possible to impose sanctions and other burdens on individuals. At the same time, due to developments in certain member states, the CJEU has accepted that EU law cannot always be applied in the manner intended. National courts have been able, accordingly, to refuse to surrender criminal suspects whose extradition has been requested through the European Arrest Warrant, and to refrain from handing over asylum-seekers in accordance with the provisions of the Dublin Regulation. In other cases it is less clear how EU rules relate to national constitutional principles, or when EU principles are to be applied instead of national ones. Reichel explores two types of situation in the chapter: decisions imposing sanctions which are taken by national authorities and courts in a cross-border setting, and cases where EU law includes rules on sanctions against individuals which are applied within a member state. In view of the results of her investigation, she concludes that the answer to the question of whether the member states can rely on the EU is strikingly often: 'it depends'. In practice, this means the content and effect of the principle of the rule of law varies from situation to situation. On the basis on this conclusion, Reichel recommends that the EU enact legislation setting limits to the exercise of public power within the scope of EU law, with a view to ensuring due process for individuals and companies.

How do the Union and the member states influence each other? Malin Stegmann McCallion discusses how Europeanization can be understood at a time when the nation-state appears to be gaining greater influence over the integration process. Her point of departure is that the member states can be influenced by the Union (top-down Europeanization), and that they can also exert their own independent influence on the Union (bottom-up Europeanization). Her chapter deals with the different strategies employed by the member states to meet pressures for change from the Union. By blocking decisions in the Council of Ministers, for instance, they can try to put a brake on common policies. Hungary and Poland have pursued such a strategy on the issue of migration, by refusing to implement the relocation mechanism for asylum-seekers.

Stegmann McCallion then considers whether differentiated integration might offer a solution to some of the problems faced by the Union. Under such an arrangement, those member states that wish to collaborate more closely may do so, while those that do not may refrain from joining in. The EMU and Schengen are examples of differentiated integration. Stegmann McCallion takes the view that, while differentiated integration can work in certain areas, it risks reducing the transparency of the EU's political system. If member states can pick and choose which areas to take part in, and to what extent, it can become even more difficult for citizens to ascertain how much influence any given member state has at the European level, or who is responsible for which decisions. Moreover, there is a risk that additional distinctions between different member states will result in their developing even more diverse interests, complicating European cooperation still further. In light of this analysis, Stegmann McCallion concludes by recommending that the EU and its member states consider carefully what type of differentiated integration is desirable. She also calls for greater nuance in the public debate on the EU. National politicians should refrain from systematically blaming the Union for unpopular decisions which they themselves have taken. Politicians and journalists should focus instead on the content of policy proposals, and explain to citizens how they can influence EU policy.

What is the connection between regional separatism and European integration? Niklas Bremberg addresses the changing nature of the relationship between the Union and subnational entities by looking at how the Union is being challenged by politicians and citizens in certain regions who wish to establish their own nation-states. Bremberg reviews the political-science literature on regional separatism, national independence, and European integration since the 1990s. He explores different ways of viewing the effects of European integration on regional separatism, as well as various interpretations of how EU law and enlargement policy can be applied and understood in the event such a region gains independence through secession.

Bremberg then turns to two cases where the question of independence and EU membership has recently arisen: Scotland and Catalonia. A comparative analysis of these cases is particularly apposite, as Bremberg sees it, in that an independent Catalonia would apparently need to apply for EU membership, even though an overwhelming majority of Catalans wish to remain part of the Union; whereas Scotland, on account of Brexit, is in the course of losing its EU membership, despite the fact that a majority of

Scots opted for Remain. Bremberg thus highlights the political and normative challenges that regional separatism poses for the EU. He concludes with a discussion of how the standing of the regions within the Union could be strengthened, and how demands for secession might be managed within the framework of the existing member states. The Commission, for example, could take the initiative for a study of the situation of the regions within the Union, with the express purpose of investigating whether democracy in the EU could be deepened by reinforcing their standing.

How, then, are we to understand the constant tension between the Union and its member states at a time when the question of which future Europe we want to see has become ever more urgent, due to the challenges from within and without which the Union faces? In his annual State of the Union address (2018), Commission President (2014–2019) Jean-Claude Juncker said: 'So let us show the European Union a bit more respect. Let us stop dragging its name through the mud and start defending our communal way of life more.' Juncker seemed to be aiming his remarks at the member states in particular, as when he said it is not just the Commission or the Parliament which must bear the blame for the fact that many of the problems the Union faces are still unsolved. The heaviest responsibility lies with the member states, in view of their inability to reach agreement in the Council of Ministers and the European Council. This connects up with the discussion of what the way forward may be for the Union at a time when the nation-state seems to be playing a greater role than previously. Is this a threat which the Union ought to meet by setting out an ambitious reform agenda, with an eye to revitalizing the European project and possibly building a federal union? Or should the EU take a step back, bide its time, and allow intergovernmental cooperation between the member states to play a greater role?

It is important for the continued discussion to recall that, as a historical matter, the EU and its member states have always had to negotiate on the balance between supranational and intergovernmental elements in the cooperative scheme. In this book, we offer several pragmatic proposals on how the EU can handle this fundamentally existential issue. All are based on the presumption that the Union cannot ignore the tensions arising from the return of the nation-state; instead it must take them seriously, whether the question be the future of the common currency, the rise of regional separatism, or threats to the rule of law. However, instead of moving towards either the supranational or the intergovernmental pole, the idea is to choose—within the bounds of the middle position that marks the EU—which democratic, legal, and economic principles should prevail. This means that the Union must concentrate on how the balance between supranational and intergovernmental interests can be calibrated so as to avoid a list in either direction, with the risk for further fragmentation within the Union that would entail. This is a delicate task.

At the same time, it is important that the EU's institutions join battle for the common values which the Union claims to defend. The Union should take a clear stand on both basic legal principles and democratic rights. It should also remind member states and citizens of the benefits of European cooperation. On the same level of importance is that the Union require that its member states honour both the formal and informal principles they have pledged to follow, and that they stop using the Union as a scapegoat for unpopular decisions (or non-decisions) for which they themselves bear a large part of the responsibility. This can help ensure that the return of the nation-state, which has set its stamp on many important areas over the last decade, does not come at the expense of all European cooperation.

References

Alter, K. J. (2001). *Establishing the Supremacy of European Law: The Making of an International Rule of Law in Europe*. Oxford: Oxford University Press.

Beyers, J. (2005). Multiple Embeddedness and Socialization in Europe: The Case of Council Officials. *International Organization, 59*(3), 899–936.

Bickerton, C. (2012). *European Integration. From Nation-States to Member States*. Oxford: Oxford University Press.

Blombäck, S. (2019). Populism as a Challenge to Liberal Democracy in Europe. In A. Bakardjieva Engelbrekt, N. Bremberg, A. Michalski, & L. Oxelheim (Eds.), *The European Union in a Changing World Order* (pp. 217–243). Basingstoke: Palgrave Macmillan.

Burgess, M. (2002). *Federalism and the European Union: The Building of Europe, 1950–2000*. London: Routledge.

Burley, A. M., & Mattli, W. (1993). Europe Before the Court: A Political Theory of Legal Integration. *International organization, 47*(1), 41–76.

Cappelletti, M., Seccombe, M., & Weiler, J. (Eds.). (1986). *Integration Through Law Europe and the American Federal Experience*. Berlin and New York: Walter de Gruyter.

Delzell, C. F. (1960). The European Federalist Movement in Italy: First Phase, 1918–1947. *The Journal of Modern History, 32*(3), 241–250.

Dinan, D. (2010). *Ever Closer Union: An Introduction to European Integration* (4rd ed.). Boulder: Lynne Rienner Publishers and London: Palgrave Macmillan.

Dinan, D. (2014). *Europe Recast: A History of European Union* (2nd ed.). Boulder: Lynne Rienner Publishers and Basingstoke, Palgrave Macmillan.

Eisenstadt, S. N. (1965). Transformation of Social Political and Cultural Orders in Modernization. *American Sociological Review, 30*(5), 659–673.

Fägersten, B. (2019). European Autonomy in a Changing World Order. In A. Bakardjieva Engelbrekt, N. Bremberg, A. Michalski, & L. Oxelheim (Eds.), *The European Union in a Changing World Order* (pp. 23–46). Basingstoke: Palgrave Macmillan.

Financial Times. (2016, April 27). Leave Camp Balks at Growing Activist Role of Europe's Highest Court. Retrieved June 26, 2018, from www.ft.com/content/98f84d76-ffff-11e5-ac98-3c15a1aa2e62.

Garrett, G. (1995). The Politics of Legal Integration in the European Union. *International Organization, 49*(1), 171–181.

Giddens, A. (1985). *A Contemporary Critique of Historical Materialism. The Nation-State and Violence* (Vol. 2). Cambridge: Polity.

Greenfeld, L. (1992). *Nationalism: Five Roads to Modernity.* London: Harvard University Press.

Grimm, D. (2015). The Democratic Costs of Constitutionalisation: The European Case. *European Law Journal, 21*(4), 460–473.

Haas, E. (1958). *The Uniting of Europe: Political, Social, and Economic Forces, 1950–1957.* Stanford, CA: Stanford University Press.

Haas, E. (1964). *Beyond the Nation-State. Functionalism and International Organization.* Stanford, CA: Stanford University Press.

Held, D. (1992). The Development of the Modern State. In S. Hall & B. Gieben (Eds.), *Formations of Modernity* (pp. 57–78). Cambridge: Polity.

Hill, C., Smith, M., & Vanhoonacker, S. (Eds.). (2017). *International Relations and the European Union* (3rd ed.). Oxford: Oxford University Press.

Joerges, C., & Glinski, C. (Eds.). (2017). *The European Crisis and the Transformation of Transnational Governance: Authoritarian Managerialism versus Democratic Governance.* Oxford: Hard Publishing.

Juncker, J. C. (2018, September 12). Speech on the State of the Union, Strasbourg. Retrieved November 6, 2018, from https://ec.europa.eu/commission/sites/beta-political/files/soteu2018-speech_en_0.pdf.

Keukeleire, S., & Delreux, T. (2014). *The Foreign Policy of the European Union* (2nd ed.). Basingstoke: Palgrave Macmillan.

Madsen, M. R., Olsen, H. P., & Šadl, U. (2017). Competing Supremacies and Clashing Institutional Rationalities: The Danish Supreme Court's Decision in the AJOS Case and the National Limits of Judicial Cooperation. *European Law Journal, 23*(1–2), 140–150.

Majone, G. (1996). *Regulating Europe.* London: Routledge.

Meseberg Declaration. (2018, June 19). Retrieved November 6, 2018, from www.diplomatie.gouv.fr/en/country-files/germany/events/article/europe-franco-german-declaration-19-06-18.

Meyer, C. (2006). *The Quest for a European Strategic Culture: Changing Norms on Security and Defence in the European Union*. Houndmills: Springer.

Michalski, A., & Danielson, A. (2019). Overcoming Dissent: Socialization in the EU's Political and Security Committee in a Context of Crises. *Journal of Common Market Studies*. https://doi.org/10.1111/jcms.12945.

Milward, A. (1992). *The European Rescue of the Nation-State*. London: Routledge.

Moravcsik, A. (1998). *The Choice for Europe: Social Purpose and State Power from Messina to Maastricht*. Ithaca, NY: Cornell University Press.

Puetter, U. (2012). Europe's Deliberative Intergovernmentalism: The Role of the Council and European Council in EU Economic Governance. *Journal of European Public Policy, 19*(2), 161–178.

Radaelli, C. (2003). *The Open Method of Coordination. A New Governance Architecture for the European Union?* Stockholm: The Swedish Institute for European Policy Studies.

Scharpf, F. W. (2009). Legitimacy in the Multilevel European Polity. *European Political Science Review, 1*(2), 173–204.

Stone Sweet, A. (2004). *The Judicial Construction of Europe*. Oxford: Oxford University Press.

Tilly, C. (1990). *Coercion, Capital, and European States, ad 990–1990*. Oxford: Blackwell.

Verdun, A., & Zeitlin, J. (2018). Introduction: The European Semester as a New Architecture of EU Socioeconomic Governance in Theory and Practice. *Journal of European Public Policy, 25*(2), 137–148.

Wallace, H. (2014). An Institutional Anatomy and Five Policy Modes. In H. Wallace, M. A. Pollack, & A. R. Young (Eds.), *Policy-Making in the European Union* (7th ed., pp. 72–112). Oxford: Oxford University Press.

Weber, M. (1978). *Economy and Society, Volume I*. New York: Bedminster.

Weiler, J. H. (1991). The Transformation of Europe. *Yale Law Journal*, 2403–2483.

Wong, R., & Hill, C. (Eds.). (2011). *National and European Foreign Policies: Towards Europeanization*. London: Routledge.

Zeitlin, J. (2005). The Open Method of Co-ordination in Question. In J. Zeiling, P. Pochet, & L. Magnusson (Eds.), *The Open Method of Co-ordination in Action. The European Employment and Social Inclusion Strategies* (pp. 24–33). P.I.E.-Peter Lang S.A: Brussels.

CHAPTER 2

The EU Hybrid: Incrementalism with Democracy?

Torbjörn Bergman and Magnus Blomgren

Introduction

What should the relationship between member states and the European Union (EU) be? How should we Europeans design the Union so that it is *effective*? Where should *power* within the Union be located? And, in particular, how should *democracy* within the Union work? The current and future relationship between the member states and EU institutions is central to all of these questions. In this chapter, we examine different member states' positions on this relationship. In particular, we analyse the positions of leading representatives from eight member states in four different policy

The authors gratefully acknowledge the contribution by Agnes Elfving, MA, with regard to the empirical work and the first translation from Swedish.

T. Bergman (✉) • M. Blomgren
Umeå University, Umeå, Sweden
e-mail: torbjorn.bergman@umu.se; magnus.blomgren@umu.se

A. Bakardjieva Engelbrekt et al. (eds.), *The European Union and the Return of the Nation State*,
https://doi.org/10.1007/978-3-030-35005-5_2

areas. The policy areas provide context and concrete examples, but our focus is on how the representatives of the member states view the relationship between member states and the EU institutions. The policy areas we consider are economy, defence, migration and social issues, all of which were significant in the campaigns leading up to the 2019 European Parliament elections.

In the debate about the future of the EU, there are two traditional positions (or approaches). The first states that European cooperation should be based on intergovernmentalism, and the second emphasises the need for a significant element of supranationalism, within which the common EU institutions have their own decision-making capacity. In this chapter, we suggest that the tension and conflict between these two positions has led the EU to develop into a hybrid regime, one which mixes features of the two classical positions. We go on to argue that there is a third approach, one that is less explicit but, in reality, equally important, namely the *incremental* one.[1] This position is considerably more complex than the other two, in terms of both how it should be explicitly designed and how it can live up to democratic ideals. The incremental position means that in EU negotiations, reforms are implemented gradually; they are gradually evaluated, and harmonisation is, to some extent, voluntary. The incremental position is a pragmatic approach and the main pursuit is political output.

Our main point in this chapter is that there is a crucial difference between these three positions. The intergovernmentalist and supranationalist views can both be associated with clearly defined models of representative democracy. In contrast, the incremental view has a much more diffuse and complex understanding of how EU democracy should work. In the latter part of the chapter, we discuss the fact that the incremental position lacks an explicit democratic model.

Our conclusion is that those who advocate supranationalism, in which parliamentary democracy is moved to the supranational (EU) level, and those who persistently advocate intergovernmentalism, where power is maintained at the national level, do so based on visions that largely lack

[1] Our use of the concept of 'incrementalism' draws, of course, on Lindblom's use of the term as something that involves policy-makers who learn and act on the basis of trial and error and who use step-by-step strategies to tackle complex situations. As pointed out by the more recent 'punctuated equilibrium' approach, this does not preclude sudden larger shifts or changes that are quite significant over time, even if they were reached in a step-by-step process (Howlett and Migone 2011).

real-world relevance in the short and medium term. Instead, it is time for a European-wide constitutional debate about how to improve the current hybrid regime from a perspective of democratic incrementalism. In this discussion, future solutions to difficult political problems must be closely linked to the issue of how citizens can be included in a functioning representative democracy. Today, this is too often missing from incrementalist debates on the future of the EU.

The remainder of the chapter is organised as follows. In the next section we describe the three positions in more detail. We then discuss our methods and material. We go on to summarise the different positions found in the policy discussions and identify the positions of specific member states on the selected policy areas. We then return to the question about democracy. In this discussion, we are inspired both by classical ideas of power sharing and Madisonian-based thinking, as well as the literature known as 'new intergovernmentalism'.

Three Positions on the European Future

According to the intergovernmentalist vision of European cooperation, the EU is an instrument for the member states. The EU should attend to the matters that the member states have agreed on, and the common institutions should implement what the member states have decided. This may require supranational institutions such as a commission and a court. However, other institutions at the European level, such as the European Parliament (EP), if they are necessary at all, should have a limited and advisory role. The governments of the member states should decide on and pursue the EU's common tasks. These governments act under the responsibility of the national parliaments, which, in turn, delegate power and demand accountability for the government's actions in European cooperation. Based on our three initial concepts of efficiency, power and democracy, this model is relatively clear. European cooperation must be based on the national parliaments; it is also within national parliaments that the power to transfer decision-making power must lie. With this model, European cooperation may not proceed that efficiently, but once the member states agree, action will follow. In this case, democracy has a robust base in the nationally elected parliaments, and hence in national democracy.

An approach that emphasises intergovernmental cooperation based on the sovereignty of national state democracy, can, if stretched, provide the basis for a 'Brexit', namely that a member state decides to leave the Union. However, in our analysis below, the intergovernmentalist position concerns the role of the member states within a union, which may have more or less supranational elements and decision-making mechanisms. This means that we highlight advocates who prefer a development in which member states retain their central role, but within the Union.

The second approach, far-reaching supranationalism, argues that member states must hand over more decision-making power to the EU institutions in order to achieve efficiency in addressing issues such as the economy, security, migration and social affairs. This approach is sometimes also referred to as federalism or new functionalism. There are subtle differences between the two, but common to both is their view that all challenges can best be met with more EU integration. One of the most important advantages of this approach is that, as with the intergovernmentalist position, it can be associated with a clear model of democracy. The idea is that integration has gone so far, and today's challenges are so great, that the time has come to create a strong central power within the Union. It should be limited. That is to say, it should not include everything, but within the areas in which the Union has been given decision-making power, there should be a strong parliament elected by popular vote and a common European government. The member states may retain some influence through an upper chamber of parliament similar to the US senate, or, more likely, a federal council similar to the German model. However, there should be no doubt that ultimate political responsibility and power lies with a directly elected parliament and a government formed on the basis of the parties in this parliament. With European political parties and all-European candidate lists, citizens will have influence over what is actually a new federal EU state.

These two positions have dominated the debate about the future of the EU, and it is possible to identify actors, for example, governments, political parties and key decision-makers that are close to one of them. An example is the group of (right wing) radical parties that are currently attracting increasing support among citizens. Even when this type of party does not advocate withdrawing from the Union, they at least want to see a development towards some kind of limited intergovernmentalism. Their emphasis on national legacy and community, and the scepticism towards tangible immigration that arises from it, is linked to a position that stresses the disadvantages of transferring additional power to the EU—doing so creates more problems than it solves. Similarly, there are actors who advocate more supranationalism, open borders and free movement within the Union. They regularly point to areas such as climate change, migration and security, where supranational solutions are seen as particularly necessary. Clearly, these two views about Europe's future are incompatible. Because of this, the EU has developed into a hybrid.

The development of the EU into a hybrid is also a result of the fact that, in practice, many actors take an incremental position. This position is a result of prevailing contradictions, but it also captures the actual debate and situation within the Union. In part, it constitutes an attempt to reconcile and balance intergovernmentalism and supranationalism. The incremental position reflects the fact that in actual negotiating situations, there is relative agreement that measures must be taken in certain areas, but there is an uncertainty (or contradicting views) about how to get there. Thus, reforms are implemented progressively; they are evaluated gradually, and harmonisation is, to some extent, voluntary. This position is not really explicitly concerned about the legitimacy of the decision-making process. Instead, as noted above, proponents take a pragmatic approach and focus on the pursuit of political output. The question remains, however, as to whether this incrementalism is compatible with democratic ideals? We will return to this in the last section of the chapter.

The Material and the Empirical Analysis

In our empirical analysis, we look at debates and positions in four different policy areas: the economy, defence and security policy, migration and the social pillar. We chose these because they are important, but also because, for each of them, it remains unclear where the locus of political power within the Union should be. We examine how eight member states relate to these policy areas: France, Germany, Hungary, Poland, Italy, Austria, Sweden and Denmark. These members were chosen because we have reason to believe that they have somewhat different views about the competences of the EU, and that these differences are connected to intergovernmentalism, supranationalism and incrementalism. Therefore, these member states can be used to illustrate these positions in a number of concrete political issues.

In order to define a member state's position in a specific policy area, we use various materials. We often rely on the expression of a position about the EU's future role in these issues made by the government as a collective or one of its representatives (minister). The material mainly comes from the official websites of the member states (i.e. government and national parliament websites) and newspaper articles. Most of the material comes from the period between 2015 and 2018 and was collected during the summer of 2018. Given that these are policy areas in flux, it should be noted that the member states' standpoints are not always stable over time. On the contrary, it is likely that policy standpoints vary over time, which is actually one of the important characteristics of the incremental position—member states try to reach agreement by compromise. Furthermore, in some policy areas, member states have not yet developed clear standpoints. In these respects, the data presented here is a snapshot of the (ongoing) debate about the future of the EU.

Actors and Positions—Poles and Middle Ground in the Debate

In Table 2.1, we outline the policy standpoints that are characteristic for the different positions in the four policy areas. The information is presented in ideal typical terms. Later, in Table 2.2, we summarise the positions using real-world arguments articulated by member state representatives and their claims about what needs to be done and who should do what. As we review each area, we will develop and contextualise the different policy standpoints, as well as identify their leading advocates.

Table 2.1 summarises the different policy standpoints that, in a clear-cut world, would arise from each of the three positions. However, as we shall see, member states' representatives do not neatly align themselves with one of the three positions about the future of the EU. On the contrary, member states often place themselves in different positions depending on policy area.

Economy

The question of the EU's role in economic policy is a long-standing controversy that has gained increased actuality due to the introduction of the euro and the serious economic crisis that began in 2008. Although the crisis affected many member states, the situation became most serious in Greece. As a consequence, cooperation on economic matters developed into the so-called Stability and Growth Pact, which had the character of

Table 2.1 Three positions about the relation between member states and EU institutions

	Intergovernmental position	*Supranational position*	*Incremental position*
Economy	Defend the right to stay outside the eurozone and claim national sovereignty in terms of taxes and government finances.	The European Commission should have greater influence over the national economy, and the eurozone must have a joint budget and finance minister. Tax systems must be harmonised and there should be some common taxes at the EU level, for example, on financial transactions.	Economic policy is largely a national affair, but some cooperation is beneficial, for example, a common monetary fund and a banking union.
Defence	Defence is a national issue. Some limited cooperation on, for example, defence equipment is beneficial, but it is critical for the EU to develop its own defence capacity	The goal is a proper defence union with a common defence budget and intervention force. In order to speed up decision-making, decisions should be taken with qualified majority in defence and security policy.	Strengthen the common defence, but do not create supranational structures. Can consider harmonising certain areas, for example, surveillance and a common structure for handling defence materials. Favour a system parallel to the EU structure, not part of the EU.
Migration	Asylum policy must be a national competence, for example, deciding common refugee quotas. Cooperation on an external border is to be decided on an intergovernmental basis.	A fully common migration policy, with common mandatory quotas that can be decided with qualified majority. A joint authority for managing the external border as well as joint asylum management. Joint programme for integrating refugees.	Member states must agree on asylum policy and on common refugee quotas. However, decisions must initially be taken by consensus and certain common systems must be established.

(*continued*)

Table 2.1 (continued)

	Intergovernmental position	*Supranational position*	*Incremental position*
Social issues	Social issues affect national welfare systems and decisions about these should not be transferred to the EU.	More effective policies in the social sphere, both common definitions and laws that determine, for example, minimum wages and other legislation on rights.	Increased cooperation on social issues, for example, through different forms of harmonisation strategies such as benchmarking, sharing experiences and government cooperation. However, decision-making must remain at national level.

intergovernmental solutions at the supranational level. Measures were also taken to strengthen the Commission's role in monitoring and coordinating national economic policies. However, some commentators claim that these measures are insufficient to ensure stable economic development over the long term. They argue that the EU system must strengthen its economic competence in order to increase its capacity to manage the economic imbalance between different areas (or member states) within the Union, which is necessary to ensure that the euro countries can achieve more effective integration. The Commission and its president, Juncker, articulate a relatively pure supranational perspective as regards this policy area. Some of its proposals call for giving the EU the authority to impose taxes, for example, on financial transactions. Increased economic resources also create a need for a common eurozone budget. Another proposal is to transform the current stabilisation mechanism into a monetary fund and to establish a new position of EU finance minister (Juncker 2017).

A crucial aspect of this policy area is, of course, whether or not a country is a member of the eurozone. Among the group of member states we are examining here, the Commission's proposals are supported by French president Macron. In his Sorbonne speech of September 2017, Macron stated that the eurozone countries need a common budget as well as a joint finance minister subordinate to the EP (Elysee 2017; Macron 2017). This would be a major step in a federal direction for (at least) the euro countries. Although Germany does not go as far as France, similar ideas

Table 2.2 Member states' positions on the future relation between member states and EU institutions

	Intergovernmental position	*Supranational position*	*Incremental position*
Economy	• Defend the right to stay outside the eurozone (**Poland, Sweden**) • Critical to an EU core of euro countries with a joint budget and finance minister (**Poland, Sweden**)	• Some common taxes (**France, Germany**) • The Stability Mechanism should be EU law (**France, Germany**) • EU finance minister, controlled by the EP (**France**) • Create a banking union (**Italy, France, Germany, Denmark**) • Common budget for the eurozone (**France, Germany, Italy**)	• In favour of a common monetary fund, but keep the intergovernmental system (**Germany, Sweden**)
Defence		• Faster decision-making, for example, by using qualified majority voting (**France, Germany**) • Common defence union and a common budget (**France, Germany**) • Common EU army (**France, Germany, Hungary**)	• Supports strengthening common defence but critical to creating supranational structures. PESCO, for example, should be controlled by the member states (**Poland, Hungary, Austria, Sweden**)

(*continued*)

Table 2.2 (continued)

	Intergovernmental position	*Supranational position*	*Incremental position*
Migration	• Asylum policy must be a national competence; EU decisions in this field must be taken by the European Council (**Hungary, Poland)** • No common quotas (**Hungary, Poland, Austria**)	• Common migration policy (**France, Germany**) • Common quotas (**France, Germany, Sweden, Italy**) • Common border control (**France, Germany, Hungary, Poland, Sweden, Italy, Austria, Denmark**) • Faster asylum process through common asylum management (**France, Germany**) • A European programme for the integration of refugees (**France**)	• Member states that want to advance cooperation in migration policy may do so, for example, by dividing incoming refugees among themselves (**France, Germany**)
Social issues	• Against making these issues supranational **(Hungary, Poland, Austria, Italy, Denmark**)	• Common definition of social justice (**France, Germany**) • Common minimum wages (**France, Germany**)	• Supports increased cooperation on social issues; power should remain with the member states (**Sweden**)

are highlighted in the so-called Meseberg Declaration, a joint statement issued by Macron and Chancellor Merkel in June 2018. Among other things, it stresses that corporate taxation must be harmonised, that the stabilisation mechanism should become EU law and that the eurozone needs a common budget (German Federal Chancellor 2018). In both France and Germany, the future of the euro is a major issue. In France, in his election campaign, Macron promised to reform the eurozone. As for Germany, the issue has been controversial since the extension of loans to Greece in the aftermath of the economic crisis of 2008. There are differences in the positions of these heads of government, but both support the view that the EU should deepen its authority over economic policy.

Italy, which is also a member of the eurozone, appears to be in favour of developing cooperation between the euro countries. In a joint statement, the finance ministers of Italy and France stressed the importance of the banking union and a common eurozone budget (Costelloe 2018). However, there are domestic political tensions in Italy. The Five-star movement, which is part of the government, has argued for a referendum on the future of the euro in Italy (EUobserver 2018; Reuters 2018a). Austria, which is also part of the eurozone, is likewise positive about the initiatives taken by the Commission in the economic sphere (Federal Chancellery of Austria 2018). The country is not in the forefront pushing for enhanced economic cooperation within the Union, but it does not oppose such developments.

The other four member states in our sample are outside of the eurozone. Two of them, in particular, have been lukewarm or even critical in their attitude towards increased EU authority in economic matters. Hungary is critical of deepening cooperation among the euro countries and defends the right not to join the eurozone. Hungary's prime minister Orbán argues that deepening the division between member states within the eurozone and ones outside is undesirable. Thus, the country is critical of the idea of the eurozone coordinating a joint budget or setting up an EU finance minister (Orbán 2018a; Reuters 2018b; Than 2017). The Swedish position also emphasises the intergovernmental element of economic policy, for example, as regards establishing a common monetary fund. Sweden has also criticised the idea of a joint finance minister (Löfven 2017; Swedish Riksdag 2017a)

The positions of the other two member states of interest here are more difficult to capture. Poland has not clearly expressed a position on these questions, but the country remains outside the eurozone and has thus far maintained a rather sceptical attitude (Reuters 2017). Denmark has a permanent opt-out from currency cooperation. However, the country is positive to the Growth and Stability Pact, and the government has said that Denmark could become a member of a banking Union in the future (Rasmussen 2018).

Defence

Issues concerning economic and fiscal policy have been controversial within the EU system for many years. Similarly, defence policy has been a policy area about which member states historically have had difficulty agreeing. However, the developments in recent years indicate that consensus has increased significantly, and defence cooperation has intensified in several areas. An important initiative is the so-called Permanent Structured Cooperation (PESCO). This defence cooperation aims at increasing coordination among member states in defence and security matters and developing a common defence capacity. PESCO is based on binding agreements, but has an intergovernmental form. Decisions are reached by consensus and activities are based on a series of joint projects concerning different aspects of the Union's defence capability. In addition to PESCO, the EU has also established a European Defence Fund aimed at coordinating member states' defence budgets, as well as purchasing defence materials. In addition, the EU conducts a joint annual review and analysis of member states' defence policy (CARD). These three initiatives are intended to increase the EU's ambitions in defence and security policy. Thus far, progress has been accomplished with an intergovernmental form of cooperation. Member states are not in agreement about all aspects of these initiatives.

Despite progress, however, some member states think that intergovernmental cooperation is insufficient. They want a larger role for EU institutions. According to these states, the EU should develop into a full-blown defence union with a common budget and joint intervention force. In order to make this possible, the Union needs a faster decision-making process in these matters. Specifically, the Council of Ministers should be allowed to make decisions using qualified majority voting. France's Macron expressed support for this in his 2017 speech at Sorbonne (Elysee 2017; Macron 2017). Germany is perhaps more cautious, but it is basically positive to the further development of EU authority as regards defence cooperation (Barigazzi 2017; German Federal Government 2017; Fleischer 2017; Manthey 2017; Robert 2016). In the so-called Meseberg Declaration, Germany and France agreed that the EU should develop its defence and security cooperation and that qualified majority voting may be needed (German Federal Chancellor 2018). The German defence minister at the time, Ursula von der Leyen (who has since become the new president of the Commission), has also clearly stated that a European Defence Union should be established as a complement to NATO (France 24 2018).

Poland and Hungary are members of PESCO, and both appear to be fundamentally positive towards enhanced defence cooperation. However, they also stress that they see NATO as the most central defence cooperation (Guyot 2018; Hungarian Government 2017, 2018a; Ministry of National Defence of the Republic of Poland 2018; Radio Poland 2017a, b; Rzeczpospolita 2017). For example, Poland opposes a military headquarters within the EU structure (Barigazzi 2016a). Thus, it is somewhat unclear how far they are actually prepared to go as regards transferring competence to the EU level. It is also not clear if they would allow qualified majority voting in defence matters. Italy is a member of PESCO and is positive to enhanced defence cooperation. The country is also in favour of a common EU army (Barigazzi 2016b, c; Gentiloni 2016; Italian Ministry of Defence 2016, 2017).

The question is a bit more complex in Austria. Although the country is also a member of PESCO, the importance of Austria's neutrality is emphasised in official statements (Hervey 2018; Neuen Volkspartei/Freiheitlichen Partei Österreichs 2017: 53). For example, the country rejects the idea of a common EU army (Vytiska 2016). This suggests that Austria would find it difficult to accept a development in which the EU increases its formal competence to act in the defence and security area.

The Swedish standpoint is similar to Austria's. Sweden also emphasises that it is alliance-free. At the same time, the country is part of PESCO and generally positive to enhanced cooperation. However, Sweden is careful to state that this cooperation must not threaten the sovereignty of member states in this policy area (Löfven 2017; Swedish Riksdag 2018). Prime Minister Löfven has clearly stated that an outright defence union is not desirable and that the development of PESCO should be governed by the member states (Löfven 2017).

Denmark has a permanent opt-out from all defence cooperation, which makes it more difficult to categorise. Denmark is not part of PESCO and clearly emphasises its membership in NATO (Danish Ministry of Defence 2018; Rasmussen 2018). At the same time, Denmark, along with nine other countries, has signed an agreement to create the European Intervention Initiative, which is outside of the EU structure (Emmot 2018). Thus, the Danish position is not about defending non-alignment per se, but rather about which defence organisation should be prioritised. At the same time, Prime Minister Rasmussen has expressed support for other EU member states who want to increase their defence cooperation, with the proviso that Denmark will not participate because of its opt-out (Rasmussen 2018).

Migration

Migration has become a central issue within the EU, a matter that might affect the future of the entire EU. The reason, of course, is the increased flow of refugees that affects Europe and, above all, the events of 2015. The basic problem related to how to allocate power between the EU and the member states is that the single market requires open borders within the Union, which leads to shared responsibility for the EU's external border. In addition, the increased flow of refugees leads to the question of how the migrants should be distributed among the member states. Is it a national issue to be decided by the members, or is it a matter that should be decided by the EU in one form or another? A number of measures have been taken, and the flow of refugees has declined, but the political crisis remains highly relevant in the EU system. EU action has primarily involved strengthening the border and the coast guard FRONTEX, establishing refugee centres in Greece and Italy to help these countries deal with the task of receiving refugees and making a deal with Turkey about how migration flows should be handled. The big stumbling block is the issue of common quotas, which involves the member states reaching an agreement about sharing the task of receiving refugees based on some reasonable principle.

Several member states think that the EU has done too little. In his speech at Sorbonne, French president Macron argued that additional action is needed to enable the EU to jointly manage border control, and that the EU needs a common migration office in order to speed up and harmonise the asylum process. Macron also supports the establishment of a common border police (Elysee 2017; Macron 2017). Germany's position is similar to Macron's. They argue that a common asylum policy is needed and that the external border must be defended better, for example, by making FRONTEX a common border guard governed by EU institutions. To make this possible, the EU must establish shared refugee criteria and a joint European asylum authority (Gutschker and Lohse 2018). Both France and Germany have also expressed support for binding refugee quotas in the EU (Gutschker and Lohse 2018; Lough 2018; Willsher and Kirchgaessner 2015). In the Meseberg Declaration, the two countries state that these issues must be handled at the EU level and not through individual agreements, which would weaken the Union (German Federal Chancellor 2018). However, since the push for common quotas has been blocked, France and Germany have changed their position. They have now launched a 'solidarity mechanism' initiative (Reuters 2019). This is an arrangement by which member states can choose to advance cooperation on migration issues, in particular to cooperate to divide the incoming refugees among themselves.

Although member states such as Hungary and Poland agree that further action is needed to strengthen the external border, they are completely opposed to the idea of common quotas. That the EU would determine the number of refugees that a member state must accept is contrary to national sovereignty and something they cannot accept (Goclowski and Than 2018; Kroet 2016; Orbán 2018b). For Hungary, in particular, this position reflects not only a view about supranationalism versus intergovernmentalism, but also the fact that the country wants to pursue a refugee policy which is in stark contrast to the policies of many other member states (Orbán 2018b). For example, in June 2018, the Hungarian Parliament adopted the so-called Stop Soros law, which among other things, makes it a crime to help illegal refugees or to work for or with NGOs that help asylum seekers or champion their cause (BBC 2018).

In Austria, as well, the issue of migration has played a major role in domestic political debates, not least the question of the EU's role. Chancellor Kurz held a speech in the EP in July 2018, in which he highlighted the fight against illegal immigration as a priority issue. He argued that strengthening control at the EU's external border is the primary way to address the problem (Kurz 2018). In other contexts, the Austrian government has argued for more effective cooperation with third countries in order to relocate immigrants (Barigazzi and Herszenhorn 2018; Federal Chancellery of Austria 2018). The government is critical of mandatory refugee quotas and the idea that these could be decided at EU level by majority decision (AFP 2017; Burns 2017). The situation in Denmark is similar. The country is strongly affected by decisions taken in other member states (primarily Germany and Sweden). In Denmark, too, the refugee issue has been a dominant issue in the domestic debate. Denmark has adopted many laws that make it more difficult for refugees to remain in the country, and the government emphasises the importance of both border controls and helping refugees outside the borders of the EU (Euractiv 2015; Rasmussen 2015; Reuters 2015, 2018c). From this perspective, Denmark is not likely to accept the proposal that refugee issues should be subject to qualified majority voting or any binding refugee quotas.

Italy is one of the member states to which refugees arrive first, and it argues that some form of compulsory distribution of refugees is required (AFP 2018). The position of Hungary and Poland, among others, puts Italy in a very difficult situation. As a result, Italy argues that there is a great need for more supranationalism in this policy area. Sweden has also argued strongly for common refugee quotas, as well as a new asylum system in Europe (Löfven 2017; Swedish Riksdag 2017a). In a speech at Uppsala University in October 2017, Prime Minister Löfven stated clearly that he favours a more common policy, and he is open to the idea of qualified majority voting on these issues (Löfven 2017). Migration is thus an area in which Sweden goes against its generally sceptical attitude towards giving EU institutions increased influence and enhanced decision-making competences.

Social Pillar

Like the others, the fourth and final policy area in this analysis has been the subject of discussion for many years. In practice, this matter concerns the consequences of the four freedoms, which led to a call for common rules. The basic problem is that without common rules in the social policy sphere, there is a risk of a 'race to the bottom', which will make it increasingly difficult for any member to maintain high labour law standards. The argument is that this is because those with higher standards must compete with members who have lower (and thus cheaper and worse) standards. So far, the Social Pillar is an agreement between the member states and the Commission, which proclaims that there should be common ambitions in this area. The starting point is a 20-principle programme and an agreement that the Commission has the right and responsibility to monitor developments within this policy area in individual member states. To date this has involved the sharing of experience, benchmarking and supporting the harmonisation process. European laws may come later, but it is still too early to say anything about what such legislation would look like. Consequently, this policy area is significantly less developed than the other three included in this analysis. Therefore, it has also been considerably harder to identify the positions of the various member states in this policy field.

Again, it is France and Macron who argue that the EU should advance in the social area. The statements are not particularly detailed, but Macron is clear that member states must harmonise policy. In his Sorbonne speech, the French president pointed out that this should mean a common lowest level for what is considered to be acceptable social standards and rules for minimum wages (Elysee 2017; Macron 2017). Germany also supports the work within the social pillar, and points specifically to the issue of harmonising the social security network and minimum wages (German Federal Chancellor 2016; German Federal Ministry of Labour and Social Affairs 2018).

Hungary and Poland also express support for efforts within the social pillar, but they are opposed to a development which leads to binding EU laws. Cooperation should instead take place on a voluntary basis and decision-making competence should not be moved to EU institutions (Government of the Republic of Poland n.d.; Hungarian Government 2018b).

Similarly, the governments of Austria and Italy also support the work within the social pillar, but are clear that they do not support moving decision-making competence to the EU level (Cooper 2017; Embassy of France in London 2017; Parliament of the Republic of Austria 2017). Denmark takes a similar position. The Danes believe that the Danish labour market system is successful and do not want it threatened by the EU. Thus, they reject the idea of mandatory rules in this area and support retaining competence at the national level. A social union is not desirable, according to the Danish prime minister Rasmussen (Rasmussen 2017, 2018).

Finally, looking at Sweden, the government has long worked to make social issues a more important issue on the EU agenda. The fact that the social pillar was dealt with at the European Council meeting in Gothenburg, which the Swedish government hosted, was not a coincidence. However, this does not mean that Sweden supports allowing these issues to be decided using supranational decision-making. Rather, Sweden favours sharing experiences and, in his speech in Uppsala, Löfven emphasised that aspect of the 20-point programme that had just been adopted (Löfven 2017; Swedish Riksdag 2017b).

Summation of the Debate on These Policy Areas

Following this review, we can now summarise how member state representatives place themselves on the different positions about the future role of EU: intergovernmentalism, supranationalism and incrementalism. Table 2.2 summarises central arguments in the respective policy areas, as well as provides examples of member states that have placed themselves in a particular position (our ambition here is illustrative; the table is not intended to be comprehensive). Note that a member state may end up in different cells within the same policy area.

The member states are not always clear about their standpoints in the various policy areas. This means that it is sometimes difficult to interpret the extent to which a member state can be defined as adhering to a specific position or as simply being close to the position. The standpoints are especially fluid between the intergovernmental and the incremental position. In some cases, the positions of an individual member state can be associated with both approaches. We have therefore tried to be particularly careful about our criteria for assigning a member state to the incremental position. Determining the positions of the member states proved to be more difficult in social affairs than the other policy areas. Thus, the differences identified in this area should not be exaggerated. It is very likely that member states which we define as occupying a position in negotiations that corresponds to intergovernmentalism, would, in practice, end up closer to an incrementalist position.

As Table 2.2 illustrates and the discussion above supports, there is no clear general pattern in the sense that the member states consistently advocate one particular position about the desired future of EU. This is true even within the same policy area. France and Germany are possible exceptions. To a greater extent than the others, they put themselves in the supranational category. Since these two member states are central for the EU, it is likely that the supranational approach will continue to have strong support in the future. The other member states analysed here tend to jump between the intergovernmental and incremental positions depending on the issue and situation.

A possible objection to our conclusion that most member states lack consistency is that the difference between the intergovernmental and incremental positions can be very small and thus a matter of interpretation. This is indeed true, but our point here is primarily another. It is that member states' standpoints, with the exception of France and Germany, do not really reflect the classic divide between intergovernmentalism and supranationalism. Instead, most of the debate in most member states shows how governments try to balance between these poles (and are sometimes torn between the two). The member states are trying to balance supranationalism and intergovernmentalism through what can be called 'the strategy of small steps'. In this way, the incremental position is the one that captures much of the debate and the actual situation in the EU today.

Given that incrementalism characterises much of what actually goes on within the Union, we need to understand the repercussions of this for the democratic governance of EU. As discussed above, one core difference between the three basic positions is their argument (or lack of argument) about democratic representation. To move beyond this conclusion, we need to look a little closer at some basic models of democracy.

The Positions and Democracy

Given that it is possible to identify three different positions about the future relations between member states and EU institutions, and one of them (the incrementalism approach) lacks a clear model of representative democracy, what does this mean for the future of democracy within the Union? We fundamentally believe that the EU system should be both effective and democratic. Sometimes it is argued that we must choose between an efficient system and a democratic one. Our position is that there is no absolute trade-off or need to choose between these values. A democratic system can very well be effective. Nonetheless, the question of how the incrementalism approach can be democratic is a difficult one.

The still dominant view is that democracy is associated with a sovereign state, which rests on a sense of national identity and community. In this representative ideal, a particular chain of representation based on delegation and accountability should dominate all others, namely national parliamentary democracy. In more specific terms, parliamentary democracy has a singular and hierarchical chain of delegation and accountability (Bergman and Damgaard 2000; Bergman et al. 2000; Bergman and Strøm 2011; Strøm et al. 2003). In a pure model, all agents report to a principal, in this case the 'people'.

In such a parliamentary democracy, the chain runs from voters to elected representatives (legislators), and from legislators to government, which controls the state. There are, of course, institutional variations. Some parliaments have two chambers, other countries are based on a federal structure, some have a directly elected head of state with certain powers and so forth. Nonetheless, the common idea of democracy is that the people elect a national parliament and the parliament appoints the government at the top of the representative chain. Thanks to this chain of delegation and accountability, people are linked to the political regime in all EU member states. Ultimately, this is about allowing people to choose their political leaders and to delegate power to them, and, not least, allowing the people to dismiss those who are in positions of political responsibility.

As we explained above, both the supranational and the intergovernmentalist approaches can claim to embrace a relatively straightforward delegation and accountability model of democracy. In contrast, representatives of the incrementalism approach are largely silent about how their position can be compatible with an explicit version of representative democracy. It is indeed difficult to see how their approach can be compatible with the idea of democracy as a single parliamentary chain. But are there perhaps alternative visions of democracy?

Since at least the 1980s, it has become increasingly common for researchers and debaters to argue that it is not enough that politicians are controlled by universal suffrage, or that democracy is primarily rooted in political parties and the government at the national level. Instead, a power distribution perspective has gained strength. In the book The *Madisonian Turn*, Bergman and Strøm (2011) and their co-authors, discuss how classical ideals of power balance have once again gained ground. According to these resurgent ideas, the political aspirations of elite politicians should be balanced against other actors' pursuit of influence and control. According to this view of representative democracy, elected politicians should also be checked and balanced. In addition, it is seen as desirable to maintain a division of power between different political levels (e.g. between a member state and a union), because this will protect citizens' rights from the abuse of a single (potentially tyrannical) political level. Thus, in this view, democracy is best realised in a political system that is based on a balance of powers.

In Northern Europe and on the British Isles, the idea of representative democracy as a singular chain is probably still the strongest democratic ideal. In this regard, the EU presents a dilemma. The problem is that the principle of a singular chain can apply either to nation-state democracy (compare with the intergovernmental position mentioned earlier) or EU democracy (supranationalism), but hardly both at the same time. However, in Madisonian-based thinking, complicated multi-level decision-making and competing delegation and accountability chains may be possible and even desirable in a democracy. Such a political system limits the influence of individual holders of power, thereby protecting citizens from abuse and tyranny. The Madisonian form of democracy, with multiple and balanced institutions and political decision-making made on a multitude of levels rather than primarily at one level (the national), might therefore inspire the development (and recognition) of the incrementalism approach to the EU. Based on such a normative perspective, the dual chains of representative democracy, both at the EU and the member state level, provide an opportunity for an explicit democracy. Balancing institutions can be a strategy to restrict the influence of elite politicians and thus avoid abuse of political power and corruption.

This changing view of democracy, that is, the movement from a widespread emphasis on pure parliamentarism to more power sharing, is compatible with the empirical analysis that we have presented. The classic positions (intergovernmentalism and supranationalism) both build on the same model of democracy, the parliamentary national state democracy. The incremental position, on the other hand, entails a more diffuse and complex political system. In the next section, we sketch a blueprint of how a Madisonian democracy model can be a reasonable alternative for developing democracy in the incrementalist approach to the relationship between member states and EU institutions.

Democracy, Efficiency and Power Within Incrementalism

The current EU hybrid is difficult to reconcile with representative democracy, in particular if it is based on the parliamentary democracy model. The hybrid is not based on a singular chain of delegation of power from citizens to political decision-makers or on a clear chain of accountability. Instead, there is a negotiating system that is obscure and constantly changing. To illustrate one consequence of this, it is difficult for potential government parties to make clear commitments about what policy they will pursue at the EU level, because their influence over the process is limited by what other member states want. Consequently, it is difficult for the voters to make a conscious choice on what policy they want to see at the EU level. In addition, there are several chains of democratic representation: the national, but also the supranational (European), the regional and the local. A de facto division of power between the supranational level and the member states is significant. All of this fits very badly with the image of an ideal parliamentary democracy.

One possible conclusion might be that development should move towards either much more supranationalism or a much stronger emphasis on intergovernmentalism. However, as we have shown, few member states consistently promote such a view. Instead, they try to find new, pragmatic, common solutions to key political issues, without creating stronger supranational institutions, and also without clearly weakening existing ones. It is also likely that they are guided by good intentions when they try to compromise and negotiate new solutions. The result is what we call a hybrid regime. But such a system of political governance is not characterised by a fundamental view of democracy, and the question is whether the 'strategy of small steps', that is, the incremental strategy, is compatible with democracy? Those who advocate incremental solutions seem to be silent on issues of democracy, or, in any case, they want to preserve the image of national democracy and not move too fast or too far in introducing supranationalism. At the same time, these advocates argue that intergovernmental policies and actions at supranational level might be needed, often on the grounds that reforms are required to address specific problems. The system must be able to deliver solutions.

A similar line of reasoning can be found in the literature that has been defined as 'new intergovernmentalism' (Bickerton et al. 2015). This perspective argues that significant political decision-making power has been transferred from the national level to the EU system in the last decade. However, instead of transferring explicit power to supranational institutions, the power shift has taken place through intergovernmental agreements (Puetter 2012). Member states have faced new challenges, including the economic crisis, food and agricultural problems, international unrest and changed migration patterns, by creating new intergovernmental institutions at the EU level rather than by authorising the (supranational) Commission to act. Instead of further empowering the Commission, member states created the European External Action Service (EEAS), the European Food Safety Authority and the European Banking Authority. This reluctance to transfer additional decision-making power and resources to supranational institutions can also be seen in the creation of the European Stability Mechanism (ESM). This fund is based on a new intergovernmental treaty rather than the provisions of the Treaty of Lisbon, which could have been used instead.

A so-called integration paradox has thus led to more and more important intergovernmental bodies at the supranational level. This, in turn, increases the need for consensus at the national level. If the perspective of *new* intergovernmentalism is taken seriously, then we understand the hybrid not simply as a compromise between the two opposing poles of intergovernmentalism and supranationalism, but also as a strategy among European leaders.

If we accept that the hybrid is the de facto political regime that we live under, how can we best design this hybrid? Can it be more democratic? As we have indicated above, we have few complete answers to this question. However, we do have some points of departure that indicate the direction in which the discussion should go. To begin with, politicians, journalists and political scientists should acknowledge that the simple parliamentary national state democracy no longer exists. Such recognition could lead to a forward-looking discussion as to what the future should be and how citizens and politicians should handle issues of efficiency, power and democracy in a multi-level system.

As we already noted above, the Madisonian perspective is a view of democratic that is potentially compatible with the EU hybrid as it has evolved. In this perspective, power sharing among institutions and levels is preferable to a single parliamentary chain. However, in itself, this Madisonian perspective does not provide a direct or simple answer to the question of what the actual relationship between member states and the EU should look like. What we need is a debate on normative consequences as well as practical solutions.

Filling the theoretical gap between the supranational and intergovernmental views here is obviously beyond the scope of this chapter. On the other hand, we believe that it is important to start this discussion. The crucial problem with the earlier integration ideas is that both take the national state as a starting point. The difference between them, of course, is that those who advocate intergovernmentalism assume (usually implicitly) that the traditional national state is largely here to stay, while advocates of supranationalism support the development of a new (national) state at the European level. However, neither of the positions provides a basis for a good analysis of the EU hybrid that has developed over the past 25 years (since the formal founding of the Union in 1993), and especially not for the developments of the last decade. Therefore, instead of discussing these two extremes and the relative benefits of one or the other, going forward, researchers, politicians and the public should primarily discuss how we can improve incrementalism in a democratic direction.

Conclusion

The focus of this chapter has not been how to form the EU's future constitution and institutions based on fine-sounding proclamations. Rather, it has been to identify the arguments and positions that member states actually articulate when they explain their views about how the work of the EU should be organised to solve important political problems. In such discussions, democratic principles are rarely in the foreground. However, we believe that future solutions to difficult political problems must be closely linked to a clear model of how citizens should be included in steering developments. Today, this is too often missing.

The current hybrid regime is a result of the difficult balancing act that goes on within the EU. A common incrementalist approach emphasises that solutions to difficult problems are found by national political elites who maintain flexibility at the national level and find solutions at the EU level. The problem with this is that such a model does not give citizens a reasonable opportunity to influence political outcomes. Perhaps if we abandon the notion of the supremacy of the simple parliamentary chain associated with nation-state democracy, we can begin to discuss how a system of more pronounced power sharing can be better developed. For example, can the role of national parliaments be coordinated more with the EP? Perhaps we should strive to develop this kind of system, rather than the parliamentarisation of the EU institutions. Based on this kind of thinking about democracy, it is reasonable to be sceptical of some of the 'reforms' that have been made and proposed in the name of democratisation. One such example is the Spitzenkandidaten system, by which the EP, in practice, appoints the president of the Commission. A Madisonian-inspired thinker could instead recommend that this system be scrapped. Since supranational parliamentarism is not possible at present, the division of powers among the institutions, as formulated in the Treaties, should be maintained and developed rather than dismantled.

In this discussion, it is of utmost importance that an analysis of EU efficiency, power and democracy takes both of the existing chains (election-legislator) into account, the one that operates through national parliaments and the one operating through the EP. An analysis of democracy and recommendations about how to strengthen it must include both chains. National democracy cannot be understood without the link to the EU and vice versa. The challenge is to conceptualise and analyse both at the same time. In this perspective, it is important to stress that EU elections are not only those that are held to elect the EP, EU elections take place every time there is a national election in a member state.

Thus, our general conclusion is that the EU is in serious need of a renewed constitutional debate. The debate should take as its starting point the de facto hybrid regime that currently constitutes the EU. Our argument is that a democratic model with stronger emphasis on power balance and power sharing should be an explicit perspective in such a debate. Our critics would argue that this is already what the EU is about. In our view, the incremental process that has resulted in the current situation lacks a cohesive and consistent view about how EU democracy should work. Much thought needs to be invested in designing rules that safeguard democratic involvement, avoid mechanisms that result in deadlocks, and promote political legitimacy. This means that while we, in democratically normative terms, might be able to justify the current regime based on a Madisonian perspective of democracy, we need to do more in order to develop an explicit democratic model founded on this perspective within an incremental system. We need concrete proposals about how the EU hybrid can be further developed in a way that balances incrementalism and democracy.

References

AFP. (2017, December 15). Austria's Chancellor-in-Waiting Sebastian Kurz Rejects EU's Mandatory Migrant Quotas. *The Local*. Retrieved August 29, 2018, from https://www.thelocal.at/20171215/austrias-chancellor-in-waiting-sebastian-kurz-sides-with-eu-countries-opposed-to-migrant-quotas.

AFP. (2018, June 6). Italy's PM Takes Aim at Migrants and Austerity in Maiden Speech. *The Guardian*. Retrieved August 2, 2018, from https://www.theguardian.com/world/2018/jun/06/italy-prime-minister-giuseppe-conte-migrants-austerity-maiden-speech.

Barigazzi, J. (2016a, September 27). Britain Digs in Against 'EU army'. *Politico*. Retrieved August 14, 2018, from https://www.politico.eu/article/britain-digs-in-against-eu-army-u-k-defense-minister-michael-fallon/.

Barigazzi, J. (2016b, September 27). The Almost-An-EU-Army Plan. *Politico*. Retrieved August 14, 2018, from https://www.politico.eu/article/italy-proposes-joint-european-military-force-schengen-of-defense/.

Barigazzi, J. (2016c, November 14). EU Backs Greater Military Cooperation. *Politico*. Retrieved August 14, 2018, from https://www.politico.eu/article/eu-backs-greater-military-cooperation-nato-donald-trump-federica-mogherini/.

Barigazzi, J. (2017, May 18). EU Pushes Joint Defense Fund. *Politico*. Retrieved August 14, 2018, from https://www.politico.eu/article/eu-pushes-joint-defense-fund-nato-security/.

Barigazzi, J., & Herszenhorn, D. M. (2018, July 11). Austria Backs Migration Centers in Non-EU Countries. *Politico*. Retrieved August 2, 2018, from https://www.politico.eu/article/sebastian-kurz-austria-backs-migration-centers-in-non-eu-countries/.

BBC. (2018, June 20). Hungary Passes 'Stop Soros' Law Banning Help for Migrants. Retrieved June 29, from https://www.bbc.com/news/world-europe-44546030.

Bergman, T., & Damgaard, E. (Eds.). (2000). *Delegation and Accountability in European Integration: The Nordic Parliamentary Democracies and the European Union*. London: Frank Cass.

Bergman, T., & Strøm, K. (Eds.). (2011). *The Madisonian Turn: Political Parties and Parliamentary Democracy in Nordic Europe*. Ann Arbor: University of Michigan Press.

Bergman, T., Müller, W. C., & Strøm, K. (2000). Introduction: Parliamentary Democracy and the Chain of Delegation. *European Journal of Political Research, 37*(3), 255–260.

Bickerton, C., Hodson, D., & Puetter, U. (Eds.). (2015). *The New Intergovernmentalism: States and Supranational Actors in the Post-Maastricht Era*. Oxford: Oxford University Press.

Burns, I. (2017, December 16). Austria's New Chancellor Says He Will Follow Eastern European Countries' Example and Reject Mandatory Migrant Quotas Set by the EU. *Daily Mail*. Retrieved August 29, 2018, from http://www.dailymail.co.uk/news/article-5182663/Austrias-chancellor-says-reject-migrant-quotas.html.

Cooper, H. (2017, March 23). Juncker Seeks to Cement Social Pillar in Rome. *Politico*. Retrieved August 14, from https://www.politico.eu/article/jean-claude-juncker-social-pillar-eu-identity-commission-welfare-policy/.

Costelloe, K. (2018, August 1). Italy Finance Minister Joins French Call for Stronger Euro Area. *Bloomberg*. Retrieved August 2, 2018, from https://www.bloomberg.com/news/articles/2018-08-01/italy-finance-minister-joins-french-call-for-stronger-euro-area.

Danish Ministry of Defence. (2018). *EU – The Danish Defence Opt-Out*. Retrieved August 3, 2018, from http://www.fmn.dk/eng/allabout/Pages/TheDanishDefenceOpt-Out.aspx.

Elysee. (2017). *Initiative for Europe: A Sovereign, United, Democratic Europe*. Retrieved June 25, 2018, from http://www.elysee.fr/assets/Initiative-for-Europe-a-sovereign-united-democratic-Europe-Emmanuel-Macron.pdf.

Embassy of France in London. (2017). *France among Countries Backing EU Pillar of Social Rights.* Retrieved August 10, 2018, from https://uk.ambafrance.org/France-among-countries-backing-EU-pillar-of-social-rights.

Emmot, R. (2018, March 6). EU Agrees First Defense Projects, Delays Decision on British Role. *Reuters.* Retrieved August 10, 2018, from https://www.reuters.com/article/us-eu-defence/eu-agrees-first-defense-projects-delays-decision-on-british-role-idUSKCN1GI1RY.

EUobserver (2018, July 30). Italian Government 'Will Not Pursue' Referendum on Euro. Retrieved August 2, 2018, from https://euobserver.com/tickers/142486.

Euractiv. (2015, December 1). Danish Opt-Out Referendum Marked by Refugee Debate. Retrieved August 9, 2018, from https://www.euractiv.com/section/justice-home-affairs/news/danish-opt-out-referendum-marked-by-refugee-debate/.

Federal Chancellery of Austria. (2018). *Programme of the Austrian Presidency.* Retrieved August 2, 2018, from https://www.federal-chancellery.gv.at/documents/333672/810683/Programme+of+the+Austrian+Presidency.pdf/39484792-93c9-42ed-aaf1-5685027eeadd.

Fleischer, J. (2017). *PESCO: Das Ziel fest im Blick.* German Federal Ministry of Defence. Retrieved August 13, 2018, from https://www.bmvg.de/de/aktuelles/pesco%2D%2Ddas-ziel-fest-im-blick-19498.

France 24. (2018, February 18). Exclusive: Germany's Defence Minister Says EU Defence Pact Will Complement NATO. Retrieved August 7, 2018, from http://www.france24.com/en/20180217-exclusive-germany-defence-minister-von-der-leyen-eu-defence-security-complement-nato.

Gentiloni, P. (2016, September 15). EU Needs 'Schengen for Defense'. *Politico.* Retrieved August 14, 2018, from https://www.politico.eu/article/italian-foreign-minister-eu-needs-schengen-for-defense-paolo-gentiloni-islamic-state-migrants-security/.

German Federal Chancellor. (2016). *Gemeinsame Erklärung zum Deutsch-Französischen Ministerrat am 7. April 2016.* Retrieved August 10, 2018, from https://www.bundeskanzlerin.de/Content/DE/Pressemitteilungen/BPA/2016/04/2016-04-07-deutsch-franz%C3%B6sischer-ministerrat.html.

German Federal Chancellor. (2018). *Meseberg Declaration.* Retrieved June 28, 2018, from https://www.bundeskanzlerin.de/Content/EN/Pressemitteilungen/BPA/2018/2018-06-19-meseberg-declaration.html.

German Federal Government. (2017). *EU Security Policy: Stronger Together Thanks to PESCO.* Retrieved August 7, 2018, from https://www.bundesregierung.de/Content/EN/Artikel/2017/11_en/2017-11-13-pesco_en.html.

German Federal Ministry of Labour and Social Affairs. (2018). *Europäische Säule sozialer Rechte.* Retrieved August 10, 2018, from https://www.bmas.de/DE/Themen/Soziales-Europa-und-Internationales/Europa/Europaeische-Sozialpolitik/soziale-saeule.html.

Goclowski, M., & Than, K. (2018, January 3). Hungary, Poland Demand Bigger Say in EU, Reject Its Migration Policy. *Reuters*. Retrieved August 6, 2018, from https://www.reuters.com/article/us-hungary-poland/hungary-poland-demand-bigger-say-in-eu-reject-its-migration-policy-idUSKBN1ES0ZW.

Government of the Republic of Poland. (n.d.). *The Position of the Government of the Republic of Poland on European Commission's Initiative: European Pillar of Social Rights*. Retrieved August 10, 2018, from http://ec.europa.eu/social/BlobServlet?docId=17268&langId=en.

Gutschker, T., & Lohse, E. (2018). *Europa muss handlungsfähig sein*. German Federal Chancellor. Retrieved August 6, 2018, from https://www.bundeskanzlerin.de/Content/DE/Interview/2018/06/2018-06-04-merkel-fas.html.

Guyot, C. (2018, March 9). Poland Defends a Europe of States. *Euractiv*. Retrieved August 15, 2018, from https://www.euractiv.com/section/future-eu/news/poland-defends-a-europe-of-states/.

Hervey, G. (2018, January 17). Sebastian Kurz: EU Lacks 'Focus' on Big Issues. *Politico*. Retrieved August 14, 2018, from https://www.politico.eu/article/sebastian-kurz-eu-lacks-focus-on-big-issues/.

Howlett, M., & Migone, A. (2011). Charles Lindblom Is Alive and Well and Living in Punctuated Equilibrium Land. *Policy and Society, 30*(1), 53–62.

Hungarian Government. (2017). *EU Ministers Sign Joint Notification on Strengthening the EU's Defence Dimension*. Retrieved August 7, 2018, from http://www.kormany.hu/en/ministry-of-defence/news/eu-ministers-sign-joint-notification-on-strengthening-the-eu-s-defence-dimension.

Hungarian Government. (2018a). *Hungary Supports the Development of European Defence Capabilities*. Retrieved August 7, 2018, from http://www.kormany.hu/en/ministry-of-defence/news/hungary-supports-the-development-of-european-defence-capabilities.

Hungarian Government (2018b, March 14). *Maintenance of Cohesion Policy Is also in Best Interests of Greece*. Retrieved August 1, 2018, from http://www.kormany.hu/en/prime-minister-s-office/news/maintenance-of-cohesion-policy-is-also-in-best-interests-of-greece.

Italian Ministry of Defence (2016). *Italy's Vision for a Stronger European Defence*. Retrieved August 7, 2018, from http://www.difesa.it/EN/Primo_Piano/Pagine/xx.aspx.

Italian Ministry of Defence. (2017). *European Defence, 23 Countries Endorse PESCO. Pinotti: A Decisive Goal*. Retrieved August 7, 2018, from https://www.difesa.it/EN/Primo_Piano/Pagine/-PESCO.aspx.

Juncker, J.-C. (2017). *President Jean-Claude Juncker's State of the Union Address 2017*. European Commission. Retrieved August 26, 2018, from http://europa.eu/rapid/press-release_SPEECH-17-3165_en.htm.

Kroet, C. (2016, August 26). Viktor Orbán Wants an EU Military Force. *Politico*. Retrieved August 14, 2018, from https://www.politico.eu/article/viktor-orban-wants-an-eu-military-force/.

Kurz, S. (2018). *Speech by Federal Chancellor Sebastian Kurz During the EP Plenary Session in Strasbourg*. Federal Chancellery of Austria. Retrieved August 2, 2018, from https://www.federal-chancellery.gv.at/-/speech-of-federal-chancellor-sebastian-kurz-at-the-european-parliament.

Löfven, S. (2017). *Vårt Europa – vårt gemensamma ansvar*. Government Offices of Sweden. Retrieved June 25, 2018, from https://www.regeringen.se/tal/2017/10/vart-europa%2D%2Dvart-gemensamma-ansvar/.

Lough, R. (2018, June 28). France Signals EU States Refusing to Take Migrants Could Tackle Crisis in Other Ways. *Reuters*. Retrieved August 29, 2018, from https://www.reuters.com/article/us-eu-summit-migrants-france/france-signals-eu-states-refusing-to-take-migrants-could-tackle-crisis-in-other-ways-idUSKBN1JO2X0.

Macron, E. (2017). *Initiative pour l'Europe – Discours d'Emmanuel Macron pour une Europe souveraine, unie, démocratique*. Elysee. Retrieved August 1, 2018, from http://www.elysee.fr/declarations/article/initiative-pour-l-europe-discours-d-emmanuel-macron-pour-une-europe-souveraine-unie-democratique/.

Manthey, F. (2017). *PESCO: Ein Meilenstein auf dem Weg zur Verteidigungsunion. German Federal Ministry of Defence*. Retrieved August 13, 2018, from https://www.bmvg.de/de/aktuelles/pesco%2D%2Dein-meilenstein-auf-dem-weg-zur-verteidigungsunion-19806.

Ministry of National Defence of the Republic of Poland. (2018). *To Effectively Use the EU Programs*. Retrieved August 14, 2018, from http://en-m.mon.gov.pl/news/article/latest-news/to-effectively-use-the-eu-programs-n2018-06-25/.

Neuen Volkspartei/Freiheitlichen Partei Österreichs. (2017). *Zusammen. Für unser Österreich. Regierungsprogramm 2017–2022*. Retrieved August 7, 2018, from https://www.oevp.at/download/Regierungsprogramm.pdf.

Orbán, V. (2018a). *Prime Minister Viktor Orbán's Speech at the Year Opening Event of the Hungarian Chamber of Commerce and Industry*. Hungarian Government. Retrieved August 1, 2018, from http://www.kormany.hu/en/the-prime-minister/the-prime-minister-s-speeches/prime-minister-viktor-orban-s-speech-at-the-year-opening-event-of-the-hungarian-chamber-of-commerce-and-industry.

Orbán, V. (2018b). *Prime Minister Viktor Orbán's Address after Swearing the Prime-Ministerial Oath of Office*. Hungarian Government. Retrieved June 21, 2018, from http://www.kormany.hu/en/the-prime-minister/the-prime-minister-s-speeches/prime-minister-viktor-orban-s-address-after-swearing-the-prime-ministerial-oath-of-office.

Parliament of the Republic of Austria. (2017). *EU will sozialer werden*. Retrieved August 14, 2018, from https://www.parlament.gv.at/PAKT/PR/JAHR_2017/PK0765/.

Puetter, U. (2012). Europe's Deliberative Intergovernmentalism: The Role of the Council and European Council in EU Economic Governance. *Journal of European Public Policy, 19*(2), 161–178.

Radio Poland. (2017a, November 13). Poland, 22 Other EU Members Sign Defence Pact. Retrieved August 6, 2018, from http://www.thenews.pl/1/10/Artykul/334875,Poland-22-other-EU-members-sign-defence-pact.

Radio Poland. (2017b, November 10). Poland to Join EU's PESCO Defence Initiative: Gov't Spokesman. Retrieved August 6, 2018, from http://www.thenews.pl/1/10/Artykul/334584,Poland-to-join-EU%E2%80%99s-PESCO-defence-initiative-gov%E2%80%99t-spokesman.

Rasmussen Løkke, L. (2015). *Prime Minister Lars Løkke Rasmussen's Opening Address to the Folketing (Danish Parliament) on 6 October 2015*. Retrieved August 9, 2018, from http://www.stm.dk/_p_14252.html.

Rasmussen Løkke, L. (2017, September 16). Go Easy on the Social, Europe. *Politico*. Retrieved August 1, 2018, from https://www.politico.eu/article/europe-future-go-easy-on-the-social/.

Rasmussen Løkke, L. (2018). *Statsminister Lars Løkke Rasmussens tale på Europadagen den 9. maj 2018*. Statsministeriet. Retrieved August 6, 2018, from http://www.stm.dk/_p_14678.html.

Reuters (2015, September 11). Denmark Says It Will Not Join EU Refugee Quotas, Has Taken Its Share. Retrieved August 9, 2018, from https://www.reuters.com/article/us-europe-migrants-eu-denmark/denmark-says-it-will-not-join-eu-refugee-quotas-has-taken-its-share-idUSKCN0RB0TJ20150911.

Reuters. (2017, October 29). Poland Wants Strong Euro Zone Before Mulling Membership – Finance Minister. Retrieved August 6, 2018, from https://www.reuters.com/article/us-eu-poland-eurozone/poland-wants-strong-euro-zone-before-mulling-membership-finance-minister-idUSKBN1CY0CL.

Reuters. (2018a, July 29). Euro Referendum not Part of Italian Government Plans – Deputy PM. *Channel News Asia*. Retrieved August 2, 2018, from https://www.channelnewsasia.com/news/world/euro-referendum-not-part-of-italian-government-plans%2D%2D-deputy-pm-10572488.

Reuters. (2018b, March 24). Hungary in No Rush to Join Euro Zone, Minister Says. Retrieved August 6, 2018, from https://www.reuters.com/article/us-hungary-euro-minister/hungary-in-no-rush-to-join-euro-zone-minister-says-idUSKBN1H0085.

Reuters. (2018c, June 6). European Leaders in Talks on Creating Asylum Center Outside EU. Retrieved August 9, 2018, from https://www.reuters.com/article/us-europe-migrants-denmark/european-leaders-in-talks-on-creating-asylum-center-outside-eu-idUSKCN1J216R.

Reuters. (2019, July 22). EU Countries Agree to New Migrant Influx Mechanism. Retrieved August 22, 2018, from https://uk.reuters.com/article/uk-europe-migrants-france/eu-countries-agree-to-new-migrant-influx-mechanism-macron-idUKKCN1UH211.

Robert, A. (2016, September 19). France Leading the Campaign for EU Military HQ. *Euractiv*. Retrieved August 13, 2018, from https://www.euractiv.com/

section/global-europe/news/france-leading-the-campaign-for-eu-military-hq/.

Rzeczpospolita. (2017). *Poland Ready to Thoroughly Engage in European Defence Policy*. Ministry of Foreign Affairs of the Republic of Poland. Retrieved August 15, 2018, from https://polska.pl/politics/foreign-affairs/poland-ready-thoroughly-engage-european-defence-policy/.

Strøm, K., Müller, W. C., & Bergman, T. (Eds.). (2003). *Delegation and Accountability in Parliamentary Democracies*. Oxford: Oxford University Press.

Swedish Riksdag. (2017a). *Onsdagen den 13 december 2017: EU-nämndens uppteckningar 2017/18:16*. Retrieved August 3, 2018, from http://www.riksdagen.se/sv/dokument-lagar/dokument/eu-namndens-uppteckningar/onsdagen-den-13-december-2017_H50A16.

Swedish Riksdag. (2017b). *Onsdagen den 15 november 2017: EU-nämndens uppteckningar 2017/18:11*. Retrieved August 3, 2018, from http://www.riksdagen.se/sv/dokument-lagar/dokument/eu-namndens-uppteckningar/onsdagen-den-15-november-2017_H50A11.

Swedish Riksdag. (2018). *Fredagen den 2 mars 2018: EU-nämndens uppteckningar 2017/18:25*. Retrieved August 3, 2018, from http://www.riksdagen.se/sv/dokument-lagar/dokument/eu-namndens-uppteckningar/fredagen-den-2-mars-2018_H50A25.

Than, K. (2017, October 12). Hungary Rejects Euro Fin Min Plan, No Rushed Entry – PM Aide. *Reuters*. Retrieved August 6, 2018, from https://uk.reuters.com/article/uk-eu-hungary-interview/hungary-rejects-euro-fin-min-plan-no-rushed-entry-pm-aide-idUKKBN1CH25D.

Vytiska, H. (2016, November 15). Divided Austria Unites in Opposition to EU Army. *Euractiv*. Retrieved August 14, 2018, from https://www.euractiv.com/section/security/news/divided-austria-unites-in-opposition-to-eu-army/.

Willsher, K., & Kirchgaessner, S. (2015, September 3). Germany and France Demand Binding Refugee Quotas for EU Members. *The Guardian*. Retrieved August 29, 2018, from https://www.theguardian.com/world/2015/sep/03/germany-france-eu-refugee-quotas-migration-crisis.

CHAPTER 3

When the Return of the Nation-State Undermines the Rule of Law: Poland, the EU, and Article 7 TEU

Andreas Moberg

Introduction

In the case of the European Union (EU), the return of the nation-state is situated at the boundary between what is decided by each member state on its own and what is decided jointly under the common rules of the Union. This boundary has been a source of conflict ever since the inception of European integration in the early 1950s. The return of the nation-state is in this chapter exemplified by the conflict between Poland and the Union, which has escalated in severity since 2015. In December 2017, the European Commission (hereafter the 'Commission') sent a reasoned proposal to the Council to ascertain whether there was 'a clear risk of a serious breach by the Republic of Poland of the rule of law' (European Commission 2017b). The Commission's proposal meant the end of a two-year dialogue between the Commission and Poland, wherein the parties maintained diametrically opposed views on how well

A. Moberg (✉)
University of Gothenburg, Gothenburg, Sweden
e-mail: andreas.moberg@law.gu.se

A. Bakardjieva Engelbrekt et al. (eds.), *The European Union and the Return of the Nation State*,
https://doi.org/10.1007/978-3-030-35005-5_3

the rule of law was respected in Poland. In the view of the Polish government, the legal changes it had made should be regarded as lustration undertaken to safeguard the rule of law; the Commission, by contrast, considered the measures taken to have put the rule of law at serious risk. Poland's refusal to accept the Commission's repeated calls is a prominent example of the return of the nation-state. The core of the conflict is whether the efforts of the Polish government to subject the country's judiciary to fundamental change constitute a breach of the rule of law—or a reinforcement of it.

As we shall see below, it is not a new problem in the history of European integration that individual member states have called commonly agreed-upon values into question. On the contrary, this has happened many times. What is new in the case of Poland—and what makes it particularly interesting to study—is that this is the first time that Article 7 of the Treaty on European Union (hereafter TEU or the 'EU Treaty') has been activated.

What makes this example of the return of the nation-state one of the most important constitutional issues in the EU today is that European integration is based on the fundamental principles of mutual trust and mutual recognition. EU member states must be able to trust in each other's legal systems, as trust is a prerequisite for respecting and maintaining the principle of mutual recognition. The principle of mutual recognition forms the basis both for the common internal market and for the joint effort to build a European area of freedom, security, and justice (Cramér 2009; Cambien 2017). It is no exaggeration to say that the EU would not be the EU without the principle of mutual recognition.

The Union has been safeguarding the rule of law both internally and externally for decades, so it is expected to act when this fundamental principle is threatened. At the same time, the EU has come in for criticism from several quarters for not having taken sufficiently effective action in this area. There is good cause to examine what this criticism consists in, and to assess whether it is justified. We ought also to analyse the potential failings of the EU when it comes to safeguarding the rule of law. How can the Union be preserved and strengthened under these conditions?

The case of Poland, then, is the first in which the Commission has applied the 'new EU Framework to strengthen the Rule of Law' (European Commission 2014). It is interesting for that reason alone. Within this new framework, the Commission takes on the role of a monitoring body. While this is not a new role for the Commission, the new framework does make for a clear shift—from an intergovernmental logic to a supranational one—in the approach taken to monitoring compliance with the fundamental values set out in Article 2 TEU.

This chapter begins with a description of the tension between supranationalism and intergovernmentalism. This tension helps frame my analysis of Article 7 TEU, which I present in the next section. A review thereupon follows of how the rule of law has become a fundamental value in European integration. Then, with these elements serving as a backdrop, I examine the Commission's framework for strengthening the rule of law. Finally, I present a number of policy recommendations as to how the Union should deal with the return of the nation-state when it takes the shape of a member state's calling into question the jointly agreed-upon fundamental values set out in Article 2 TEU.

The Tension Between Supranationalism and Intergovernmentalism

The EU Treaty is an intergovernmental agreement, in the form of an international treaty. Through this agreement, the parties have jointly decided to create a number of institutions, to which they have assigned certain competences.[1] The parties have also, in several different situations, committed themselves to following the decisions which these institutions make—a fact perhaps best exemplified by the undertaking of the parties to respect the judgments of the Court of Justice of the European Union (hereafter, the CJEU or the 'Court') (Article 19 TEU). Most of the decisions taken by the Council, as well as by the European Parliament (EP), are taken as majority decisions. The 'majority' in question is defined in different ways, but the interesting thing is that the parties to the EU Treaties have chosen to let the institutions make binding decisions on a majority basis—not just on a unanimous one.

Unanimity is otherwise the most common method under public international law for decisions that bind sovereign states. It follows naturally from the principle of sovereignty, according to which states can decide on their own whether or not to accept a legal obligation. The distinction between majority decisions and unanimous ones can therefore be used as

[1] Cf. Article 4 TEU and Articles 2-6 TFEU as well as Title III TEU.

an effective indicator of the line between supranationalism and intergovernmentalism.

Within the EU, however, this difference has become even clearer. Due to decisions taken by the Court in the early 1960s, in cases such as *Van Gend* and *Costa* (Court of Justice of the European Union 1963, 1964), two crucial principles have been enshrined: Union law enjoys primacy, and it has direct effect. These two principles mean that each member state, under certain conditions, is legally obliged to apply EU law even in cases where national legal rules are applicable. This holds true both for provisions in the Treaties and for provisions in acts adopted by the institutions created by the Treaties—in all situations where member states exercise authority (in their courts) in relation to all categories of norms defined by the national legal system.

The combination of primacy and majority decision gives the EU's institutions a supranational character on issues where the member states have granted them the power to act. However, the member states are 'masters of the Treaties' and can thus, by altering their text, both extend and reduce the degree of supranationalism characterizing the Union's institutions. The most common method is to choose between majority decision and unanimity in the Council. It is common for unanimity to be chosen in areas where national interests are strong. By means of the veto, national control is maintained. Another (significantly less common) method used by the member states to maintain control over sensitive matters is by limiting the influence of the CJEU. Accordingly, the influence of the latter on the Common Foreign and Security Policy (CFSP) is very limited.

The latter variant of the tension between supranationalism and intergovernmentalism is evident in Article 7 TEU. That is my focus in this chapter, wherein I analyse the legal procedure for dealing with breaches of the fundamental values set forth in Article 2.

Article 7 TEU: A Hybrid of Supranationalism and Intergovernmentalism

Article 7 stipulates how the Union is to handle two different situations arising in connection with breaches of Article 2. The ultimate sanction which a member state may suffer for infringing Article 2 is to have its voting rights in the Council curtailed (see Article 7(3)). It is certainly not uncommon for the Union's institutions to make decisions that bind the member states: they do so daily, both in legislation and in legal judgments. What is remarkable in the case of Article 7 is that it is the Council and the European Council—not the Court—which are charged with examining alleged violations and deciding upon sanctions.

Article 7 involves three steps. In the first, the task is to determine whether 'there is a clear risk of a serious breach by a Member State' of any of the values enshrined in Article 2. This review is initiated (under Article 7(1)) 'on a reasoned proposal by one third of the Member States, by the European Parliament or by the European Commission'; and the decision rests with the Council. In the second step, the European Council determines whether a member state has committed 'a serious and persistent breach' of said values. It should be added that the second step is not dependent on a decision's having been made in the first step (i.e., under Article 7(1)). The third step is the decision on whether to impose sanctions (this does require, however, that the European Council take a decision under Article 7(2)). The determination of whether the values set out in Article 2 are at risk of being breached (Article 7(1)), or have been persistently and seriously breached (Article 7(2)), is thus carried out by the Council (Art. 7(1), by a four-fifths majority) or by the European Council (Art. 7(2), on the basis of unanimity). The consent of the EP is required under Article 7(1) and Article 7(2), but not under Article 7(3). Normally, the EP votes on the matter before the Council does. When the EP votes under Article 7(1) and Article 7(2), a two-thirds majority is required and at least 50% of its members must vote (Article 7(5)).[2] When the European Council has made a decision under Article 7(2), the Council, acting by a qualified majority in accordance with Article 7(3), may decide to suspend some of the rights of the designated member state under the Treaties. The decision on whether to impose this strong sanction is made by the Council by qualified majority, which in this case means 72% of the members representing the participating states comprising at least 65% of the population of the states voting.[3]

Certainly, decision-making by qualified majority is a clear sign of supranationalism; however, in order for a sanction to be imposed, a unanimous decision must be taken by the European Council, that is, by the heads of state or government. This is a procedure which displays a clear intergovernmental logic. What is interesting in light of the distinction between

[2] The procedure is regulated in Article 354 TFEU.

[3] Cf. Articles 7(5) TEU and 354 TFEU.

supranationalism and intergovernmentalism is not just the size of the majority required, or whether the Council or the European Council votes on the matter. The really striking thing is that it is not the CJEU that determines whether or not the values set out in Article 2 have been violated.

Article 7 is thus a procedural provision. It sets out how the Council or the European Council is to decide whether the conduct of a certain Council member is contrary to a pre-established norm—that of the rule of law and the other fundamental values. It is very rare that positions are taken in such a way in the Council. The foundations of intergovernmentalism are shaken when one state sits in judgment on another. It is much more common for conflicts to be settled through negotiation. In cases where states are put on trial, it is considerably more common for independent third parties to make the legal assessments involved. The reasons for this are many, but one of the more obvious ones is that an independent third party is less likely to have any interests engaged in the case.

It should also be pointed out that Article 2 is a proclamation intended to communicate an image of the fundamental nature of European cooperation and integration. It is not a provision that commits contracting states to one another. It is only when it is read in conjunction with Article 7 that it becomes clear that it imposes obligations on the member states. The obligation in question is to respect and uphold all of the fundamental values mentioned in Article 2. In this chapter, however, my focus is on the 'rule of law'.

The Union and the Rule of Law

There were no references to the rule of law in the early days of European integration. The Paris Agreement (1952) and the Treaty of Rome (1957) do not mention this particular value. When the European Union saw the light of day, with the entry into force of the EU Treaty on 1 November 1993, the protection of the rule of law became one of the objectives of the CFSP as well as an objective of Community development cooperation. However, no explicit references were made to the rule of law regarding EU internal relations. The first such reference appeared as a result of a revision of the EU Treaty introduced by the Treaty of Amsterdam in 1999. Thus ended 47 years of cooperation without an explicit reference to the rule of law. The first paragraph of Article 6 TEU (which revised Article F) stated: 'The Union is based on the principles of liberty, democracy, respect for human rights and fundamental freedoms, and the rule of law, principles common to the Member States.'

In 2019, Article 6 celebrated its 20th anniversary. Nowadays, following the changes brought by the Lisbon Treaty—which entered into force in December 2009—the rule of law is no longer termed a 'principle'. Instead, the *value* of the rule of law is cited as one of six values in Article 2 TEU. Furthermore, in an effort to highlight the inherent obligation involved, the language was changed from descriptive to normative: '[t]he Union is based on' (the wording from 1999) became '[t]he Union *shall* be based on', and the values in question '*shall* be common' to the member states.[4]

One might wonder why the reference to the rule of law was introduced in 1999, and also why the descriptive statement of the 1990s became a normative injunction ten years later. Erik Wennerström (2019) highlights the EU's forthcoming eastward enlargement and a number of individual events—in Austria (1999) and in Italy (2001)—as contributing causes. He also points out that the changes to Article F.1 TEU/Article 7 TEU brought by the Treaty of Nice, which entered into force on 1 February 2003, enhanced the Council's ability to sanction a member state for breaching any of the principles set out in Article 6 TEU. In the earlier wording, the member state had to have committed a 'serious and persistent breach' of the principle in question. The amendment introduced by the Treaty of Nice meant that the Council now had the opportunity to state that there was 'a clear risk' of a breach by a member state. This change was a direct consequence of the fact that, in the two cases mentioned (Austria and Italy), the member states concluded that the sanction mechanism could not be invoked because no breaches had (yet) occurred.

These revisions—of Article 6 of the Amsterdam Treaty and Article 7 of the Nice Treaty—are examples of how the management of conflicts between the member states is gradually becoming less intergovernmental and more supranational.

I argue here that the shift from intergovernmentalism to supranationalism is closely linked to juridification. According to Gunther Teubner (1998), enhanced sanctions are one of several clear features of juridification. He identifies three different perspectives on juridification: 'the juristic view', the 'sociologist of law' view, and the 'political science perspective' (Teubner 1998: 396). These correspond respectively to 'a flood of norms', to 'conflict expropriation', and to 'restricting the room for manoeuvre of social movements and interest groups' (ibid.). Teubner uses Weber's distinction between formal and material legal rationality to explain how

[4] Emphasis added in both quotes.

formal law is changing due to societal demands for the materialization of law (Teubner 1998: 399ff).[5] It is this, he contends, that drives juridification. Teubner's account of juridification fits nicely with the changes made to Article 7 TEU. For purposes of the present inquiry, Teubner's work is highly illuminating, since it makes plain that there are many different kinds of juridification. However, the different kinds all have one central thing in common: the law expands, colonizes, and incorporates that which is non-law.

One clear marker of juridification can be seen in the limitation on actors' freedom of action due to increased regulation; another is evident in the tendency to move conflict resolution to an independent third party (typically a court). Seen from a legal perspective, it is analytically reasonable to see increased juridification and increased supranationalism as converging tendencies. This means that the markers used to identify a process of juridification also work to identify a movement towards increased supranationalism at the expense of state sovereignty. One important reason why the connection is so strong lies in the aforementioned principles of the primacy and direct effect of EU law. Simply put, more regulation at Union level means more supranationalism. This applies both to EU citizens and to the member states.

The main reason for the Treaty changes, of course, was that a more credible threat of sanctions was thought to encourage greater respect for, and thus closer compliance with, the principles proclaimed by the Union. It is impossible, of course, to establish whether the effort has had its intended effect; however, there would seem to be ample grounds for scepticism. In numerous cases, individual member states have openly defied the principles in question. This has supplied several opportunities to invoke Article 7 TEU, and thereby to establish whether there has been a clear risk of a breach of said principles.[6]

In hindsight, it seems clear that the changes have not had their intended effect. The explanation for this would appear to be that a decision under Article 7 TEU must be taken by the Council by a majority of four-fifths, after the consent of the EP has been obtained. So, even though the process of juridification has introduced the possibility of imposing sanctions

[5] Teubner (1998: 399) makes reference to Weber, M. (1978). *Economy and Society*. Berkeley: University of California Press.

[6] Denmark 2001, the Netherlands 2010–2012, France 2010, Hungary 2011 and Romania 2012 are pertinent examples, see Wennerström (2019).

in the case of a 'clear risk of a serious breach', the process as such is firmly located in the intergovernmental and less legalized arena, because the decision is taken by the Council and not by an independent third party (such as a court) (Cf. Closa and Kochenov 2016).

In his annual speech to the EP in 2012, the Commission's then-president, José Manuel Barroso, confirmed that he too was frustrated that the available mechanisms were not effective enough to counter threats to the rule of law. He returned to the same theme the following year, and then promised as well that the Commission would develop a framework to further streamline efforts to avert threats to the rule of law in the Union. It is not really a remarkable thing, but it bears stressing in this context that Barroso's proposal strengthens the link between legalization and supranationalism further, inasmuch as it proposes legislative action aimed at regulating the member states, rather than their citizens or markets.

A New EU Framework for Strengthening the Rule of Law

In March 2014, the Commission submitted a communication to the EP and the Council entitled: 'A New EU Framework for Strengthening the Rule of Law' (European Commission 2014; Crabit and Bel 2016). The Commission made clear in the communication that it was setting up the framework in response to a direct request from both the EP and the Council (European Commission 2014: 3).

The new framework is the Commission's internal procedural regime, or framework, for how it will work to strengthen protection for the rule of law in the member states. The framework is intended to deal with threats to the rule of law which are of a 'systemic nature' (ibid., 7). It is thus not intended for use in response to single events that entail violations of basic values; its purpose, rather, is to deal with structural problems. The Commission emphasizes that the aim of the framework is to devise early solutions to such threats to the rule of law, so as to avoid any necessity of activating either of the mechanisms of Article 7 TEU (ibid., 6). Furthermore, the framework is not intended to prevent the Commission from initiating infringement proceedings, under Article 258 TFEU, in situations where the rule of law is being undermined by a member state's breach of EU law, including the Treaties (ibid., 3).

In the communication presenting the new framework, the Commission emphasizes the special importance of the rule of law for the Union. If individual rights, for instance, are to be safeguarded adequately, then the rule of law must obtain. In addition, however, the Commission puts particular emphasis on how important it is that all EU citizens and national authorities have confidence in the legal systems of other member states. Without this confidence, namely, the Union will not be able to maintain the area of freedom, security, and justice without internal frontiers (ibid., 4).

The communication begins with a definition of the rule of law. This is a positive approach, and it must be said that it is not a simple task to specify the principle in question. The Commission chooses to break it down into six basic principles, which are derived from the case law of both the CJEU and the European Court of Human Rights, as well as the Council of Europe through its advisory body—the European Commission for Democracy through Law (the Venice Commission). The six principles are lawfulness, legal certainty, equality before the law, independent and impartial courts, prohibition of arbitrary exercise of executive functions, and effective judicial review (including respect for fundamental rights) (ibid.).

Following this definition of the rule of law, the Commission describes the new procedure. It is a three-step process: the Commission's assessment, the Commission's recommendation, and the follow-up to the Commission's recommendation (assessment—recommendation—follow-up). In the first step, the Commission compiles and analyses information indicating a systemic threat to the rule of law. If this initial assessment confirms the perception that the rule of law is threatened, the Commission then initiates a dialogue with the member state in question, expressing its 'opinion on the rule of law' and proposing measures that can be taken to strengthen it. If the parties fail to reach consensus on how to handle the issues, and/or if the authorities of the member state refrain from taking appropriate action, the Commission sends a 'rule of law recommendation' to the member state concerned. Unlike the opinion, the recommendation is published. It specifies and clarifies the Commission's reasons for identifying the situation as a systemic threat to the rule of law. It also sets a deadline, and requires the member state to take action and to report to the Commission. In the third step, the Commission monitors whether the member state follows the recommendation. If the member state does not do so to the satisfaction of the Commission, the latter body then considers activating either of the mechanisms of Article 7 TEU.

On 27 May 2014, on behalf of the General Affairs Council, the Council Legal Service delivered its opinion on the Commission's communication.

It offered a thin analysis, which really comes down to one point—that by creating the above-mentioned framework, the Commission has violated the fundamental principle of conferral. This conclusion has two parts: first, that Article 7 TEU is the sole procedure through which the EU's institutions can deal with infringements of Article 2 TEU; and second, that Article 7 TEU does not confer on said institutions the competence to develop this procedure further (The Council of the European Union 2014a).

The Council Legal Service thus reaches its conclusion by emphasizing that the Commission's role as 'guardian of the Treaties' does not include Article 2 TEU, notwithstanding the fact that said Article grants the Commission the right to submit a reasoned proposal to the Council.[7] In my view, it is not unreasonable to expect the Commission to design a procedure for the exercise of that very right[8]; however, the Council Legal Service does not concur. It is unfortunate that two Union institutions fail in such a flagrant way to cooperate on the issue. Indeed, I would argue, it is open to doubt whether the Council's actions here are consistent with the duty of the institutions to cooperate loyally (Article 3 TEU) (Oliver and Stefanelli 2016).

Why is it so difficult for the Council and the Commission to cooperate on this issue?[9] The explanation for this can be found in the tension between supranationalism and intergovernmentalism—between a low and a high degree of juridification. Two different legal logics are in play within Article 7 TEU, and they are impossible to reconcile fully. It is hardly surprising, in fact, that the Council represents the one logic, while the Commission advocates the other. The Council Legal Service wants to ensure that conflicts within a member state regarding protection of the rule of law are resolved through intergovernmental negotiation, not through negotiation between an individual member state and the supranational Commission. In its statement, the Legal Service outlines a possible mechanism for designing the dialogue with member states that do not respect the rule of law (The Council of the European Union 2014a: 7–8).

[7] For a similar view, see Kochenov and Pech (2015). These authors also point out that, already in 2003, the Commission had declared that the EU's institutions were required to monitor compliance with Union law. No objections were heard from the Council Legal Service at the time.

[8] For a concurring opinion, see Crabit and Bel (2016: 205).

[9] Cf. Schusterschitz (2016) for a similar, but distinctly different approach to the general problem.

In December 2014, the General Affairs Council decided to establish its own mechanism for safeguarding the rule of law. In a joint decision by the Council and the member states, it was agreed that an annual dialogue on the rule of law would be arranged (The Council of the European Union 2014b). It would be interesting to know what the Council Legal Service makes of this mechanism, in light of the principle of conferral. As of yet, however, it has issued no opinion on the subject.

Is the EU Doing Enough?

Many scholars have criticized the EU's institutions for not doing enough to counteract the backsliding on the rule of law which we have witnessed over the last decade (see, e.g., Sadurski 2010; Hillion 2016; Kochenov and Pech 2016; Closa and Kochenov 2016a; Jakab and Kochenov 2017). It would appear, however, that some of this criticism overlooks the fact that the situation has involved two different actors operating according to different legal logics, and with no coordination. The intergovernmental approach in this area is prone to be significantly less effective than the supranational approach, which ultimately ends in the Court. Most of the criticism assumes that the Commission's (supranational) approach constitutes the preferred way to deal with the conflict, and that the Council should simply execute what the Commission has proposed. This critique is seriously flawed. It neglects the fact that Article 7 of the EU Treaty leans strongly towards an intergovernmental solution, as shown above. It should therefore be stressed that the Commission's transparent supranational approach, in combination with the intergovernmental logic of Article 7 TEU, is likely to have made the Council's decision under Article 7 TEU more difficult than it might have been. The Council has been criticized for not acting, and rightly so; but in view of how the member states designed the Treaty, there is not even an obligation for the Council actually to determine that there is a 'clear risk of a serious breach by a member state'. The criticism recalls that directed at the UN Security Council when one of the five permanent member states vetoes a proposal. It is, of course, anyone's prerogative to criticize the design of the Treaty, but to criticize the Council for acting according to a traditional intergovernmental logic when dealing with a reasoned proposal under Article 7 TEU is not entirely fair. The Council did not design Article 7 TEU.

An unfortunate effect of this kind of criticism is that the divide between the Commission and the Council grows deeper. Whether or not this furthers the rule of law remains to be seen. The member states are not likely to revise Article 7 TEU, and that means the decision on respect for the values in Article 2 TEU will remain within the intergovernmental arena—that is, in the hands of the Council. One might think this a bad thing, and one could argue that the Union needs a more federal structure in order to handle this type of conflict better. But such criticism, no matter how sharp, does not change the wording of the Treaty. It may be wiser to focus our criticism on the failure of the Council and the Commission to appreciate that they must cooperate loyally on the issue.

2015—The Year the Reform of the Courts Began in Poland

The Commission's reasoned proposal, which it sent to the Council on 20 December 2017 (European Commission 2017b), is based on three previous recommendations to the Polish government (European Commission 2016b, 2016c, 2017a). The three recommendations review the Commission's dialogue with Poland and justify the measures it proposed. They provide, along with the 'reasoned proposal', a clear picture of threats to the rule of law in Poland during the previous two years.

The introduction to the reasoned proposal spells out the basis for asserting the existence of a clear risk of Poland's seriously infringing the rule of law within the meaning of Article 7(1) TEU. For one thing, the country lacks an 'independent and legitimate constitutional review'; for another, the Polish legislature has significantly increased the systemic threat to the rule of law by adopting new legislation on the judiciary. The Commission mentions four specific pieces of legislation: the Supreme Court Act (15 December 2017), the General Court Organization Act (28 July 2017), the National Court of Justice Act (15 December 2017), and the National Judicial School Act (13 June 2017) (European Commission 2017b: 2). In short, the Commission considers that the Polish government has severely reduced the independence of the judiciary in general, by taking control of how judges are trained, appointed, supervised, and organized; and of the Constitutional Court in particular, by dismantling its powers of constitutional legal review. In the course of two years, the judiciary has been fundamentally reformed.

The Polish government does not deny it has reformed the country's judiciary. It claims, however, that the changes represent a necessary lustration of the judiciary, because the judges it has now replaced all share a long past as officials at the time when Poland was a communist state and judges were politically appointed.

Let us now look in more detail at the events which led, on 20 December 2017, to the activation of Article 7 TEU for the first time ever. On 25 October 2015, elections were held to the Polish Sejm, the lower house of the Polish parliament. Prior to these elections, the outgoing Sejm had decided to nominate five new judges to the Constitutional Court, in order to fill chairs left empty by retiring judges. According to the Polish constitution, judges are appointed by the president—a decision which, however, is usually considered a formality. When the election results were in, it was clear that PiS (Prawo in Sprawiedliwość, 'Law and Justice') would receive a majority of the seats in the Sejm. On 19 November, PiS introduced a change to the Constitutional Court Act, allowing the five appointments to be cancelled and five new judges to be nominated. Two cases were filed against this change. Shortly thereafter, on 3/12 and 9/12, the Constitutional Court issued two judgments, to the effect that the outgoing Sejm had not had a mandate to nominate five judges (but instead only three), and that the newly elected Sejm had not been mandated to cancel the five nominations. Prior to the Constitutional Court's judgment, however, the president of Poland had appointed the five new judges.

These actions on the part of the Polish government exemplify the type of conduct which led the Commission, on 13 January 2016, to initiate the process in the EU framework for protecting the rule of law. The decision gave Commission Vice-President Frans Timmermans the mandate to begin a dialogue with the Polish government. The content of the talks that were conducted have not been made available to the public, but the Commission has published the main positions it took and how they were received by the Polish government (European Commission 2017a). Timmermans visited Warsaw on two occasions, and met both with ministers and with judges at the Constitutional Court. He also received the deputy prime minister of Poland in Brussels. In addition, a number of meetings were held between representatives of the Polish government and the Commission.

After almost six months of investigation and dialogue with the Polish authorities, the Commission decided to send a 'rule of law opinion' to the Polish government. It did so on 1 June 2016 (European Commission 2016a). An opinion of this kind is the result of an assessment by the Commission (step 1 of the EU framework). The opinion requested that

Poland respond to the circumstances which the Commission considered to threaten the rule of law. In a letter dated 24 June 2016, the Polish government confirmed having read the opinion. In the same letter, the said government announced to the Commission that it would adopt an amendment to the Constitutional Court Act, and that this amendment would enter into force after approval by the president on 30/7.

Poland's response to the Commission's 'rule of law opinion' likely did not fill Timmermans with joy, and the legislative amendments passed in July probably made his mood worse still. On 27 July, the Commission published a recommendation on the rule of law in Poland (European Commission 2016b). A recommendation of this kind constitutes step 2 in the EU framework, and it is only taken if the opinion in step 1 has not produced the intended effect. The recommendation proposed that the Polish government take five concrete measures, all of which had to do with the Constitutional Court (European Commission 2017b: para. 74).

The Commission gave the Polish government three months to 'solve the problems identified in this recommendation' (European Commission 2017b: para. 76). Three months to the day after the Commission published its recommendation, the Polish government replied that it disagreed with the Commission on all of the items reported, and that it did not intend to take any of the measures proposed.

In the autumn of 2016, the Polish government continued with its lustration process. In particular, the laws on the organization of the Constitutional Court were subject to changes. On 19 December, the Polish president appointed Julia Przyłębska, a judge appointed by the newly elected Sejm, as acting president of the Constitutional Court. Her first action was to allow the three judges who had been appointed in breach of the December 2015 Constitutional Court ruling to take up their posts. She then called on all the judges to vote in the election of a new president of the Court. Of the 15 called to do so, six—the three judges which the Commission considered to be unlawfully appointed, together with three judges that the new Sejm installed—cast their vote. Two candidates were then brought forward: Julia Przyłębska and Mariusz Muszyński. The next day, the Polish president appointed Julia Przyłębska president of the Constitutional Court (European Commission 2016c: paras. 24–26 of the preamble; 2017a: paras. 6–9).

On the same day, 21 December 2016, the Commission adopted a second recommendation on the rule of law in Poland (European Commission 2016c). This recommendation repeated its call for measures from the previous recommendation, which Poland still had not taken, as well as adding its criticism of measures taken during the autumn—of which the procedure for appointing a new president of the Constitutional Court was particularly emphasized. In this recommendation, the Commission gave Poland two months to take action.

On 20 February, the Polish government responded. In addition to contradicting the Commission's assessments, the reply contained an interesting explanation for the appointment of new judges. According to the Polish government, the legislative changes it had made were necessary in order to enable the Constitutional Court to start functioning again, having been paralysed by political strife (in which the former president of the Court had been involved). Prior to this, moreover—on 20 January—a major reform of the country's judiciary had been announced, to be implemented in 2017 (European Commission 2017a: paras. 8 and 13 of the preamble).

The reform did not take long to carry out. A number of changes in the composition of the courts were adopted and implemented in the spring. Among other things, the vice-president of the Constitutional Court was replaced as well, by Mariusz Muszyński (one of the judges whom the Commission and the previous Constitutional Court considered to be unlawfully appointed). Thus, on 26 July, the Commission adopted a third recommendation on the rule of law (European Commission 2017a). In this recommendation, the Commission stated that it considered the threat to the rule of law to have been significantly aggravated since its second recommendation. This time, the Commission gave Poland a month to take action in line with its proposals. Furthermore, the Commission expressly threatened in this recommendation, for the first time, to activate Article 7 TEU if the Polish government did not take appropriate action. In particular, the Commission demanded that the Polish authorities refrain from any efforts to force Supreme Court judges to retire.

As we already know, however, the threat was of little help. Thus on 20 December 2017, the Commission submitted a reasoned proposal to the Council for a decision under Article 7(1) TEU (European Commission 2017b). Consisting of just over 40 pages, the reasoned proposal is a very thorough report. It contains a meticulous review of a large number of events, over the preceding two years, due to which the threat to the rule of law in Poland went from being alarming to posing a clear risk that Poland was seriously breaching the rule of law.[10]

According to Article 7(1) TEU, if the EP consents, the Council may determine by a majority of four-fifths of its members that there is a clear risk of a member state's seriously infringing the rule of law. In a resolution dated 1 March 2018, the EP welcomed the Commission's decision to activate Article 7(1) TEU (European Parliament 2018a). The same resolution calls on the Council to act swiftly on the issue. In December 2019, the Council has not yet taken a decision. What could possibly be the reason for this long wait?

Advantages and Disadvantages of Supranational Legal Dialogue for Safeguarding the Rule of Law Under the EU Treaties

The Council has not yet taken a position on the issue of whether there is a clear risk of Poland's seriously violating the rule of law. The dialogue that has been conducted has not left any concrete imprint at all. When discussing this further, we should bear a couple of points in mind. First, Article 7(1) TEU states that, on a proposal from the Commission, the EP, or one-third of the member states, the Council may 'determine' a clear risk. Second, the Treaty states that this requires a four-fifths majority. The Treaty does not explain what the rule of law is; the explanation for that must be sought from other sources. The procedure laid down in the Treaty is strongly influenced by an intergovernmental logic, where all of the member states are in fact in the same boat as the culprit (in this case Poland).

There is a significant difference here from the default procedure specified in Article 258 TFEU for a member state which fails to fulfil an obligation. Although the Commission is in a position to challenge the offence in both cases, the other member states do not decide under Article 258 TFEU whether or not the member state concerned has infringed the Treaty. That decision is taken instead by an independent third party—the

[10] Kochenov and Pech (2016: 1071) argue that, quite a long time before the Commission submitted its reasoned proposal, the Polish government had actually violated the rule of law systematically and on several occasions. In their view, therefore, the Commission ought to have activated Article 7(2) TEU instead. They emphasize, moreover, that the Commission can in no way be said to have exaggerated the situation.

CJEU—whose only function is to interpret and apply the rules of the Treaty.

Article 7 TEU and Article 258 TFEU provide two very different paths to determining whether a member state has breached its obligations under the Treaties. If we are to understand (and perhaps also to reformulate) the criticism of the Council's inaction, we must bear this critical difference in mind. Both articles form part of the Treaties, and thus both are part of international law. However, they operate according to very different logics.[11]

International law has many different tools for resolving conflicts. Several of these lack third-party involvement. This means they are often deemed 'politicized', which is hardly surprising, as that is a commonly drawn (and somewhat flawed) conclusion regarding most legal instruments that place the sanctioning decision with a collective that does not isolate the potential target of the sanction.[12] The famous injunction in the Bible—'Let he who is without sin cast the first stone!'—bears recalling here, as does the impact on future cooperation between the one casting the stone and the others.

Furthermore, in the context of Article 7 TEU, all of the states involved already seem persuaded that an investigation under Article 7(2) TEU is pointless, inasmuch as the Hungarian prime minister, Viktor Orbán, has stated that he will not assent to such a proposal. Thus, there is even less incentive to determine whether there is a clear risk of a serious breach under Article 7(1) TEU. If instead we had an independent third party, with a prosecutor function and a court, the issue would most likely already have been settled. The matter would have come to trial, and we would already have gotten an answer (within a reasonable space of time).

Back in 2014, when the Commission decided—in response to criticism of the ineffectiveness of Article 7 TEU—to adopt the EU framework (and with it the procedure that could lead to the activation of Article 7 TEU) the tension between intergovernmentalism and supranationalism that was already inherent in the article was reinforced. The EU framework furnished

[11] Cf. Closa and Kochenov (2016b: 188). Closa and Kochenov describe the difference as 'judicial versus political procedures'. In my view, labelling the Article 7 procedure as 'political' is unfortunate, since it draws on the classical assumption of positivist legal theory that a distinct line can be drawn between law and politics. Having said that, I fully agree with the essence of what Closa and Kochenov argue in the cited section.

[12] The representative of the member state in question does not take part in the vote, Article 354 TFEU.

the Commission with a useful definition of the rule of law, as well as with a much more transparent procedure than that set out in the Treaty. Furthermore, the Commission took on the role of prosecutor under Article 7 TEU, by almost copying its own way of working with infringement proceedings. Thus, the whole process diverged several steps away from the intergovernmental procedure set out in Article 7 TEU, towards a substantially more supranational procedure. Yet, all the while these significant changes were being made, one thing remained the same: the decision rested with the Council.

The transparency engendered by the Commission's framework—and especially the name-and-shame opportunities it has afforded—has made for a very effective demonstration that the Polish government is violating the rule of law. However, for the Council, this only makes the situation more difficult since it significantly impairs a negotiated, diplomatic, solution to the situation.

Once Again, the Commission Turns to the CJEU

On 2 July 2018, following further reforms of the Polish judiciary, the Commission initiated a procedure potentially leading to an action against Poland under Article 258 TFEU. This time the Polish government intended to reduce the retirement age for judges. The proposed law was meant to have retroactive effect, meaning it would also apply to judges already in office, whereby a 'significant number' of the judges on the Supreme Court risked being forced to retire (European Commission 2017b). On 14 August, the Commission sent a reasoned opinion to Poland, giving its government one month to prevent the law from taking effect.

Importantly, the Commission did not claim the law meant that Poland was in breach of Article 2 TEU; rather, it averred, Poland was failing to respect its obligations under Article 19(1) TEU and Article 47 of the Charter of Fundamental Rights of the European Union. As Poland failed to convince the Commission of the converse, the latter body, on 2 October 2018, brought a suit against Poland at the CJEU.

Interestingly, it took no more than 17 days for the action against Poland to bear fruit. At the same time the Commission filed the lawsuit, it also petitioned the Court to take interim measures against Poland. The Commission requested that the CJEU order Poland to suspend the implementation of the law lowering the retirement age of the Supreme Court judges. The Court upheld the four measures proposed by the Commission on 19 October, whereupon the Polish government confirmed that it intended to comply with the Court's decision (Court of Justice of the European Union 2018d).

The decision taken by the vice-president of the Court, Rosario Silva de Lapuerta, came as quite a surprise. The reasons for it were many, but above all it should be recalled that decisions on interim measures are unusual in EU law. In most cases, they are used to postpone the enforcement of Union acts under constitutional review, thereby targeting the EU's own institutions. In this case, however, the decision was directed at a member state, which is always a much more sensitive matter from a political point of view. It should also be noted that the decision was taken without Poland's having been given a chance to respond to the Commission's claims.[13]

It is possible the Commission felt that the Court's recent case law clearly indicated that questioning of the 'rule of law' by member states cannot be tolerated. There are several cases where this line of argument has appeared, two of which concern Poland and one of which concerns Portugal.[14] Commenting on the decision, the president of the Court, Koen Lenaerts, clearly stated that a member state which does not respect a decision of the CJEU places itself outside the legal order of the Union. It seems the Commission has a more attentive audience on the supranational Court than in the intergovernmental Council.

The Commission Should Choose Its Battles and Cooperate Better with Its Allies

The Commission has thus chosen to act against Poland's dismantling of the rule of law, using both Article 7 TEU and Article 258 TFEU. As mentioned earlier, these alternatives operate according to different logics. It would be advisable for the Commission to reduce its presence in the highly politicized intergovernmental arena of Article 7 TEU, and to increase its use of the more supranational instruments at its disposal, of which Article 258 TFEU is the main one. The CJEU's ruling on the case also supports this view (Court of Justice of the European Union 2019). On 24 June, the

[13] Cf. Article 160 (7) of the Rules of Procedure of the Court.

[14] See, for example, Court of Justice of the European Union *Associação Sindical dos Juízes Portugueses* v. *Tribunal de Contas* (2018a), *European Commission* v. *Republic of Poland* (2018b), *LM* (2018c).

Court ruled that the Polish government had failed to fulfil the obligation set out in Article 19(1) TEU, due to its having ordered that the lowered retirement age be applied to judges in office, as well as its having granted the president of the Republic the power to extend the mandates of individual judges beyond the fixed retirement age.

In light of the findings and arguments presented in this chapter, the Commission would be well-advised to leave the EU framework behind, in favour of the traditional mechanisms for addressing a member state's failure to fulfil its obligations, as set out in Article 258 TFEU. It is unfortunate that the Commission did not opt to use the extremely well-prepared material gathered from two years of investigation and dialogue, which had resulted in four recommendations on the rule of law and a reasoned proposal, to include Poland's violation of Article 2 TEU as separate grounds in the case as well. The Commission shares the view of the Council that Article 2 TEU falls outside the scope of Article 258 TFEU,[15] but it is clear from the EU Treaty (Article 344 TFEU) that the only institution that can decide that particular issue on an authoritative basis is the Court. Had this matter too been included in the Commission's infringement case, the question would have elicited a definite answer.

This does not mean, it bears emphasizing, that the Council should refrain from acting under Article 7 TEU. When member states, whether individually or on a coordinated basis, challenge the jointly agreed-upon fundamental values of the Union, this needs to be addressed by all of the EU's institutions in all of their respective capacities. Since the Council handles these problems through dialogue and intergovernmental negotiation, any criticism of the Commission's more supranational actions can be balanced out. If each institution focuses on the role assigned to it (by the member states) in the Treaties, this will serve to reinforce the legitimacy of the actions undertaken by the institutions overall. This in turn will enhance the effectiveness of the EU's efforts.

In conclusion, the first case in which the Commission's new EU framework has been used has shown that the procedure set out in Article 7 TEU has been significantly juridified, thereby pushing the process in a supranational direction. The Commission's framework thus complicates the Council's work on taking an intergovernmental decision under Article 7 TEU. In light of these experiences, it would be wise of the Commission and the Council to cooperate better on issues relating to the protection of

[15] This view is also supported by Schroeder (2016: 28).

the Union's fundamental values.[16] Complicating the issue further, a reasoned proposal from the EP under Article 7(1) TEU against Hungary (European Parliament 2018b) is also pending, and more cases may be initiated in the near future. This means that, within the next few years, the Council will have to assess in more and more cases whether member states are violating the fundamental values set out in Article 2 TEU. In view of the fact that the Council seems unable to decide in these cases, and since increased transparency (through juridified procedures in both the Commission and the EP) is likely to make the Council's efforts at intergovernmental negotiation more difficult, it would be unfortunate if the Commission continued to choose the intergovernmental Article 7 TEU over the supranational Article 258 TFEU.

References

Cambien, N. (2017). Mutual Recognition and Mutual Trust in the Internal Market. *European Papers, 2*(1), 93–115.

Closa, C., & Kochenov, D. (Eds.). (2016a). *Reinforcing Rule of Law Oversight in the European Union*. Cambridge: Cambridge University Press.

Closa, C., & Kochenov, D. (2016b). Reinforcement of the Rule of Law Oversight in the European Union: Key Options. In W. Schroeder (Ed.), *Strengthening the Rule of Law in Europe: From a Common Concept to Mechanisms of Implementation* (pp. 173–196). Oxford: Hart Publishing.

Court of Justice of the European Union. (1963). NV Algemene Transport- en Expeditie Onderneming van Gend & Loos v Netherlands Inland Revenue Administration, C-26/62. ECLI:EU:C:1963:1.

Court of Justice of the European Union. (1964). *Flamino Costa v. E.N.E.L*, C-6/64. ECLI:EU:C:1964:66.

Court of Justice of the European Union. (2018a). *Associação Sindical dos Juízes Portugueses* v *Tribunal de Contas*, C-64/16. ECLI:EU:C:2018:117.

Court of Justice of the European Union. (2018b). *European Commission* v. *Republic of Poland*, C-441/17. ECLI:EU:C:2018:255.

Court of Justice of the European Union. (2018c). *LM*, C-216/18 PPU. ECLI:EU:C:2018:586.

Court of Justice of the European Union. (2018d). *Commission* v. *Poland*, C-619/18 R. ECLI:EU:C:2018:1021.

Court of Justice of the European Union. (2019). *European Commission* v. *Republic of Poland*, C-619/18. ECLI:EU:C:2019:531.

[16] This is also the Commission's new approach, although it has been expressed in a slightly less self-aware way. See European Commission (2019).

Crabit, E., & Bel, N. (2016). The EU Rule of Law Framework. In W. Schroeder (Ed.), *Strengthening the Rule of Law in Europe: From a Common Concept to Mechanisms of Implementation* (pp. 197–206). Oxford: Hart Publishing.

Cramér, P. (2009). Reflections on the Roles of Mutual Trust in EU Law. In M. Dougan & S. Currie (Eds.), *50 Years of the European Treaties: Looking Back and Thinking Forward* (pp. 43–62). Oxford: Hart Publishing.

European Commission. (2014). Communication from the Commission to the European Parliament and the Council. *A new EU Framework to strengthen the Rule of Law*, COM (2014) 158 final, 19 March 2014.

European Commission. (2016a, June 1). Commission adopts Rule of Law Opinion on the situation in Poland. Press Release MEMO/16/2017. Retrieved September 2, 2019, from https://europa.eu/rapid/press-release_IP-16-2015_en.htm.

European Commission. (2016b). Commission Recommendation (EU) 2016/1374 of 27 July 2016 regarding the rule of law in Poland, OJ L 217/53, 12/08/2016.

European Commission. (2016c). Commission Recommendation (EU) 2017/146 of 21 December 2016 regarding the rule of law in Poland complementary to Recommendation (EU) 2016/1374. OJ L 22/65, 21/01/2017.

European Commission. (2017a). Commission Recommendation (EU) 2017/1520 of 26 July 2017 regarding the rule of law in Poland complementary to Recommendations (EU) 2016/1374 and (EU) 2017/146.

European Commission. (2017b). Reasoned Proposal in Accordance with Article 7(1) of the Treaty on European Union Regarding the Rule of Law in Poland, 20 December 2017. COM (2017) 835 final.

European Commission. (2019). Communication from the Commission to the European Parliament, The European Council, The Council, The European Economic and Social Committee and the Committee of the Regions, *Strengthening the rule of law within the Union A blueprint for action*, 17 July 2019. COM (2019) 343 final.

European Parliament. (2018a). Resolution of 1 March 2018 on the Commission's decision to activate Article 7(1) TEU as regards the situation in Poland (2018/2541(RSP).

European Parliament. (2018b). Resolution of 12 September 2018 on a Proposal Calling on the Council to Determine, Pursuant to Article 7(1) of the Treaty on European Union, the Existence of a Clear Risk of a Serious Breach by Hungary of the Values on Which the Union Is Founded (2017/2131(INL)), P8_TA(2018)0340.

Hillion, C. (2016). Overseeing the Rule of Law in the European Union, *European Policy Analysis*. Stockholm: Sieps 2016:1epa.

Jakab, A., & Kochenov, D. (Eds.). (2017). *The Enforcement of EU Law and Values: Ensuring Member States' Compliance*. Oxford: University Press.

Kochenov, D., & Pech, L. (2015). Monitoring and Enforcement of the Rule of Law in the EU: Rhetoric and Reality. *European Constitutional Law Review, 11*(3), 512–540.

Kochenov, D., & Pech, L. (2016). Better Late than Never? On the European Commission's Rule of Law Framework and Its First Activation. *JCMS: Journal of Common Market Studies, 54*(5), 1062–1074.

Oliver, P., & Stefanelli, J. (2016). Strengthening the Rule of Law in the EU: The Council's Inaction. *JCMS: Journal of Common Market Studies, 54*(5), 1075–1084.

Sadurski, W. (2010). Adding Bite to a Bark: The Story of Article 7, EU Enlargement, and Jörg Haider. *Columbia Journal of European Law, 16*(3), 385.

Schroeder, W. (2016). The European Union and the Rule of Law – State of Affairs and Ways of Strengthening. In W. Schroeder (Ed.), *Strengthening the Rule of Law in Europe* (pp. 3–27). Oxford: Hart Publishing.

Schusterschitz, G. (2016). The EU and the Rule of Law – The Unavoidable Question of: Who Controls It? In W. Schroeder (Ed.), *Strengthening the Rule of Law in Europe* (pp. 243–255). Oxford: Hart Publishing.

Teubner, G. (1998). Juridification: Concepts, Aspects, Limits, Solutions. In R. Baldwin, C. Scott, & C. Hood (Eds.), *A Reader on Regulation* (pp. 389–440). New York: Oxford University Press.

The Council of the European Union. (2014a). *Opinion of the Legal Service of the Council 10296/14, 27 May 2014.*

The Council of the European Union. (2014b). *Note from the General Secretariat of the Council to Delegations, 17014/14, 16 December 2014.*

Weber, M. (1978). *Economy and Society.* Berkeley: University of California Press.

Wennerström, E. O. (2019). Can the EU Protect Its Fundamental Values? In A. Bakardjieva Engelbrekt, N. Bremberg, A. Michalski, & L. Oxelheim (Eds.), *The European Union in a Changing World Order* (pp. 245–272). Basingstoke: Palgrave Macmillan.

CHAPTER 4

The Refugee Crisis and the Reinvigoration of the Nation-State: Does the European Union Have a Common Asylum Policy?

Magnus Henrekson, Özge Öner, and Tino Sanandaji

Magnus Henrekson and Özge Öner gratefully acknowledge financial support from Jan Wallanders och Tom Hedelius stiftelse.

M. Henrekson (✉)
Research Institute of Industrial Economics, Stockholm, Sweden
e-mail: magnus.henrekson@ifn.se

Ö. Öner
Research Institute of Industrial Economics, Stockholm, Sweden

Department of Land Economy, University of Cambridge, Cambridge, UK
e-mail: oo263@cam.ac.uk

T. Sanandaji
Institute for Economic and Business History Research, Stockholm School of Economics, Stockholm, Sweden
e-mail: Tino.Sanandaji@hhs.se

A. Bakardjieva Engelbrekt et al. (eds.), *The European Union and the Return of the Nation State*,
https://doi.org/10.1007/978-3-030-35005-5_4

Introduction

One of the fundamental debates in the European Union (EU) concerns the appropriate degree of federalism for the Union, and the ensuing question which policies should be conducted at the EU or the national level for the 28 member states. A core component of the EU project is the free movement of workers and students across member states. This freedom is supported by a majority in all member countries (European Commission 2018a). By contrast, a far more contentious issue is the ambition of the EU to lay down and enforce a common asylum policy. The representatives of the EU as well as the member states officially claim that the Union does have a common asylum policy. However, existing agreements give considerable room for maneuver to the individual member states. This discretion enables them to individually regulate the intake of refugees and still comply with international agreements.

In this context, it is important to clearly distinguish between different types of migration. The factors that determine migration from within Europe and high-skilled migration from non-EU countries differ from factors determining migration by refugees and asylum seekers. In this chapter, we focus on refugees and asylum seekers from outside of Europe. The refugee crisis in the fall of 2015 revealed an inherent weakness of the EU as a federal project, while at the same time reemphasizing the continued dominance of sovereign European nation-states. The crisis also showed the ineffectiveness of a common migration policy for all EU member countries coordinated from Brussels, as the EU failed to deal with the sharply increased flow of asylum seekers. Instead, several individual member states began to introduce border controls by referring to the possibility of exemption from the Schengen Agreement if countries experience a serious threat to public order and internal security. The member states are given considerable scope to decide whether this is the case, and thus whether an exemption may be renewed. Not least Sweden, the country that has received the largest number of refugees per capita, has made use of this opportunity. Border control to other Schengen countries was introduced in November 2015, and following several extensions such control was still effective in August 2019.

This chapter shows that the cross-country differences in the reception of refugees are so large and systematic that it is not meaningful to speak of a common EU asylum policy. The asylum policy is governed by a number of policy tools and since the extent to which countries coordinate their asylum policies at the EU level is largely voluntary, it is mainly determined by domestic politics. When there are large refugee flows and tensions between members, the tendency to stick to a domestic political agenda is amplified. Even though there is a *de jure* asylum system equally applicable to all EU countries, we argue that no such system exists in practice. Nation-states continue to control border enforcement, asylum application agencies, and welfare state policies that determine the degree of generosity toward refugee migrants, which means that the *de facto* commitments of EU member countries based on existing agreements are largely symbolic. After having shown that the EU lacks a common asylum policy, we discuss whether policies pertaining to refugees are most appropriately determined at the national level, or whether the role of the EU ought to be strengthened.

In the following section, we make a brief presentation of the core principles underlying EU cooperation with respect to migration. In Section "Public Opinion and Euroscepticism", we discuss the public opinion vis-à-vis asylum policy and the skepticism against the EU project more generally that has been fueled by the recent refugee crisis. In Section "EU Asylum Law", we present the international agreements pertaining to the treatment of refugees as well as the specific EU asylum legislation. This is followed by Section "Worlds Apart: Variation in Refugee Flows in the EU", which deals with governance problems that arise as a result of the fact that responsibilities for decisions and integration measures involve multiple actors on different interconnected levels. In Section "Striking a Balance Between Asylum Policy at the National and EU Levels", we analyze the large cross-member differences with respect to refugee intake and labor market integration. This is followed by a section where we discuss the conflict between the federal and the national governance level and the risks for the EU project at large if the EU forces its member countries to harmonize their respective refugee policies to an extent that lacks public support. In the concluding section we offer our policy recommendations on how the EU can identify the optimal level of federalism versus nation-state sovereignty in immigration policy.

A Common EU Asylum Policy in Theory and Practice

Although there is no formal definition of the EU as a federal state, the Union has gradually developed some basic federal features (Kelemen 2007). The EU has been endowed with supranational power in several policy areas, notably with respect to the monetary union and its 19 member states (see Andersson in this volume). The purview of the Union's power is increasingly extending into the core of traditional national responsibilities—such as internal security, notably through visa rules and immigration. The most important aspect that differentiates the EU from federal states—such as the United States, Belgium, and Australia—is the fact that the Union does not have the power of enforcement by its own police, security, and defense forces. Such power belongs to the individual member states, and the Union relies on its member states to enforce the regulations and policies made at the Union level. In this respect, the EU is much more decentralized than a typical federal state.

Free movement of labor and capital is an essential component of the foundation of the EU. The emphasis on free movement is linked to the ideal to create a European identity and integrate the European nations. One important development in order to create an EU with open borders between the member states is the Schengen Agreement. The agreement was signed in 1985 by five of the then ten member states (France, West Germany, the Netherlands, Belgium, and Luxembourg). The agreement entailed the complete elimination of internal border controls between the signatories and the establishment of a common visa policy. The fact that only five countries initially signed the agreement also meant that the borders of the Schengen Area have undergone a sizable expansion as the number of member states increased. At the beginning of 2019 the Schengen Area consisted of 26 European countries: all EU countries except the United Kingdom, Ireland, Cyprus, Bulgaria, Romania, and Croatia, plus Norway, Iceland, Switzerland, and Liechtenstein. In total it encompasses a population of over 400 million people and an area of 4.3 million square kilometers.

However, the enlargement of the EU through the addition of eleven former Eastern Bloc countries resulted in sharply increased differences in average incomes as well as in the overall quality of institutions of the member states (Elert et al. 2017, 2019; Dilli et al. 2018). In the absence of borders and strict rules concerning immigration across the member states, these large cross-member differences induced large-scale labor migration from poorer to richer EU countries.

Terms such as refugees, migrants, and asylum seekers are sometimes used interchangeably, but it is useful to be clear about the distinctions in order to avoid confusion. Not all asylum seekers will be granted asylum, and some choose to withdraw their application. At the same time, many immigrants do not obtain legal residence permit as asylum seekers, but instead through family reunification, labor migration or as students. It is also not unusual for asylum seekers, who are denied asylum, to become immigrants through these channels—notably as labor migrants or as students. Additionally, some asylum seekers, who are initially denied asylum, eventually obtain asylum after appealing in court or after filing a new application. Even for those who are granted asylum as refugees, there is usually a lag of one to two years from the point of applying for asylum until the person becomes registered as an immigrant.

The Schengen Agreement lays down common rules regarding the treatment of asylum seekers. After the acute refugee crisis in the fall of 2015, the public discourse shifted in many European countries—international solidarity was downplayed, while issues of national identity were given increased weight. This tendency was strengthened when the EU failed to agree on and implement efficient measures to deal with the crisis. The Schengen Agreement allows individual members to reinstate internal border controls in case of an emergent 'public policy or national security' reason. If the emergency continues, the controls can be extended. These exceptions are intended to be temporary and exceptional, but this possibility has been used broadly by several countries which have continually renewed and extended the internal border controls. In August 2019, six Schengen countries still had such controls in force.[1]

Public Opinion and Euroscepticism

The political importance of migration policy has grown both at the European level and at the level of individual member states. At least to some extent, this is also true for the issue of free cross-country mobility within the Union. Surveys indicate that voters overall see both a role for the EU and for individual member states in migration policy. In the spring 2018 Eurobarometer, 68 percent of Europeans supported a common European policy on migration. Regarding irregular migration, for example, during a refugee crisis, 38 percent of respondents reported that additional measures should be taken 'preferably at an EU level', and an additional 23 percent reported that additional measures should be at both EU and member state levels (European Commission 2018b). However, the nation-state is seen as having the superior role by most respondents. A

[1] Norway, Sweden, Denmark, Germany, Austria, and France; see European Commission (2019a).

2017 Pew Survey showed that the majority of citizens in all surveyed European countries (nine countries were included in the study) believed that national government rather than the EU should make decisions about migration. The median share of respondents who said that decisions regarding the migration of non-EU citizens should be made in Brussels was 23 percent, while 74 percent said such decisions should be taken by the respective national governments (Stokes et al. 2017).

While the gradually increasing federalization of the EU has been a voluntary process, strong Eurosceptic sentiments have recently arisen among many member states, particularly related to the migration crisis. Although Eurosceptic views came under the spotlight following the Brexit referendum, its historical roots are much older. This critique is found both on the left and the right side of the political spectrum in virtually all member states.

The ultimate example of EU skepticism is the British decision to leave the Union following a referendum in 2016. But the United Kingdom is not alone. According to the Eurobarometer, the share of respondents who express trust in the EU and its institutions has declined strongly since its peak of 57 percent in 2007, and while recovering somewhat in recent years this share has since then remained below 50 percent (European Commission 2018a). Country differences are large: trust is greatest in Lithuania, Portugal, and Denmark and lowest in Greece, the United Kingdom, and France. Issues the EU is most criticized for include the Common Agricultural Policy, onerously regulated labor markets, and the deflationary bias of the European Central Bank. However, after 2015 these issues are eclipsed by the EU's management of the refugee inflow.

Sweden is an extreme case by having accepted more refugees per capita than any other EU country. However, there is no strong political force pushing for a Swedish exit from the EU. While demands for a more restrictive immigration policy have grown considerably, support for the Union has also increased. Despite the failure of the common EU migration policy, people in Sweden seem able to appreciate the fact that the economic integration achieved through EU membership impacts positively on growth and job creation and thus on the potential for successful integration of immigrants. This view is confirmed by results from SVT's (the Swedish public service television company) poll of 12,000 voters on election day (September 9, 2018), where numerous questions were asked (SVT 2018). Regarding the proposal to 'accept fewer refugees into Sweden', 26 percent said that this was a bad proposal, 52 percent that it was a good proposal, while the remaining 22 percent expressed no opinion. Thus, two-thirds of those who expressed an opinion wanted Sweden to accept fewer refugees. At the same time, 69 percent said that it was a bad idea for Sweden to leave the EU, and in contrast a mere 15 percent thought it was a good idea. It is obvious that there is strong support in the Swedish electorate for continued EU membership while at the same time many voters favor a more restrictive asylum policy.

Immigration is by far the issue that is most contentious and thus has the greatest centrifugal potential. According to a press release by the European Commission that summarizes the findings of the spring 2018 Standard Eurobarometer, European citizens consider immigration as the number one challenge for the EU to tackle, followed by terrorism (European Commission 2018a). While 65 percent express positive feelings toward migration of people from other EU member states, only 41 percent express positive feelings toward immigration from outside the EU. It should moreover be noted that this question on sentiments toward migration is fairly general; it does not specifically address refugee migration.

An analogy can be made between the challenges of a common asylum policy and the problems of the eurozone. The discussion among economists about the euro has focused on the question whether Europe is an optimal currency area composed of regions symmetrically affected by external disturbances (Mundell 1961; Andersson in this volume). Many analysts maintain that the economic structure of the countries and regions that have a common currency is not sufficiently similar for this arrangement to be appropriate. The imposition of a common asylum policy may be even more inappropriate; not only economic differences but also differences in religion, culture, social norms, and levels of education speak against policy harmonization in this area.

More importantly, many of the problems that arise and need to be resolved by a country are pushed downward from the national to the regional and local/municipal level. These lower levels of governance often lack the economic resources and institutions required to successfully manage lengthy and complex integration processes. Nevertheless, one should not forget that the EU has achieved some results when it comes to the common migration policy, notably through the establishment of the European Border and Coast Guard Agency (Frontex) and reaching an agreement to guard the EU border with Turkey.

EU Asylum Law

In order to understand why there are such large differences in refugee flows across member states despite that these states are subject to the same (or a similar) legal framework, we will now summarize the legal roots of the Asylum Law in the EU and review the legal efforts made by the EU following the 2015 surge in refugee immigration.

The Geneva Convention from 1951 is the first international treaty regulating the right of asylum. The Convention broadly defines a refugee as someone who (Cherubini 2014: 9):

> As a result of events occurring before 1 January 1951 and owing to a well-founded fear of being persecuted for reasons of race, religion, nationality, membership of a particular social group or political opinion, is outside the country of his nationality and is unable, or owing to such fear, is unwilling to avail himself of the protection of that country; or who, not having a nationality and being outside the country of his former habitual residence as a result of such events, is unable or, owing to such fear, is unwilling to return to it.

This universal acknowledgment of an individual's status as a refugee does not mean that refugee status is conferred in practice; determining someone's refugee status, in theory, is not sufficient to determine the right of asylum. Countries receiving refugees have considerable leeway when it comes to the methods and criteria for determining refugee status, which in turn influences whether a person will be granted asylum (Cherubini 2014). Despite the extreme variation in refugee flows to the countries that recognize and abide by the Geneva Convention, this point is often ignored in the public discourse.

The legal criteria that need to be fulfilled for refugee status have changed considerably over the years. Since the Geneva Convention was instituted in response to the post-World War II population movements *within* Europe, it was designed to apply to the individuals affected by the events that took place prior to 1951, and only within Europe. However, the amendment to the Convention in the Protocol Relating to the Status of Refugees, ratified in 1967, removed these restrictions. This made the Convention applicable at a universal scale. Today only a few states still maintain the geographical restriction. Among these is Turkey, which gives them the right to pass asylum seekers and refugees on to other countries.[2]

The Refugee Convention's definition of a refugee can be broken down into several elements, which pertain to potential reasons for seeking asylum (Lenzerini 2009). Two key elements are a well-founded fear of persecution and being unable to (or unwilling to) return to the country of citizenship (or residence). Since *fear* is subjective, the definition of an individual requesting recognition as a refugee should follow the same subjective line of practice according to the UN refugee agency UNHCR. However, the argument has been made in the legal literature that the notion of 'well-founded' suggests that an objective measure, that is, a measure that does not make room for the alleged state of mind of the individual, should be used to determine the refugee status (Cherubini 2014: 13). Obviously, such an objective measure would be ideal, but unfortunately, there exists no unequivocal way of identifying a foolproof practice to arrive at such a measure. Nevertheless, decisions will be taken by national courts and agencies, but there will continue to be room for substantial variation in how the law is interpreted over time and across countries.

Despite that human rights violations are highly relevant when judging whether an individual should be granted refugee status, this does not mean that every human rights violation automatically suffices to grant that person refugee status. The breach needs to be sufficiently severe to be characterized as persecution (Lenzerini 2009: 247). The Refugee Convention broadly restricts the reasons that justify recognition of an individual as a refugee to the following five reasons: persecution because of (1) race, (2) religion, (3) nationality, (4) membership of a social group, or (5) political opinions.

As clearly defined as these reasons may seem, there is considerable room for debate whether an individual satisfies the requirements to be recognized as a refugee, or how these five reasons should be interpreted. For example, the Convention initially does not address persecution due to sexual orientation (Wessels 2011). However, 'membership in a social group' is sometimes interpreted to cover homosexuality when this is adduced by individuals coming from countries that criminalize homosexuality and/or have sodomy laws (McGhee 2001). However, there are still a

[2] Removing the geographical restriction has been imposed as one of the requirements on Turkey in its EU membership accession process (Edsbäcker 2011).

number of cases where an individual coming from countries where homosexuality is illegal is not granted refugee status. The reasoning is that even if the country may deem homosexuality illegal, the requirement remains that the person claiming to be persecuted because of his or her sexual orientation is able to prove a well-founded fear of this persecution.[3] Individual assessment, therefore, is important in deciding the refugee status and in many cases the claims are considered insufficient. Against this, UNHCR (2002) maintains that

> during a mass exodus such as occurred from Kosovo or Africa's Great Lakes, it may not be possible to carry out individual screening. In such circumstances, particularly when civilians are fleeing for similar reasons, it may be appropriate to declare 'group' determination of refugee status, whereby each civilian is considered as a refugee, prima facie—in other words, in the absence of evidence to the contrary.

The criteria applied by the EU legal framework for the recognition of an individual as a refugee adhere closely to the conditions stated under the Geneva Convention. Since 1999, the EU has been striving to create a Common European Asylum System (CEAS) and to improve the related legal framework. Between 1999 and 2005, several legislative measures harmonizing common minimum standards for awarding asylum were adopted. Moreover, the European Refugee Fund was established to facilitate the reception of asylum seekers and refugees, which was a means to pave the way for a common asylum policy and the creation of a federal asylum system.

In 2001, the EU adopted the directive on temporary protection in the event of a mass influx of displaced persons, the aim of which is to ascertain that all member countries harmonize their actions in such situations. The applicability of the EU Directive on the right to family reunification has also been extended to refugees. The current EU Qualification Directive of 2011 is intended to (European Commission 2018b):

- Clarify the grounds for granting and withdrawing international protection.
- Regulate exclusion and cessation grounds.

[3] One such example is *F. v. United Kingdom* 2004: 11.

- Improve the access of beneficiaries of international protection to rights and integration measures; better take into account the specific practical difficulties faced by beneficiaries of international protection.
- Ensure that the best interest of the child as well as gender-related aspects are taken into account in the assessment of asylum applications, as well as in the implementation of the rules on the content of international protection.

In order to further strengthen and harmonize CEAS rules, the Commission submitted a draft proposal for a new Qualification Regulation in July 2016 that covers three additional essential features (European Commission 2016; italics added):

- Ensuring that protection is granted *only for as long as the grounds for persecution or serious harm persist* without affecting the refugee's integration prospects.
- Addressing secondary movements of beneficiaries of international protection.
- Further harmonizing the rights of beneficiaries of international protection.

The EU's official site on Common European Asylum System (CEAS) states:

> Asylum must not be a lottery. EU Member States have a shared responsibility to welcome asylum seekers in a dignified manner, ensuring they are treated fairly and that their case is examined to uniform standards so that, no matter where an applicant applies, the outcome will be similar.[4]

The Dublin Regulation (European Parliament and the Council of the EU 2013) determines the EU member state responsible for examining an application for asylum seekers seeking international protection under the Geneva Convention and the EU Qualification Directive from 2011. The Dublin Regulation applies to all member countries except Denmark. In July 2017, the European Court of Justice declared that the Dublin Regulation still stands, giving EU member states the right to deport migrants to the first country of entry to the EU.

[4] See European Commission (2019b).

Although all member states ostensibly follow the Geneva Convention and the same EU directives for asylum migration, a shared responsibility and a unified legal treatment are far from the reality of the EU today. The legal wiggle room at the national level in identifying what constitutes a refugee, the capacity of countries to control their own borders, thereby making it more difficult for refugees to enter and apply for asylum, and national discretion regarding the economic incentives facing refugees implies that the asylum policy is *de facto* determined at the national level.

The Tensions Related to Multilevel Governance

Multilevel governance is a concept developed in the early 1990s in political science and public administration studies of European integration (Hooghe and Marks 2001). Many governance problems emanate from the fact that the mandate to command and control is both hierarchically structured and split up across different levels of aggregation: the federal (EU), national, regional, and municipal levels. However, decisions taken at the various levels often interact in complex ways that are not strictly hierarchical. Migration policy and how immigration and integration can be handled in a system of nation-states is an archetypical example. How the different levels and their respective competencies can best be coordinated has not been laid down at the EU level despite the fact that the EU is supposed to have a common migration policy. Instead, each member state is expected to resolve this complex issue in its own way. Because of this lack of strategy, the recent refugee crisis has given rise to formidable governance challenges in the member states.

An OECD report following the refugee crisis specifically addressed the challenges emanating from variation in multilevel governance across the member states (OECD 2018). After conducting surveys across different levels of government of the member states, they identify a great degree of variation in the way refugee placement and integration policies are implemented. Without going into detail country by country, we list here some of the major concerns related to the multilevel governance in the EU regarding the recent refugee crisis.

First, the OECD study reports that 80 percent of the 72 respondent cities all over Europe state that 'there is a lack of co-ordination between different levels of government regarding migrant integration'. Two-thirds of the respondents identify that this problem is particularly severe with respect to the asylum and refugee population. The overwhelming majority of the respondent cities argued that there exists a large information gap. The report puts forward 'institutional mapping' as a potential tool to clarify which governance level is responsible for which public service provision and has the power to implement integration policies. However, such unified mapping is not practicable as the power of local governments as well as their responsibilities regarding which public services they should provide differ greatly across member states.

Related to local governance of migrants and refugees, a number of objectives are identified in the report. These are (1) matching migrant skills with economic job opportunities, (2) securing access to adequate housing, (3) providing social welfare measures aligned with migrant inclusion, and (4) providing educational opportunities that counteract segregation and offer equitable paths to professional growth. The practical implementation of these objectives is far from unproblematic. At times, different objectives are in conflict with each other; this problem is particularly severe in some member states due to the massive and unprecedented scale of immigration. In this regard, Sweden can serve as a salient example of conflicting objectives concerning the matching of migrant skills with economic job opportunities and providing access to adequate housing. In Sweden, the problem is particularly severe as there is a strongly negative relationship between housing availability and job opportunities at both the local and regional level. Municipalities in economic decline have greater housing availability, but in these municipalities job opportunities are scarce, and unemployment is high. In practice, the national government has prioritized the provision of 'a roof over their head', while the objective of matching refugees to job opportunities has been largely disregarded. A significant share of the refugees has been placed in rural municipalities, and this tendency was intensified in the 2010s when the flow of asylum seekers increased sharply (Wennström and Öner 2018).

Toward the end of the 2010s, this is clearly a serious impediment to successful integration. This problem can be expected to grow in the medium term as a result of the high rate of asylums granted in the 2006–2017 period, which amounted to approximately 3 percent of total population in that period. The annual inflow of immigrants in the years to come is likely to remain at that level as a result of the immigration in the form of family reunification that will ensue (Swedish Migration Agency 2018).

Funding is another important matter related to multilevel governance. A sharp increase in the influx of migrants and asylum seekers financially overburdens the system of local service provision. The Swedish example shows that municipalities with greater economic problems tend to opt for accepting a greater number of refugees, either in the hope that they may recover these costs in the long run when the immigrants become self-reliant taxpayers, or thanks to the transfers they receive from the national government.

There is little evidence that those immigrants that were placed in municipalities with a declining native population, and who manage to become self-reliant, remain in that municipality. On the contrary, immigrants with good labor market prospects sort themselves into larger labor markets with better opportunities for finding a job (Faggian and Öner 2018). Looking at the EU as a whole, the short-run financial support municipalities get from the national government for receiving refugees varies substantially in duration and size across member states. An obvious alternative would be supranational funding provided by the EU to the member states that assume a disproportionate share of the burden. However, there is no empirical evidence suggesting that EU funds directly target migration-related activities at the municipal level (OECD 2018: 100).

Worlds Apart: Variation in Refugee Flows in the EU

The EU has harmonized many policy areas and has long been working toward a common European migration policy. In the political rhetoric, both the European Commission and many national governments often refer to what is described as a comprehensive migration policy common to all member states. While the EU plays an important role with respect to the Dublin Regulation and the external border control, asylum policy is mainly determined at the national level. The 28 EU member states differ greatly in terms of migration rates, immigrant outcomes, and asylum policy. These differences in part reflect varying rates of economic development between Southern, Eastern, and Northern Europe. However, there are also large differences when comparing wealthy member states. Some wealthy EU countries, such as Sweden and Germany, have accepted many refugees, whereas other wealthy EU countries, such as the United Kingdom and Ireland, have taken relatively few.

Eurostat, the statistical agency of the EU, compiles high-quality data on immigration in general and refugee migration in particular. Eurostat (2018) defines immigration as establishing one's chief residence in an EU member state for a period of at least 12 months. Net migration is defined as the difference between the number of immigrants (persons receiving asylum or residence permit) and the number of emigrants who leave the country. Eurostat collects and publishes data on asylum seekers for most of the EU since 1985 and provides comprehensive data for almost all member states since 1990. Eurostat also publishes data on the employment rates of migrants of varying backgrounds. Here we report statistics on non-European immigrants. It should be noted that this is not synonymous to asylum seekers, since many immigrants from outside Europe are not refugees. Nevertheless, the employment outcomes for non-European immigrants illustrate the point that there is great variation among EU countries in their ability to absorb non-European immigrants in the national labor market.

Typically, the share of approved asylum applications ranges from 30 to 60 percent, but the share varies substantially between countries and over time, and it also depends on which country the asylum seekers come from. During the 2010s, the share of granted asylums has been higher than in the past. This is partly explained by the fact that more asylum seekers were from Syria or unaccompanied minors. These categories were granted asylum to a higher degree.

The reasons for this variation are complex and driven by many factors. As expected, periods of conflict—such as the wars in the former Yugoslavia, Iraq, and Syria—give rise to greater flows of refugees to Europe. The member countries also differ with respect to pull factors that attract immigrants: geography, welfare rights, ease of being granted family reunification, the threshold for being granted status as a refugee, and the willingness to welcome refugees signaled by the country. This leads to stronger inflows of refugees to some countries and cross-country differences in the proportion of approved asylum applications.

Since all EU countries have signed international treaties that oblige them to grant refugees protection under certain conditions, a member state does not fully control the number of refugees it will have to take. The right of being granted refugee status only applies to those asylum seekers that make it into the territory of EU member states. In practice, EU member states regulate refugee inflows through border control that make it difficult for asylum seekers to enter any EU country in the first place (Sanandaji 2017). Thus, although the member states have signed similar international treaties, they may choose to interpret the letter and, even more importantly, the spirit of the law differently. Although international refugee treaties grant asylum seekers certain rights, individual countries still have the right to regulate the inflow of refugees. Perhaps most importantly, the right of asylum only applies to those who make it to the country in the first place and does not require countries to grant immigrants entry visas.

In addition, member states can make it less attractive to apply for asylum by applying more austere economic policies toward refugees such as high thresholds to qualify for financial assistance and social benefits, by only granting temporary asylum, limiting family reunification, and other measures that are within the letter of the law. This policy stance is viewed by many voters in various member states as ungenerous and against the perceived moral right of asylum. The degree of generosity is therefore a contested political issue that varies depending on the political preferences of the electorate and the ideology of the political parties in power.

Those who manage to cross the border into an EU country have the right to apply for asylum, but the country in question has substantial discretion in assessing whether the applicant's need of protection is sufficiently great to warrant asylum. Thus, the large cross-country variation in the rate at which asylum applications are approved is no proof that countries with low approval rates violate international agreements. Instead, it is the result of the great scope for differing interpretations that these agreements allow for. Cross-national differences can also be magnified by economic and geographic factors, and the fact that refugee policies vary over time within countries is a further indication that the observed cross-country differences are largely explained by variation in national policies.

Thus, while the refugee inflow is not a discretionary choice, countries have a wide room to maneuver within the framework of international treaties. Differences in asylum policy among EU countries are staggering and make clear that *de facto* there is no common EU policy. Figure 4.1 shows the number of persons applying for asylum in the EU countries per thousand inhabitants between 2006 and 2017. In addition to the 28 EU member states, we also include Norway and Switzerland. Countries are ranked according to the number of asylum applications relative to their population (see also column 1 in Table 4.1). Country differences in this respect are extremely large. For example, relative to population, the number of asylum seekers to Sweden was 100 times greater than that to Portugal. The time period 2006–2017 was chosen to be able to present data for all countries, but results are similar if we were to look at a wider time window, such as 1985–2017 (Sanandaji 2018a, b).

The countries that receive the largest number of refugees per capita tend to be either wealthy welfare states such as Sweden and Austria, or small countries in the Mediterranean such as Malta and Cyprus. In the latter case, the large number of asylum seekers is readily explained by the proximity to common transit routes. The countries that receive the lowest number of refugees per capita are either Eastern or Southern European countries. In fact, all Eastern European countries are below the EU average, including relatively wealthy countries such as Estonia and Slovenia. There is also considerable variation among the wealthy Western European countries.

The low figures for Southern Europe are interesting as Southern European Mediterranean countries, such as Portugal and Spain, are more easily accessed by asylum seekers than Scandinavia or Germany. Similarly, Eastern Europe is also more accessible than Northern Europe. One important explanation is economic circumstances as Northern European countries not only have higher average income but offer refugees far more benefits compared to countries such as Portugal and Croatia.

The United Kingdom is among the Western European countries that receive few refugees, and it did not experience a large inflow during the 2015 crisis either. Nevertheless, the fact that migration policy contributed to the Brexit decision may indicate that dissatisfaction with EU migration from Eastern Europe played an important role (see Forslid and Nyberg in this volume).

Even excluding Eastern Europe, the variation in refugee flows is extremely large—far larger than one would expect based on differences in economic characteristics. GDP per capita is roughly three times higher in the richest Western European country compared to the poorest, while the top countries in terms of refugee intake per capita, Malta and Sweden, have acceptance rates that are more than 250 times higher than the country that has the lowest acceptance rate, Croatia (column 2 in Table 4.1). The differences are also huge among the largest European countries: in relation to its population, Germany has granted asylum to four times as many refugees as France and Italy, five times more than the United Kingdom, and 35 times more than Spain. Given these stark differences, it is not surprising that the EU has found it nearly impossible to agree on a common asylum policy by 2019.

There is also variation over time. For instance, Denmark used to take many refugees but the country has tightened its policy and significantly reduced its refugee intake during the 2010s. Some of the countries that used to be the most generous, such as Austria and Denmark, are in 2019

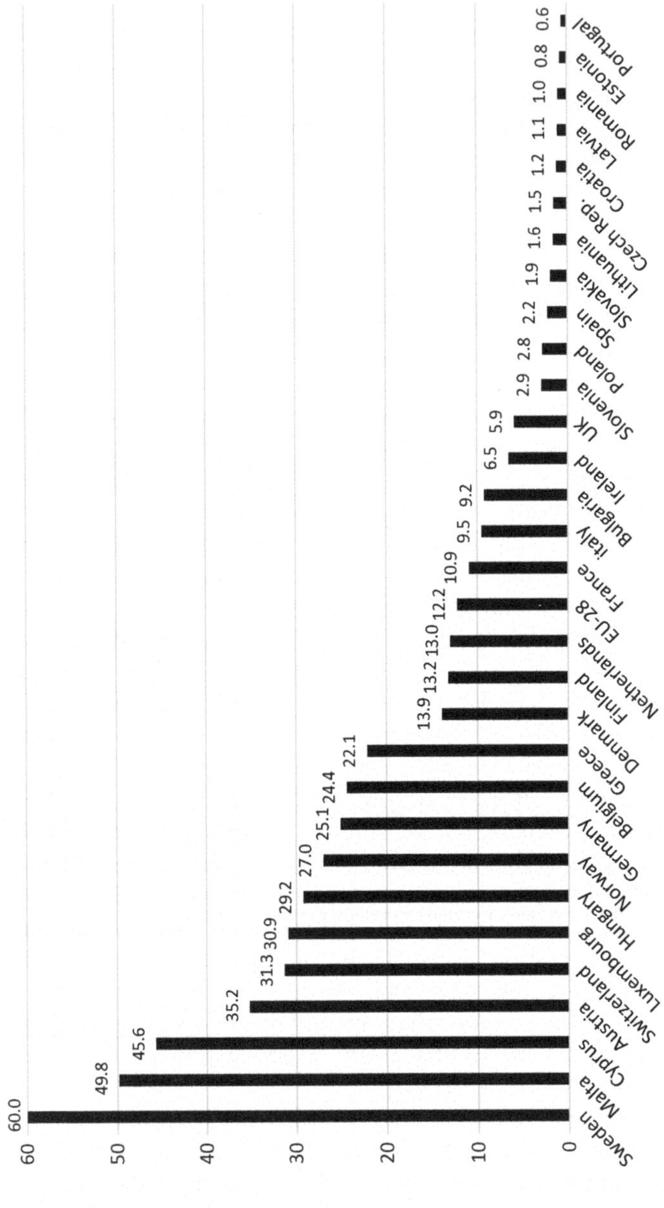

Fig. 4.1 Asylum applications 2006–2017 per thousand inhabitants (Source: Eurostat)

Table 4.1 Variations within Europe in asylum seeking, per capita income, and employment gaps of non-EU migrants and refugees

	Asylum appl.[a]	*Granted asylum appl.*[b]	*Share of granted appl. %*	*GDP per capita*[c]	*Gov't spending, % of GDP*	*Employment gap, non-EU-28 (2017)*[d]	*Employment gap, refugees (2014)*[d]
Sweden	60.0	30.3	50.5	33,600	50.6	19.3	25.2
Malta	49.8	31.1	62.5	23,000	40.8	7.6	N.A.
Cyprus	45.6	10.3	22.7	24,800	40.9	3.4	N.A.
Austria	35.2	15.6	44.3	34,400	51.1	16.9	15.4
Switzerland	31.3	14.1	44.9	43,100	30.2	N.A.	6.5
Luxembourg	30.9	7.5	24.1	70,100	42.0	6.6	N.A.
Hungary	29.2	0.5	1.8	17,600	49.1	1.6	N.A.
Norway	27.0	14.2	52.8	46,300	45.0	15.0	21.6
Germany	25.1	13.1	52.3	32,600	44.6	17.1	20.2
Belgium	24.4	7.9	32.4	31,800	52.9	19.0	23.8
Greece	22.1	3.1	14.0	21,200	51.9	4.0	N.A.
Denmark	13.9	6.7	48.4	33,900	54.1	17.9	N.A.
Finland	13.2	4.6	34.9	30,700	53.8	18.8	27.7
Netherlands	13.0	6.6	50.5	35,600	45.3	20.5	N.A.
EU-28	**12.2**	**4.9**	**40.1**	**26,800**	**47.4**	**10.0**	N.A.
France	10.9	3.1	28.4	28,700	55.9	16.9	13.6
Italy	9.5	3.6	37.3	27,200	49.5	0.2	−1.5
Bulgaria	9.2	2.7	29.1	12,000	36.9	6.7	N.A.
Ireland	6.5	1.1	17.1	39,900	39.3	6.6	N.A.
United Kingdom	5.9	2.6	43.2	29,100	43.7	8.2	25.1
Slovenia	2.9	0.3	9.8	22,600	47.7	5.4	−4.6
Poland	2.8	0.4	14.7	16,900	43.2	−2.1	N.A.
Spain	2.2	0.4	17.4	25,500	43.4	4.4	20.5
Slovakia	1.9	0.3	13.7	19,800	40.8	0.3	N.A.
Lithuania	1.6	0.3	21.4	18,200	37.2	6.1	N.A.
Czech Rep.	1.5	0.4	26.0	22,700	41.9	−0.9	N.A.
Croatia	1.2	0.1	10.4	16,200	47.0	6.6	8.5
Latvia	1.1	0.3	26.7	16,000	38.7	8.6	N.A.
Romania	1.0	0.3	34.8	14,100	36.7	−7.0	N.A.
Estonia	0.8	0.3	35.2	19,200	39.1	8.3	N.A.
Portugal	0.6	0.2	25.8	21,100	48.0	−1.5	14.6

(*continued*)

Table 4.1 (continued)

Source: Eurostat statistical database

Note: The countries were sorted in descending order based on asylum applications per thousand inhabitants (column 1). The table includes all 28 EU member states in 2018 plus Norway and Switzerland regarding the inflow of asylum seekers and the granted share relative to population in 2006–2017, and average PPP-adjusted GDP per capita and government spending as a share of GDP are calculated for the period 2006–2017. The employment gap among refugees and non-European immigrants relative to the native population is for 20–64-year olds. The native population is defined as all persons where both parents were natively born

[a]Asylum applications per thousand inhabitants, 2006–2017

[b]Granted asylums per thousand inhabitants, 2006–2017

[c]Measured in PPP-adjusted USD

[d]In percentage points and latest available year

among those countries that have shifted the most toward a restrictive asylum policy. However, few countries have shifted from restrictive to more generous polices. The most notable exception is Germany, which increased its share of granted asylums from around 15 percent of the total EU intake in 2007 to 61 percent in 2017, but since then Germany has instituted a more restrictive policy. On the other hand, Spain has moved toward a more generous asylum policy following a change in government in 2018. This illustrates the importance of internal political sentiments within member states vis-à-vis migration policy.

In most instances, the ranking of countries is similar for the number of applications and the number of granted applications relative to population. There are a few exceptions, notably Hungary, that received a great number of applications but granted rather few. Malta, Germany, Sweden, the Netherlands, and Norway can be found at one extreme, approving over 50 percent of the submitted asylum applications between 2006 and 2017. By contrast, Hungary at the other extreme approved less than 2 percent of the applications. It is important to note that this percentage may not exactly equal the share of applicants being granted asylum, since there is a lag between applying and being granted asylum, and since some individuals appeal a negative decision. Still, over long periods the ratio of the number of granted asylums to the number of applications gives a good approximation of the share of approved asylum applications. The cross-country differences in this ratio are massive within the EU. Since the countries that have higher ratios also tend to be those that take more asylum seekers, the gap between EU countries becomes even larger when comparing granted asylum.

Table 4.1 shows that wealthier countries and those with a larger public sector tend to have a more generous asylum policy, but also that the variation in asylum policy is far greater than what can be accounted for by per capita GDP or the size of government. Furthermore, the table shows that there is a large employment gap in most European countries between refugees and the native-born population. In the labor market statistics, country of birth is recorded more often than the reason for migration. Needless to say, many migrants from outside the EU are not refugees. Some are labor migrants from countries such as China, India, and former Soviet republics.

It is possible to report the employment gap between the native-born population and migrants from outside the EU for all countries in 2017. However, the employment gap for refugees can only be presented for some countries (with a lag of some years). Figure 4.2 presents this gap for Western European countries. Again, we can see that non-EU immigrants are less likely to be employed than the native-born population in all included countries, with the exception of Portugal. The reasons for this state of affairs are complex but can partly be explained by migrants' background and skills. While the differences are smaller once one controls for education, country of origin, and other factors, the EU is far from homogenous when it comes to the labor market performance of migrants (Sanandaji 2017).

The large and persistent differences in asylum policy amongst countries at fairly similar levels of economic development likely reflect strong underlying differences in culture, ideology, politics, and institutions.[5] Attempts by countries with more generous refugee policies, such as Sweden and Germany, to convince countries that take fewer refugees to increase their intake have thus far failed and caused tensions.

The Tension Between the National and the Federal Level

Our analysis so far shows that the policies, migration flows, and how well refugees are integrated into the labor market differ immensely across member countries, and there is little public support for a common European asylum policy. Unlike many other policy areas, policies related to refugee migration were never successfully harmonized. The EU countries are simply too far apart in several key respects—such as per capita

[5] For studies trying to explain cross-country differences in migration policies, see Chin and Cortes (2015), Hatton (2016), Keogh (2013), and Toshkov (2014).

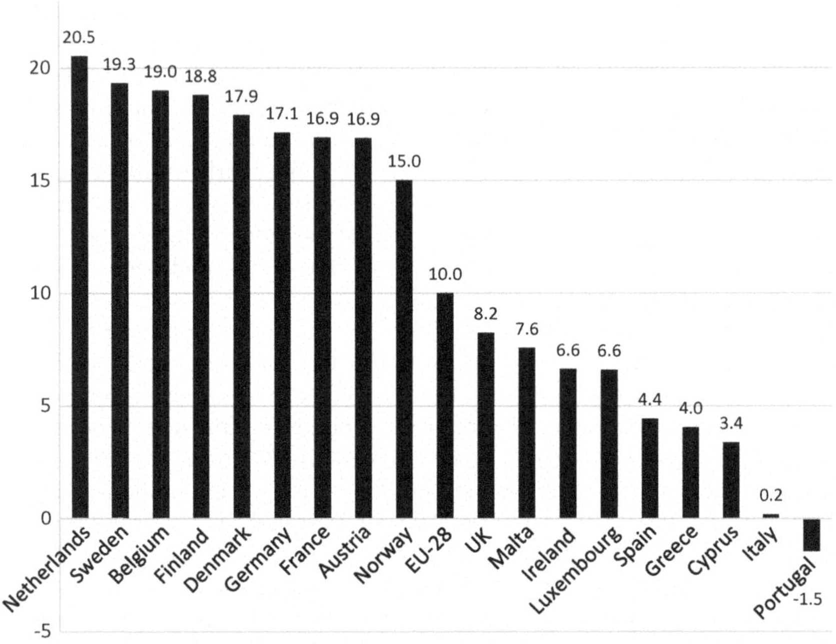

Fig. 4.2 Gap in employment rate between native born and non-EU-28 migrants, 2017 (percentage points) (Source: Eurostat)

income, employment opportunities, size and effectiveness of government, political history, and culture—for a meaningful convergence. This has caused tensions, as there were attempts to push countries to adopt similar policies, which has undermined support for the EU as a whole in several countries.

A salient example of the rising political tension within the EU is reflected in the June 2018 meeting in Budapest between the Austrian Chancellor Sebastian Kurz and 'the Visegrád four' (Poland, the Czech Republic, Slovakia, and Hungary). The leaders of these five countries expressed their dissatisfaction with the disregard of national identities, rapid centralization in the EU, and imposition of what they deemed to be unreasonable immigration quotas (cf. Stegmann McCallion in this volume).

On December 4, 2018, the European Commission in a press release called on member states and the European Parliament prior to the December European Council to 'consolidate the significant progress made by adopting the outstanding reform proposals'.[6] Three regulatory and practical issues are emphasized in the report: (1) cooperation between partners, (2) stronger border management, and (3) the management of internal migration within the EU. In his statement, Vice President Frans Timmerman emphasizes the need for 'switching from reactive ad hoc responses to completing the reforms for a sustainable future proof migration and asylum system', acknowledging the ad hoc nature of the asylum process throughout the crisis. In the statement the importance of protecting external borders is repeatedly emphasized, implicitly recognizing the failure in border security during the peak of the crisis. Interestingly, this is one of the few times where the focus is also on improving cooperation with external partners to increase return and readmission.

Moreover, there are two other important issues raised in the press release. First, the need to address the root causes of asylum immigration and the *innovative funding instruments* that are put in place to manage to do so (e.g., the EU Trust Fund for Africa). Second, the need to expand the existing partnerships built between the EU and the countries in distress. In particular, the return and readmission practices are explicitly mentioned in the press release, including the new arrangements that have been instituted since 2016 with countries such as Afghanistan, Guinea, Bangladesh, and Ethiopia.[7]

The EU's refugee crisis challenge relates to the academic debate on the durability of EU federalism. Kelemen (2007: 54) argues that federalism is inherently unstable, and that federations may fail either through *implosion* or *explosion*. Implosion refers to over-centralization of power at the federal level, which has been at the core of the Eurosceptic debate. Explosion refers to the thinning out of cooperation at the federal level, where members start pursuing their own objectives in opposition to the federal level, which in the worst-case scenario can result in gradual disintegration and the eventual demise of the federal system. Even if there were only a few countries that opted out of the system, or if the increased frictions only result in further polarization within the system, that would still indicate that a common EU asylum policy may be detrimental. Hence, every decision at the federal level aiming at furthering the harmonization and

[6] See European Commission (2018c).

[7] See European Commission (2018c). A complete list of readmission agreements and related return-migration practices can be found at the Migration and Home Affairs site of the European Commission (2019c).

decreasing the variation in refugee policies across member states should be thoroughly evaluated prior to implementation. Failing to do so runs the risk of taking ill-conceived policy decisions that would lead to further discontent with the EU, and increases the likelihood that the Union disintegrates.

Striking a Balance Between Asylum Policy at the National and EU Levels

If one accepts our premise that Europe currently does not have a common asylum policy, more than on paper, it is also worth asking whether the EU in the future should strive for such a policy and federalism in the refugee area. If a common asylum policy is economically and politically rational, the case could be made that the EU and national governments should push harder to make the political rhetoric of a common asylum policy a reality. On the other hand, if attempts to force federalism are not viewed as desirable by a large share of EU citizens, it could backfire and undermine the confidence in the EU cooperation. This type of resistance is likely if there is great variation in EU refugee inflows that reflect underlying economic, cultural, and political factors.

The European Commission has attempted to move toward a more common asylum policy, but the more far-reaching proposals have met with strong political resistance in several member countries. This resistance against a common EU asylum policy is sometimes interpreted as a sign of parochialism and national selfishness, but this stance may just as well reflect a rational assessment. The fact that the refugee issue has given rise to such tension and conflicts between member states strongly suggests that the EU may not be a region for which it is optimal to impose a common asylum policy. The opposition to such an idea thus has a fundamental basis that needs to be weighed in when the European Commission and/or the European Parliament considers various alternatives. Failing to do so, the entire EU project may be jeopardized. Therefore, refugee policies should for the most part be decided upon at the national level. This needs to be done in cooperation with the regional and local levels where the integration measures in the form of education, job matching, provision of housing, health, and so forth are implemented.

The fact that the EU has succeeded in achieving free movement of labor within the Union does not suggest that it should impose a common asylum policy for the movement from external countries on all its members. The 2015 refugee crisis showed that nation-states are capable of regulating asylum policy, whereas the EU was incapable of doing so. However, there may well be an important role for the EU. One difference between a refugee union and a currency union is that asylum policy is far more multilayered, both vertically and horizontally. It is fully possible for member states to retain elements of asylum policy at the national level, while coordinating on other elements at the federal level. Examples of the latter include refugee aid to countries afflicted by war and natural disasters, treaties with non-member countries for readmission and resettlement, rescue missions in the Mediterranean, as well as external border control. Although such objectives have already been clearly stated by the European Commission,[8] there are still considerable disagreements around them in the public debate of the respective member states. Therefore, it is important that the objectives of the Union regarding a common asylum policy should be better communicated to its member states.

The central policy tools and the agencies that decide on and implement the relevant measures, such as agencies in charge of border controls and assessment of asylum applications, should remain at the national level. This guarantees that their actions are aligned with the interest and political preferences of citizens to regulate migration. The nation-state is the unit within which migration and integration policy is conducted and remains the most appropriate unit also for regulating inflows, the asylum process, and upholding border controls. Moving forward, refugee migration policy should learn from this experience and acknowledge the important role still played by the nation-state.

References

Cherubini, F. (2014). *Asylum Law in the European Union*. New York: Routledge.

Chin, A., & Cortes, K. E. (2015). The Refugee/Asylum Seeker. In B. R. Chiswick & P. W. Miller (Eds.), *Handbook of the Economics of International Migration* (Vol. 1, pp. 585–658). Amsterdam: North-Holland.

Dilli, S., Elert, N., & Herrmann, A. M. (2018). Varieties of Entrepreneurship: Exploring the Institutional Foundations of Different Entrepreneurship Types Through 'Varieties-of-Capitalism' Arguments. *Small Business Economics, 51*(2), 293–320.

[8] See, for example, European Commission (2019d).

Edsbäcker, K. (2011). *Turkey's Asylum Policy in the Light of EU Accession – The Impact of Its Geographical Limitation to the Geneva Convention*. Master's thesis, Lund University, Lund, Sweden. Retrieved from http://lup.lub.lu.se/student-papers/record/2063509.

Elert, N., Henrekson, M., & Stenkula, M. (2017). *Institutional Reform for Innovation and Entrepreneurship – An Agenda for Europe*. Cham, CH: Springer International Publishing.

Elert, N., Henrekson, M., & Sanders, M. (2019). *The Entrepreneurial Society: A Reform Agenda for the European Union*. Cham, CH: Springer International Publishing.

European Commission. (2016, July 13). *Proposal on Standards for the Qualification of Third-Country Nationals or Stateless Persons as Beneficiaries of International Protection [...] Amending Council Directive 2003/109/EC of 25 November 2003 Concerning the Status of Third-Country Nationals Who Are Long-Term Residents*. COM(2016) 466 final 2016/0223 (COD), Brussels.

European Commission. (2018a). Spring 2018 Standard Eurobarometer: One Year Ahead of the European Elections, Trust in the Union and Optimism About the Future Is Growing. Retrieved September 18, 2018, from http://europa.eu/rapid/press-release_IP-18-4148_en.htm.

European Commission. (2018b). Who Qualifies for International Protection. Retrieved September 18, 2018, from https://ec.europa.eu/home-affairs/what-we-do/policies/asylum/refugee-status_en.

European Commission. (2018c, December 4). *Managing Migration: Commission Calls Time on Asylum Reform Stalling*, Brussels [Press release]. Retrieved from http://europa.eu/rapid/press-release_IP-18-6627_en.htm.

European Commission. (2019a). Temporary Reintroduction of Border Control. Retrieved August 7, 2019, from https://ec.europa.eu/home-affairs/what-we-do/policies/borders-and-visas/schengen/reintroduction-border-control_en.

European Commission. (2019b). Common European Asylum System. Retrieved August 7, 2019, from https://ec.europa.eu/home-affairs/what-we-do/policies/asylum_en.

European Commission. (2019c). Return & Readmission. Retrieved August 8, 2019, from https://ec.europa.eu/home-affairs/what-we-do/policies/irregular-migration-return-policy/return-readmission_en.

European Commission. (2019d). Migration. Retrieved August 8, 2019, from. https://ec.europa.eu/home-affairs/what-we-do/policies/irregular-migration-return-policy/return-readmission_en.

European Parliament and the Council of the EU. (2013). Regulation (EU) No. 604/2013 of the European Parliament and of the Council of 26 June 2013 Establishing the Criteria and Mechanisms for Determining the Member State Responsible for Examining an Application for International Protection Lodged in One of the Member States by a Third-Country National or a Stateless Person (Recast). *Official Journal of the European Union, L 180*, 31–59.

Eurostat. (2018). *Glossary: Migration*. Statistics Explained. Retrieved August 7, 2018, from http://ec.europa.eu/eurostat/statistics-explained/index.php/Glossary:Migration.

F. v. United Kingdom. (2004, June 22). Application no. 17341/03, Council of Europe: European Court of Human Rights. Retrieved from https://www.refworld.org/cases,ECHR,4ee21ffd2.html.

Faggian, A., & Öner, Ö. (2018). *Location Decision of Refugees in the Receiving Country: The Swedish Case*. Mimeo. Cambridge and Stockholm: Department of Land Economy, Cambridge University and the Research Institute of Industrial Economics.

Hatton, T. J. (2016). Refugees, Asylum Seekers, and Policy in OECD Countries. *American Economic Review, 106*(5), 441–445.

Hooghe, L., & Marks, G. (2001). *Multi-Level Governance and European Integration*. Lanham, MD: Rowman & Littlefield.

Kelemen, R. D. (2007). Built to Last? The Durability of EU Federalism. In S. Meunier & K. R. McNamara (Eds.), *Making History: European Integration and Institutional Change at Fifty* (Vol. 8, pp. 51–66). Oxford: Oxford University Press.

Keogh, G. (2013). Modelling Asylum Migration Pull-Force Factors in the EU-15. *Economic and Social Review, 44*(3), 371–399.

Lenzerini, F. (2009). *Asilo e Diritti Umani: l'Evoluzione del Diritto d'Asilo nel Diritto Internazionale* (Vol. 10). Siena: Giuffrè Editore.

McGhee, D. (2001). Persecution and Social Group Status: Homosexual Refugees in the 1990s. *Journal of Refugee Studies, 14*(1), 20–42.

Mundell, R. A. (1961). A Theory of Optimum Currency Areas. *American Economic Review, 51*(4), 657–665.

OECD. (2018). *Working Together for Local Integration of Migrants and Refugees*. Paris: OECD Publishing.

Sanandaji, T. (2017). *Massutmaning – ekonomisk politik mot utanförskap och antisocialt beteende* [Mass Challenge: Economic Policy Against Social Exclusion and Antisocial Behavior]. Stockholm: Kuhzad Media.

Sanandaji, T. (2018a). *Les Suédois et l'Immigration, Fin de l'Homogénéité?* [The Swedes and Immigration: End of Homogeneity?]. Paris: Fondation pour l'innovation politique. Retrieved from http://www.fondapol.org/wp-content/uploads/2018/08/130-SUEDE-IMMIGRATION_I_2018-08-27_web-1.pdf.

Sanandaji, T. (2018b). *Les Suédois et l'Immigration, Fin du Consensus?* [The Swedes and Immigration: End of Consensus?]. Paris: Fondation pour l'Innovation Politique. Retrieved from http://www.fondapol.org/wp-content/uploads/2018/08/130-SUEDE-IMMIGRATION_II_2018-08-27_web.pdf.

Stokes, B., Wike, R., & Manevich, D. (2017). Post-Brexit, Europeans More Favorable Toward EU. *Pew Research Center.*

SVT. (2018). SVT's Vallokalsundersökning: Riksdagsvalet 2018 [SVT's Election Survey: The Swedish Parliamentary Election 2018]. Retrieved September 27, 2018, from https://www.svt.se/omoss/media/filer_public/5c/17/5c17fc91-31c4-4e0a-a17f-b42318edf4a4/valuresultat_riksdagsval_pk_2018_vagda_0912.pdf.

Swedish Migration Agency. (2018). Verksamhets- och utgiftsprognos 2018-07-29. Dnr. 1.1.3-2018-929. Norrköping: Migrationsverket.

Toshkov, D. (2014). The Dynamic Relationship between Asylum Applications and Recognition Rates in Europe (1987–2010). *European Union Politics, 15*(2), 192–214.

UNHCR. (2002). Protecting Refugees: Questions and Answers. Retrieved September 1, 2018, from http://www.unhcr.org/afr/publications/brochures/3b779dfe2/protecting-refugees-questions-answers.html.

Wennström, J., & Öner, Ö. (2018). *Political Hedgehogs: The Geographical Sorting of Refugees in Sweden.* IFN Working Paper, no. 1266. Stockholm: Research Institute of Industrial Economics.

Wessels, J. (2011). *Sexual Orientation In Refugee status Determination.* Refugee Studies Centre Working Paper, no. 73. Oxford: Oxford Department of International Development, University of Oxford.

CHAPTER 5

Brexit and the Survival of the Union

Rikard Forslid and Sten Nyberg

Introduction

After a long period of advancing internationalization—manifested in freer trade, the enlargement of the European Union (EU), and increasingly internationalized value chains in production—we seem now at the end of the 2010s to be witnessing a backlash. Negotiations on the Transatlantic Trade and Investment Partnership (TTIP) agreement on free trade between the EU and the US have stalled, Britain is on its way out of the EU (Brexit), and the fissure between Catalonia and the central government in Spain has grown ever deeper. The political life of many countries reflects a more and more pronounced focus on national interests. Issues such as migration, crime and punishment, and the threat to jobs posed by international competition have come to the fore. The spirit of the times, which these developments express, may have many and complex causes; moreover, some of the dramatic changes we have seen—such as Brexit—have been decided by small margins. The outcome was not decreed by history; things could well have turned out differently. However, underlying economic conditions may shed some light on the trend towards increased nationalism and on the British decision to leave the Union.

R. Forslid • S. Nyberg (✉)
Department of Economics, Stockholm University, Stockholm, Sweden
e-mail: rikard.forslid@ne.su.se; sten.nyberg@ne.su.se

A. Bakardjieva Engelbrekt et al. (eds.), *The European Union and the Return of the Nation State*,
https://doi.org/10.1007/978-3-030-35005-5_5

In this chapter, taking our point of departure in the economic literature, we discuss certain countervailing forces: on the one hand, those that impel countries to move towards increased economic and political integration and, on the other, those that prompt them to seek to disengage from supranational unions and systems of cooperation. The main question is how the EU can be saved and even strengthened in light of the signals that Brexit has sent. We also examine the anatomy of the divorce in view of the ongoing Brexit process, which is disclosing major differences between the parties in their expectations of how separation is to occur. We seek to answer a series of questions: Which expectations are reasonable? What rhetorical moves reflect the self-interest of the parties? How can the parties avoid a bad outcome? What factors lay behind the outcome of the British referendum? Finally, how great is the risk that additional states will opt to leave the Union?

This chapter is arranged as follows. In the next section, we discuss how the EU emerged in competition with European Free Trade Association (EFTA).[1] Although cooperation within the EU involves a degree of supranationalism, of which several of the former EFTA countries were sceptical, the benefits arising from a large integrated market weighed most heavily in the end. In view of the economic benefits of a large market, we might then ask whether there are any limits at all to the size to which a union such as the EU can grow. This question is analysed in the political-economy literature on optimal state formation, which is the theme of the next section. We then discuss what happens if a country leaves the EU, taking our point of departure in the ongoing Brexit negotiations and the questions of trade and migration. We highlight the incentive of the parties to position themselves politically and rhetorically, and we proffer some concrete advice on how negotiations can be conducted in order to minimize the damage caused by Brexit. The fact that the British referendum had the result that it did is also bound up with the fact that groups in the UK—as indeed in other countries—see themselves as having lost out from globalization and from the market integration entailed by the single market. In the subsequent section, we discuss what trade theory has to say about this. We then proceed to examine how attitudes towards the Union have developed in different countries. British scepticism of the EU is of long standing, but we find no similar patterns in other countries. Finally, based on our own

[1] For ease of exposition, we use the term 'EU' in this chapter to refer not just to the EU strictly speaking, but to its predecessor organizations as well—that is, the EEC and the EC.

research and that of others, we present some policy recommendations for how the Union can be preserved and additional exits avoided, in light of experiences from the Brexit process.

A United Europe—But How? Supranationalism Versus Intergovernmentalism

> We must build a kind of United States of Europe. In this way only will hundreds of millions of toilers be able to regain the simple joys and hopes which make life worth living.
>
> Winston Churchill, University of Zurich, 19 September 1946

Seen from the vantage point of 2019, it is somewhat ironic that a British prime minister was the first to speak publicly about the importance of a united Europe and the possibility of forming some kind of European federal state.

The Cold War, which broke out very soon after the end of the Second World War, made it necessary to create an economically and militarily strong and united Europe amongst the countries outside the Warsaw Pact. Already from the outset, however, there was a tension between those who envisaged cooperation of a supranational kind—where the ultimate goal might be some kind of federal state—and those who sought intergovernmental cooperation between independent states.

The European Coal and Steel Community (ECSC), formed in 1951 by Belgium, France, Italy, Luxembourg, the Netherlands, and West Germany, was the seed from which the current EU grew. When, in 1958, these countries deepened their cooperation and formed a customs union, the European Economic Community (EEC), several federal elements were already present. For example, the EEC had a court (the Court of Justice of the European Communities) and a parliament (the European Parliamentary Assembly). Furthermore, a customs union as such involves a degree of supranationalism, inasmuch as countries in a customs union can no longer determine and set their own duties (see, e.g. Cramér 2019)

By contrast, EFTA—formed in 1960 by Austria, Denmark, Norway, Portugal, Sweden, Switzerland, and the UK—was a free-trade agreement. That is to say, it was an arrangement for cooperation between independent states that could also set their own customs duties. One might say that EFTA and the EEC (in time the EU) embodied two different visions of how European cooperation should look. However, having two different free-trade areas in Europe made for economic instability, due to the differing size of the two areas.

All else being equal, it is better for a company to have access to a bigger market than to a smaller one; and already at the outset, the market represented by the EU was about twice as large as that of EFTA. It is true there were trade agreements between EFTA and the EU, but the companies within each association nonetheless enjoyed a certain competitive advantage within their own free-trade area over companies from outside it. Thus, market size gave the EU an advantage. This in turn gave countries an incentive to switch from EFTA to the EU, due to the larger market to which membership in the latter afforded access. Now, suppose a country finds it advantageous to leave EFTA and to join the EU. If it does so, the difference in market size grows still greater. This may in turn prompt more countries to switch from EFTA to the EU. A domino effect may then result, and the smaller association may collapse (see, e.g. Baldwin 1999). Indeed, that is just what happened.

When Britain, the largest country in EFTA by far, applied to join the EU in 1961, a strong domino effect was triggered. Several of the smaller EFTA countries then hurried to apply for EU membership as well. Surprisingly, however, Britain's application was met with a 'no' (or rather a 'non'). De Gaulle, who saw British membership as a Trojan horse for American influence, blocked Britain from joining throughout his presidency. It was not until 1973 that the UK, together with Denmark and Ireland, became a member. The EU continued to deepen and to expand; and the larger and more integrated its market became, the greater was the disadvantage suffered by countries left outside. It is therefore natural that almost all of EFTA's members eventually joined the Union.

The years from 1973 to 1986 were marked by Euro-pessimism. After the oil shocks of 1973 and 1979, the European economy had difficulty getting up to speed. Economic growth was weak and the labour market developed poorly, and Europe's economy seemed particularly sluggish compared to that of the US. This was the background when, in 1986, the Union decided to adopt the Single European Act (also referred to as the 1992 programme). This entailed sweeping liberalization of the economy. The 1992 programme established the single market, with its freedom of movement for goods, services, capital, and labour. Many non-tariff barriers to trade were removed at the same time: technical standards were harmonized, border formalities simplified or taken away, rules for public procurement rewritten to allow companies from other EU countries to gain access, etc. The next step, once the single market was completed, was to introduce the common currency through the Treaty of Maastricht in 1992. Moreover, even as the Union deepened in this way, it expanded as well. Portugal and Spain joined in 1986; the former EFTA states of Austria, Finland, and Sweden did so in 1995.

The fall of the Berlin Wall in November 1989 meant that, all in one go, the countries of Eastern Europe became candidates for EU membership too. Opinion within the Union was divided over whether it would be best first to deepen the Union and then to enlarge it, or to do the converse instead. In the end both deepening and enlargement took place, and at about the same time. In 2004, the Union underwent a major eastward enlargement, with the admission of Cyprus, the Czech Republic, Estonia, Hungary, Latvia, Lithuania, Malta, Poland, Slovakia, and Slovenia. Bulgaria and Romania joined in 2007. The most recent country to be admitted is Croatia, which joined in 2013. The Union has thereby become more heterogeneous, which poses a problem in itself.

Is the Union Too Big or Too Small?

The EU consisted originally of six countries: Belgium, France, Italy, Luxembourg, the Netherlands, and West Germany. It now includes 28 countries, and several others are waiting their turn to join. One fundamental question, then, is how large the Union can or should become. Will the EU fall apart if it gets really big, or is large size rather a prerequisite for its survival?

Successful states, according to the traditional view in research on political and economic history, are characterized by good conditions for the collection of taxes (see, e.g. Brewer 1989). Subsequent research by Acemoglu et al. (2005) and Besley and Persson (2009) has stressed the importance of institutions that facilitate international trade and functioning markets. The EU primarily concerns the latter: the establishment of a well-integrated and functioning market in Europe. Where collecting taxes is concerned, on the other hand, the prerogatives of the Union are very limited. Its revenues derive largely from customs duties and from an annual fee of about 1 per cent of the collective GDP of the member states.

As for the optimal size of countries, Alesina and Spolaore (1997) point to a trade-off between economic efficiency and a country's ability to satisfy the different preferences of its citizens. First of all, a large state or country has an advantage when it comes to producing so-called collective goods characterized by economies of scale. Examples include national defence, physical and intangible infrastructure, and branches associated with these. Second, a larger state—or a union—also means a larger market, especially if trade and movement across national borders are otherwise restricted. The EU, like a nation-state, is a free-trade area, and the value of this trait increases with the size of the area. A larger market without significant barriers to trade also allows for greater specialization and generates stronger competitive pressures. These factors tend to lead to lower costs, higher quality, and a more varied offering of products.

At the same time, it is harder for a government (or the Commission in the case of the EU) to take into account special preferences amongst certain groups in a country with a large population, or amongst certain countries in a union with many member states. Due to the EU's principle of subsidiarity, at least some attempt is made to limit supranational decision-making. Nevertheless, the impact of various EU regulatory frameworks is palpable. This impression is reinforced, of course, if national politicians cite the need to comply with EU policy in order to justify enacting unpopular legislation—legislation which may have been necessary even if the country in question had been outside the EU.

Politics typically focuses on the median voter. In a hypothetical country with just one resident, the policies enacted are perfectly adapted to that person's preferences. However, as the population becomes larger and not least more heterogeneous, more and more individuals will have preferences far from those of the median voter. The preferences of voters on redistribution and redistributive taxes are an example. Bolton et al. (1996) and Bolton and Roland (1997) show how growing differences in such preferences can lead to political tension and polarization, which moreover may—if these differences have a clear ethnic or geographical dimension—be reflected in stronger political support for separatist movements. It bears noting that migration within a union can also reduce such tensions.

Thus, policies in a large country or in a large union will tend to be less well-adapted to the preferences of voters. It need hardly be said that this problem has not diminished as the EU has grown. Moreover, some of the recently admitted states have displayed political preferences far from those common in the Union's core countries.

Under such circumstances, Alesina and Spolaore (1997) point out in their theoretical analysis that democratic decision-making can result in states which are too small. Gancia et al. observe, in an expanded analysis from 2016 of the effects of globalization, that the state provides both an institutional framework for the market and public services to the population—and that there may be synergies between these activities. They find that, initially, globalization can impel the formation of large states, which have often been associated with armed conflicts historically. At later stages, however, the desired reduction in trade costs can take place peacefully, within the framework of economic unions. The economic benefits of market integration, combined with the heterogeneity of services demanded within a union, can then justify a division of responsibility for the market's institutional framework and for the provision of services between the union and its member states, even if this takes place at the expense of the aforementioned synergies.

In the case of the EU, the economies of scale resulting from a large union have mainly been manifested through the single market, which entails free trade, freedom of movement for capital, and freedom of movement for labour. In some other areas, however—such as a joint defence—the Union has not been able to exploit economies of scale. In this area, apparently, the EU has some limitations compared with a nation-state. Alternatively, one could say the EU has untapped potential here.

The EU's principle of subsidiarity represents an effort to reduce the friction between the drive towards standardization and differences in member states' preferences. At the same time, examples are not lacking of policy areas which are controversial in this regard. Agricultural policy is such an area. The introduction of the Union's social pillar may also involve far-reaching changes in areas that member states regard as important.

The fact that Britain has voted to leave the Union could be interpreted as evidence that the EU has come close to its maximum size, where the disparities between member states have become so great that it becomes difficult for the Union to hold together. It is not uncommon for Union policies to come into conflict with the preferences of individual member states. In recent years, for instance, such conflicts have arisen in relation to Hungary, Italy, and Poland. However, it is only in the case of Britain that the benefits of a large market seem to have been outweighed by the drawbacks of supranational decision-making when it comes to satisfying national preferences.

One important factor in such an assessment, of course, concerns expectations of what leaving the EU means. Ideally, a nation that is withdrawing would retain the benefits of a large market while gaining autonomy on issues where major conflicts have arisen vis-à-vis the Union—that is, it would have its cake and eat it too. And sure enough, the UK has expressed a clear desire to retain relatively free trade with the rest of the Union, even as it seeks greater control over migration and legislation. British confidence in this regard may reflect the success Britain has enjoyed as a member state in negotiating special conditions for its membership. However, it may also reflect insufficient appreciation of the reduction in bargaining power that a country suffers if it chooses to leave the Union—a point we touch on in the next section.

Brexit may also affect how cooperation between the remaining member states develops in the future. One response to Brexit from France and Germany, for instance, has been to stress that integration must now be deepened. The following statement by the president of France, Emmanuel Macron, at the EU summit in Sofia 2018 (cited in Herszenhorn 2018), may serve to illustrate this:

> It is also a historical battle for our Continent and I will put all my energy to lead it and to win it. I think since the Second World War, there has never been a moment of such historical importance, where our traditional alliances are being made fragile, where the issue of the global order is being reconsidered, where the issue of European sovereignty including on defense matters is so strongly at stake, and we'll see that on the occasion of the next NATO summit. There is also an issue of our own internal solidarity. So those who had doubts or thought they could walk away from these issues. Well, history is back. And it is now time for decisions.

Thus, the Union may develop in a more federal direction after the UK has left. This may help to ensure that unused economies of scale within the Union are utilized. At the same time, however, it means more supranationalism, which several of the smaller member states will find difficult to digest. The division within the Union over the extent of supranationalism is of long standing, and in many ways central to Brexit.

The Nation-State Leaves the Union—Brexit

The balance between the standardization needed to achieve the benefits of a common market and the adjustments necessary to accommodate differences in national preferences is not a precise or uniform affair. It is possible, for example, for nation-states to assert themselves within a union as well. Within the EU, various exemptions have been granted and special solutions devised for individual countries (the UK not least). At the same time, there is a core of commitments within the Union that is more difficult to disregard. Pursuing greater autonomy and leaving the Union, as the UK is doing, is a big step. We discuss different possible outcomes of Brexit below, and how they are likely to be affected by the manner in which Brexit negotiations are conducted.

The decision to withdraw also affects the negotiating situation vis-à-vis the Union. The EU's motivation to make concessions in order to prevent a member state from leaving disappears if exit has already been decided. For the remaining countries, moreover, the market within the Union will be much more important than the trading relationship with the country that is leaving. The Union may then seek to penalize the state which is withdrawing, in order to deter others from attempting the same.

The effects of Brexit depend on where the negotiations over it end up. Several different outcomes are possible. The simplest will be if the UK, along Norwegian lines, stays within the single market without being an EU member. This, however, is unlikely, because Britain will then have to accept the free movement of labour. The most costly outcome will be if the UK and the EU fail to conclude any trade agreement at all. WTO tariffs will then apply between them—that is, basically the same trading relationship as that which applies between the EU and the US today. That will hurt European consumers, for whom British goods and services will become more expensive; and European companies as well, since they will find it harder to export to the UK. The most serious effects, however, will likely be felt in Britain.

A group of researchers at the London School of Economics has calculated what the costs of Brexit are likely to be for the UK, as well as for other EU countries (Dhingra et al. 2016). They put the annual costs for the UK at 1.3–2.6 per cent of GDP, depending on which trade agreement is reached. Over the long run, however, the effects may be two to three times greater, when account is taken of the effects on growth and on foreign direct investment. The cost for the EU from reduced trade will be about the same—in absolute terms, that is. However, since the economy of the Union is ten times larger, the cost in relation to GDP will be about ten times smaller. The EU, then, is far more important as a trading partner for Britain than Britain is for any individual EU country.

Negotiations over Brexit are also complicated by the fact that political and economic considerations are intertwined. The referendum on Brexit, and the political positions taken within the campaign as well as afterwards, has reduced the room for manoeuvre on the British side a great deal. The

EU, for its part, has staked out a position on the indivisibility of the four freedoms which also serves to narrow the scope for fruitful negotiations. The result is what Putnam (1988) calls a two-level game—that is, the political game within national arenas interacts with and influences the outcome of negotiations between nations. Actors that make ironclad political commitments—such as to their own voter base—may find it costly to make concessions in negotiations and to achieve more favourable results thereby. Then, if both parties take a hardline position, there is a risk that negotiations will fail, or at least issue in a worse outcome for both sides. We examine this problem in a study from 2017. On the basis of that study, we analyse the Brexit negotiations below in terms of a sequential game in which the parties may commit themselves to certain positions on migration and access to the common market (Forslid & Nyberg 2017).

The British nation-state must continue to deal with the Union even after it leaves it. The Brexit negotiations determine how this future relationship is going to look. In what follows, we leave the problem of the Irish border aside; instead we focus on trade and migration. These two questions differ from each other fundamentally. When it comes to labour mobility, the interests of the EU and the UK are diametrically opposed. Where trade is concerned, on the other hand, the economic interests of the two sides would seem to coincide, in favour of free trade. As previously mentioned, however, the Union has clearly stated that the four freedoms are indivisible. It is also worth noting that the parties can unilaterally impose restrictions on the movement of goods and labour; by contrast, maintaining free trade or freedom of movement requires the consent of both parties. As a result, the party wishing to pursue the most restrictive policy is decisive, and can enforce its position unilaterally. Accordingly, we limit our analysis to the UK's position on labour mobility and to possible EU restrictions on British access to the common market.

EU proclamations on the indivisibility of the four freedoms may reflect a genuine preference, such as a desire to avoid opening the gates to a myriad of special solutions for different member states, to the detriment of market integration. The different freedoms may be complementary in this respect. This in turn means that heavier restrictions on labour mobility on the part of the UK will make the EU more inclined to restrict British access to the common market. If mobility is already low, then trade barriers are perceived as less costly.

Another purpose may be to demonstrate to other member states that might consider exiting that such a move will inevitably result in restricted access to the common market. According to De Vries (2018), Brexit is a reference point regarding the economic and political consequences of exit, so it affects support for the Union amongst the member states that remain. De Vries (2017: 51) reports results in line with this, noting: 'They suggest that it will be crucially important for the EU and the national governments of the remaining 27 member states to make sure that the British example does not set a positive precedent'.

The rhetoric on the indivisibility of the four freedoms could also be an empty threat used by the EU to press Britain on other issues. In such a case—that is, if more trade is better than less trade for the EU, notwithstanding some restrictions on freedom of movement—then a stubborn British line on the issue of migration may be successful. If the rhetoric in question is not an empty threat, on the other hand, then a stubborn British line can lead instead to a collapse of negotiations or at least a bad outcome.

We must also stress the importance of the sequence in which issues are decided. In our study from 2017, we argue it is best to negotiate first on issues where the parties have directly opposed interests (migration), and only thereafter to proceed to matters where their interests more nearly coincide (trade).

If access to the common market is decided first, then Britain will have no reason to take the EU's wishes on labour mobility into account in the next phase. Moreover, this is likely to be evident to the Union from the start, whereupon access to the common market will be decided against the background of very low expectations on labour mobility. Therefore, if the EU regards the four freedoms as indivisible, a negotiating sequence of this kind may result in significant restrictions on trade. However, if labour mobility is decided first instead, then Britain's behaviour will affect its prospects for achieving free trade. The UK will then have good reason to consider how its stance on migration affects the EU's attitude on free trade, whereupon the outcome will likely be greater labour mobility and freer trade. The more inclined Britain is to regard the Union's declarations on the indivisibility of the freedoms as credible, the greater will be its incentive to give ground on labour mobility. However, this may in turn prompt the Union to ramp up its rhetoric and to put undue emphasis on the indivisibility of the four freedoms. In our study from 2017, we show how the Union always has an incentive to proclaim the indivisibility of the freedoms, even though it actually sees more trade as always better than less. The EU can even win by committing itself to a line at variance with its true preferences, if it is able thereby to influence the UK's position in a sufficiently favourable direction.

It may be worth noting that a strong complementarity between the freedoms means the EU will react more strongly against restrictions on labour mobility. This may in turn have a restraining effect on Britain's policy on migration. But this does *not* entail a stronger desire to punish the UK for withdrawing or to deter other member states from leaving. The Union has nothing to gain from stoking a desire to punish Brexit any more than might be necessary in order to minimize the risk that other member states will leave.

The more strongly the EU regards the four freedoms as indivisible, the more important it is to reach agreement on migration first. From this point of view, the EU seems to have taken the most rational approach to the negotiations so far. While the UK would have liked to talk about the future trading relationship, the EU has demanded that negotiations first be concluded on some stumbling blocks over which the parties have wholly conflicting interests, and here the Union has had its way. If migration issues can be resolved first, the prospects for ensuring relatively free trade between Britain and the EU will be more favourable.

According to the account above, restrictions on free trade have served partly as a means by which to deter other member states from leaving the Union, and partly as a means by which to persuade the UK to minimize restrictions on labour mobility. However, trade barriers are a blunt instrument of deterrence in both cases, since they also harm the EU itself. By contrast, imposing a hefty divorce bill on Britain for leaving—requiring it to make a significant contribution to the Union budget—can have the desired deterrent effect, even while benefitting the Union financially and having no distorting effect on trade. Freer trade and a higher divorce bill can thus benefit both parties.

Winners and Losers on the Single Market

Following the introduction of freedom of movement, the Union has unsurprisingly seen an increase both in trade and in labour migration, not least after the Union's enlargement to the east. Britain in particular has experienced a sharp increase in labour migration from the rest of Europe, as Fig. 5.8 shows. What economic effect might an increase in trade and migration have on different groups, and to what extent can this explain the increase in nationalism and resistance to integration? We provide a brief overview below of certain simple economic mechanisms which may have a bearing on this.

Integration and reduced trading costs are economically favourable on the whole, but they also tend to entail both winners and losers. The problems are less pressing when countries at the same level of development trade with each other. For example, when Sweden exports Volvos to Germany and imports BMWs from said country, profits are made in both nations and there are no direct losers. The theory on this type of trade, commonly referred to as intra-industry trade, was first developed by Paul Krugman in two articles in 1979 and 1980. On the other hand, when countries at different levels of development trade with each other winners and losers are created in both countries. This is usually illustrated with the simplest conceivable trade model, which features two countries, two commodities, and two production factors. The production factors can be high- and low-skilled labour, with more of the former being used in producing one of the commodities than in producing the other. In the absence of trade, the countries focus their production on a mix that best meets local demand. With free trade, on the other hand, they gain by concentrating on producing the commodity for which they enjoy a comparative advantage. That is to say, the country with better access to high-skilled labour, which we can call the rich country, concentrates on producing the commodity which requires more in the way of such labour. The poor country does the opposite. This 'globalization' results in higher overall production, but in a way that benefits high-skilled groups in the rich country and low-skilled groups in the poor one. Both benefit from the exports that trade entails. On the other hand, low-skilled persons in the rich country and high-skilled persons in the poor one see their wages fall, as a consequence of competition from imports. Trade leads to an equalization of factor prices between the countries in question. In view of this, we can expect resistance to globalization and demands for trade barriers to display the same pattern. Within the EU, there is much intra-industry trade between the richest countries, while trade between the older member states and some of the newer and poorer ones is based on comparative advantage (please note that this example solely illustrates trade; it says nothing about the impact of migration).

When a country imports a commodity, however, it imports more than just the material from which the commodity is made; it also imports the labour that went into making it. For example, importing clothing from low-wage countries means importing not just the material in question, but also the low-paid labour that went into producing the product. One consequence of this is that free international trade has the same effect as labour migration. In principle, importing goods that embody a high proportion of low-skilled labour has the same effect as moving the low-skilled workers in question to the importing country. Free trade means that labour need not move geographically. Freedom of movement in either dimension is theoretically sufficient to equalize wages and other factor prices between countries. The world, however, does not really work that way. There are plenty of examples of persistent wage differentials between countries that can hardly be explained by corresponding differences in productivity. One reason for this is that not all goods and services are subject to trade. In a country with highly productive labour in sectors which are exposed to international competition, the wages accruing to such labour will be high, and this will have spill-over effects on sectors which are not exposed to such competition. Economists call this the Balassa-Samuelson effect.

From an economic point of view, therefore, we can expect labour migration to have a somewhat broader impact than trade, since it affects the domestic labour force both in sectors which are exposed to competition from trade and in sectors which are not. Take construction for example. For practical reasons, housing and home repairs cannot be traded to any great extent. The construction branch is thus largely protected from foreign competition through trade. However, when construction workers are able to migrate within the EU, the effect is the same as it would be if trade in housing and home repairs were in fact possible. That is to say, it results in lower prices for construction services in the high-wage countries to which the building workers move. There may thus be broader resistance to migration than to trade in rich countries, if it primarily involves an influx of low- or medium-skilled workers who compete for low-skilled jobs. Moreover, as Mayda (2008) shows, there is some evidence of a corresponding difference in attitudes towards migration between workers in sectors which are exposed to competition from trade and workers in sectors which are not.

Another aspect of the single market concerns the impact of trade and migration on the location of industry. Trade leads to international specialization, which in turn leads to changes in the industrial structure of countries. Production in export industries increases, while it declines or disappears in some industries that compete with imports. In the richer EU countries especially, services and high-tech industries have increased in importance. The restructuring of industries affects their placement.

Companies in advanced service industries, for example, are attracted to areas where highly qualified workers are in plentiful supply, and where they can benefit from technological transfer from other companies in their industry. That is to say, they are drawn to the service-industrial clusters which are located almost exclusively in or near the major cities and the university towns. This trend has resulted in a widening gulf between city and countryside, and many residents of the latter feel they have lost out.

Migration, moreover, entails encounters between different cultures that can both enrich social life and lead to friction; and, for this reason too, attitudes towards migration may differ from attitudes towards trade. Within the EU, the sharp increase in refugee immigration in recent times may well influence views on labour migration and freedom of movement within the Union.

In a study of the Brexit referendum published in 2017, Becker et al. examine what distinguishes Leave voters. They find that exposure to the EU in terms of trade and migration explains relatively little of the variation in voting results. Instead, they claim, certain basic characteristics of a locality are central for explaining the share of voters within it that opted for Leave: low incomes, high unemployment, low educational levels, and a historical dependence on jobs in manufacturing. These results indicate, they suggest, that policy issues relating to migration and cuts in social spending were linked particularly closely with a high level of support for Leave in cases where local socioeconomic conditions were difficult (with low incomes and high unemployment), and where the local population was not well-equipped—due to low levels of education—to adapt to negative shocks.

The authors also explore the extent to which similar patterns explain the share of the vote going to Marine Le Pen in the French presidential election, in view of the prominent part played in both elections by populist currents (UKIP in the UK and the Front National (now Rassemblement National) in France). Limitations in available data make the comparison somewhat tricky, but the pattern in the two cases proves to be similar; in particular, a low level of education is central. A prediction of Le Pen's share of the vote in the French election based on the coefficients estimated for Brexit explains about half as much of the variation as the best prediction based on French coefficient estimates.

A further example can be seen in Sweden, where one parliamentary party in particular—the Sweden Democrats—has staked out positions of both a nationalist and a Eurosceptical kind. A study by Dal Bó et al. (2018)

examines the characteristics of both the party's representatives and its voters. The study considers the impact of two economic changes: firstly, a series of reforms that increased income gaps between insiders and outsiders on the labour market; and, secondly, the financial crisis, which doubled the risk of unemployment for vulnerable groups. The authors find that Swedes who have lost out in both these respects are over-represented among representatives of the Sweden Democrats, as compared with their counterparts in other parties. Furthermore, increased income inequality at the local level is associated with increased support for the party, as is a higher proportion of vulnerable insiders.

Attitudes Towards the Union in Different Member States[2]

After the launch of the single market in 1992, the disadvantages of being left outside the Union became very palpable, and there was a strong concern within the business community in the EFTA countries about the consequences of being excluded from the single market. Large companies responded by making sure they had a foot in the single market. In many cases, they achieved this through direct investment and company acquisitions in the EU. For a brief time, for example, companies from Sweden were among the very largest investors in the EU, as the *Economist* noted in an issue adorned by a Viking ship bearing large Swedish companies to Europe.

When most of the EFTA countries then joined the EU, this was due in part to strong pressure from the business community. At the same time, the rest of the population showed a fairly high level of scepticism towards the Union. Figure 5.1 shows how residents of the 15 EU member states in 1995 answered the question in the Eurobarometer of whether membership was a good thing for their country. It is striking how widespread Eurosceptical attitudes were among people in the former EFTA countries (Austria, Denmark, Finland, Portugal, Sweden, and the UK). People in those member states were among the most sceptical in the Union. Swedes were the most sceptical at the time, followed closely by Austrians and Britons. In time this would change, however.

[2] Unless otherwise specified, the data in this section comes from the European Commission's database on the Standard Eurobarometer, see European Commission (2019).

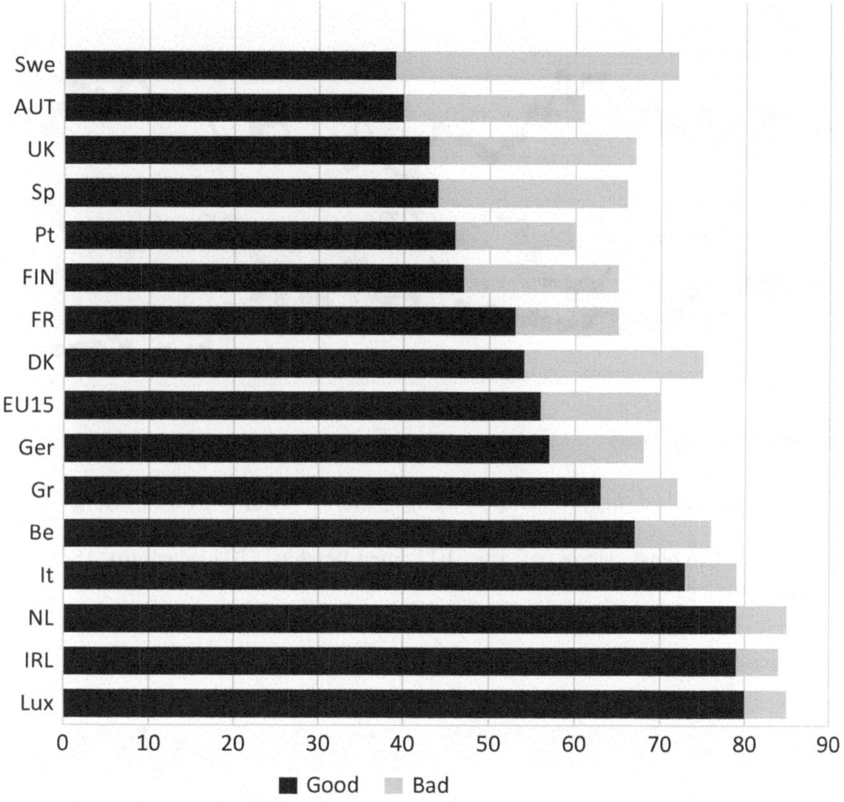

Fig. 5.1 Support for EU membership 1995 (Source: Eurobarometer)

Figure 5.2 shows how attitudes towards EU membership developed up to 2011 (Eurobarometer). For the EU as a whole, there was a stable predominance throughout the 1983–2011 period for the view that EU membership has benefitted the country. This can be seen in Fig. 5.2; however, it bears recalling here that the number of member states has grown over time, making it harder to interpret this average. In the case of the most Euroscеptical country, Sweden (Fig. 5.3), public perception of the Union grew much more positive over time, after a dip in the first two years. Over 50 per cent were positive around 2011; slightly more than 30 per cent were negative. The UK (Fig. 5.4) shows a completely different pattern. In that country Euroscepticism dominated for most of the period; and from

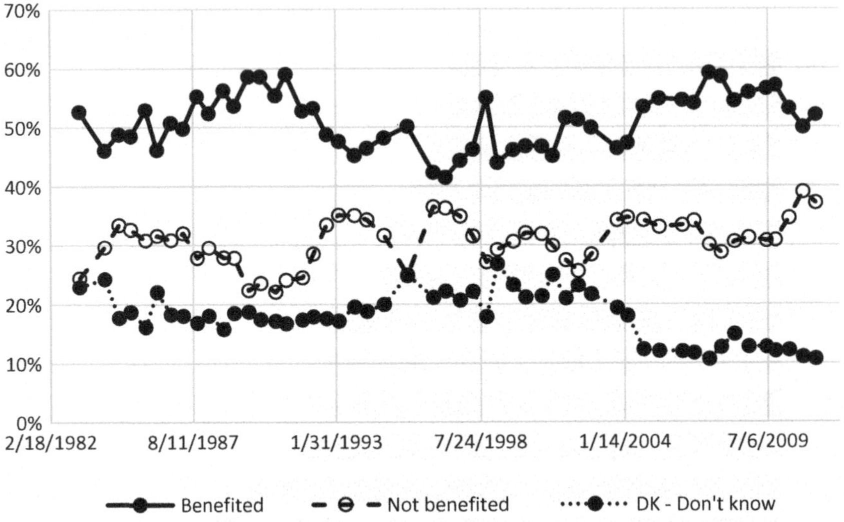

Fig. 5.2 Citizens' views of the EU membership (EU average) (Source: Eurobarometer)

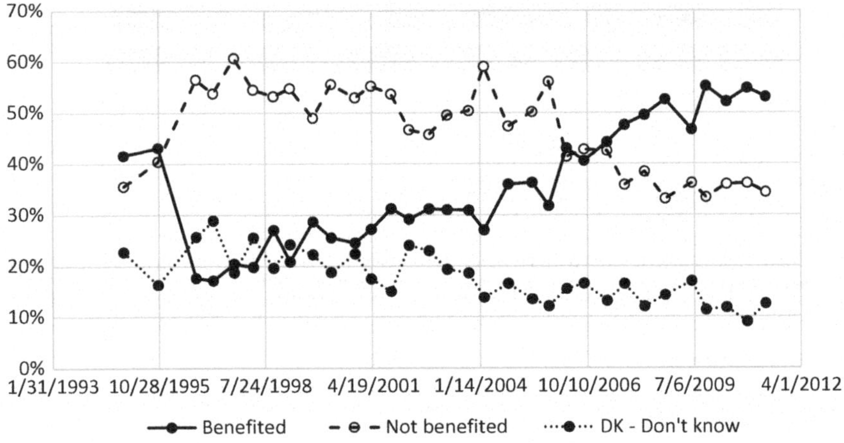

Fig. 5.3 Citizens' views of the EU membership (Sweden) (Source: Eurobarometer)

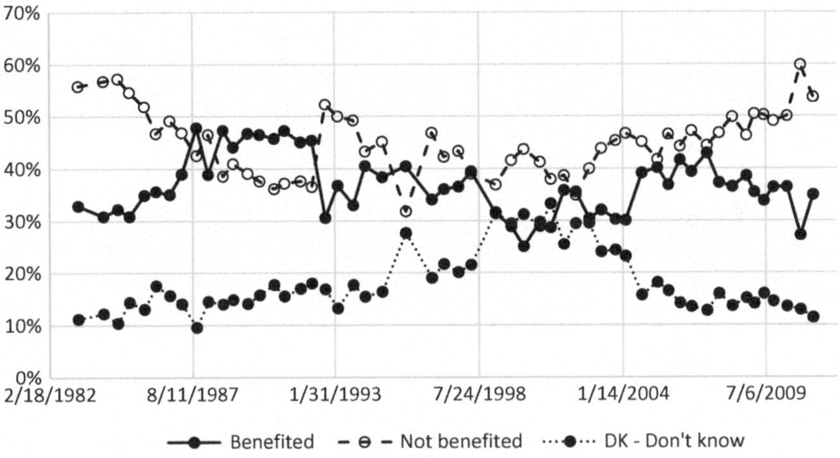

Fig. 5.4 Citizens' views of the EU membership (UK) (Source: Eurobarometer)

the beginning of the 2000s it increased and reached over 50 per cent in 2011. The rising scepticism in the UK from the beginning of the 2000s coincided with the Union's enlargement to the east. Sweden and the UK were very positive towards eastward enlargement, and together with Ireland they were the only countries that did not introduce special rules slowing the influx of labour from the countries of the former East bloc. Ironically enough, it is precisely the migration from Eastern Europe which champions of Brexit cite today as a strong argument for leaving the Union. There are some three million immigrants from other EU member states in the UK currently.

Another angle on how attitudes towards the Union have evolved can be seen in Eurobarometer's annual question about how much trust people have in the EU, which can be compared with how much trust they have in the government of their own country. Figure 5.5 shows the percentage of respondents in the EU as a whole who have trust in the Union and in their own national governments. Here we see that, on average, the level of trust in the EU is always higher than the level of trust in national governments; but the curves have converged to some extent since 2010. However, this figure conceals great differences between the member states.

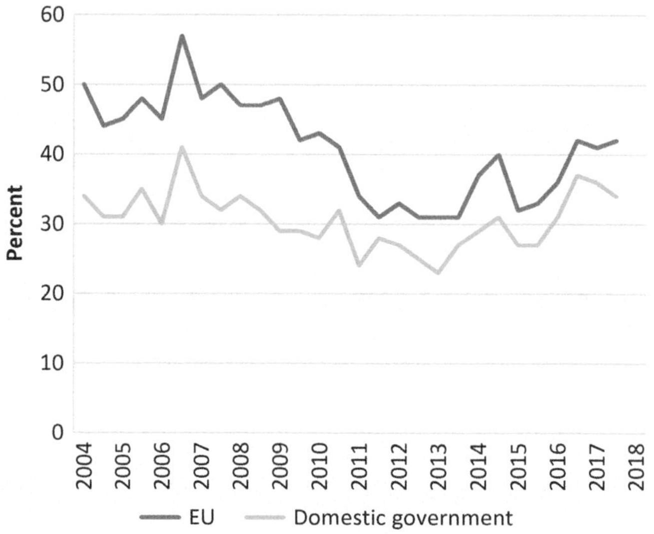

Fig. 5.5 Citizens' trust in the EU and the domestic government 2004–2018 (Source: Eurobarometer)

In Fig. 5.6, we have taken the difference between the percentage of respondents who have trust in their national government and the percentage of respondents who do not. We have done the same calculation in relation to levels of trust in the EU (i.e. the Commission). We have taken our data from Eurobarometer in 2017 and 2018. The bars in Fig. 5.6 are sorted by level of trust in the EU. Greeks have the lowest level of trust in the EU; it should be noted, however, that they have even less trust in their own national government. The British come next, with a very low level of trust in the Union and about the same level of trust in their national government.

Among several of the richest countries in the Union—among them Austria, Germany, Luxembourg, the Netherlands, and Sweden—trust in the national government exceeds that in the EU in varying degrees. However, respondents in several eastern member states—including Bulgaria, Hungary, Latvia, Lithuania, Romania, and Slovakia—have a very low level of trust in their own government but a high level of trust in the Union.

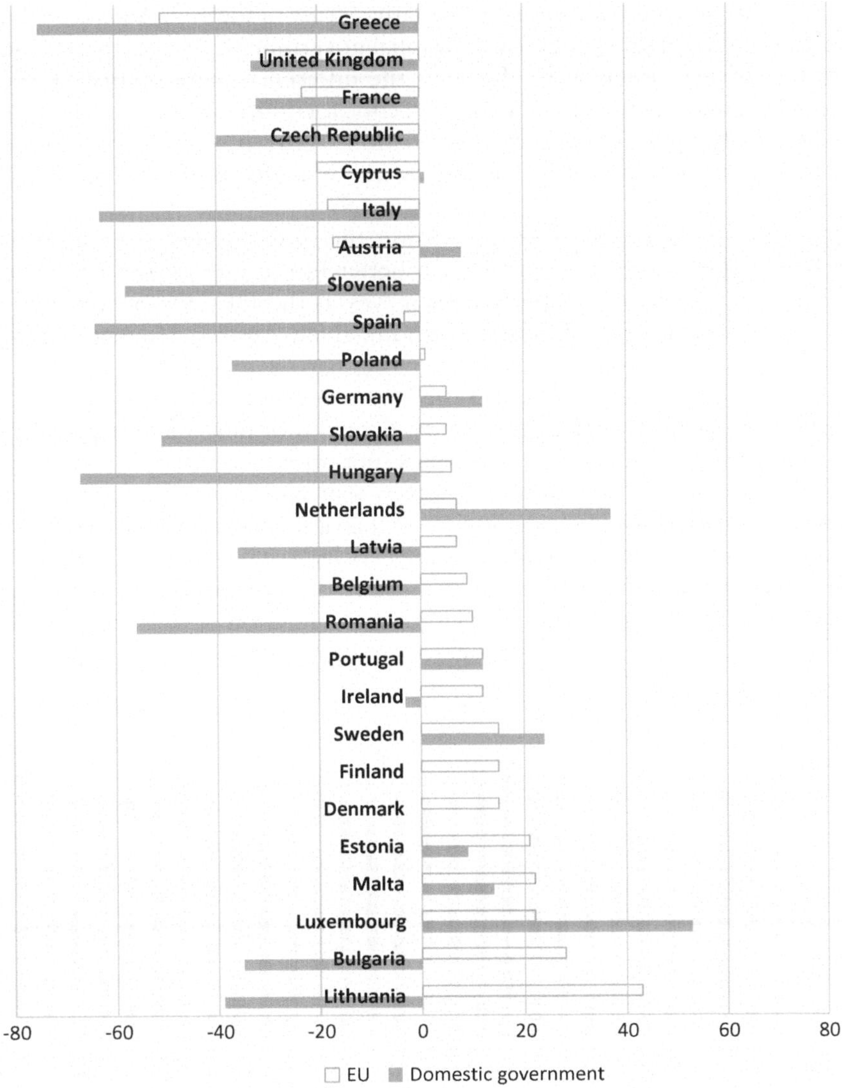

Fig. 5.6 Differences in trust in the EU and the domestic government (2017/2018) (Source: Eurobarometer)

Finally, all countries showing 'negative' trust in the EU, Austria aside, have even less trust in their own national government. In fact, this is true in the British case as well, although the difference there is small. Only Austria stands out as a rather Eurosceptical country whose inhabitants have much higher trust in the own national government. In sum, these figures give no indication of any wave of nationalism in the member states.

Figure 5.7 shows how people answer the Eurobarometer question of whether their country would have a better future outside the EU. The only country where a majority answer 'yes' is the UK; however, respondents in several other countries—among them Austria, Hungary, Italy, and Slovenia—answer 'no' by only a rather narrow majority.

One of the greatest challenges the Union faces is how to deal with freedom of movement within its bounds. Freedom of movement is popular: more than eight out of ten Europeans support it, according to the latest Eurobarometer. It is possible, however, that enthusiasm for one's own freedom to move is substantially greater than any appreciation for an influx of workers from other countries. At the very least, it is evident that support for freedom of movement is lower in some of the main labour-receiving countries, including Britain. The large-scale migration of workers into the UK was also one of the strongest arguments proffered by advocates of Brexit.

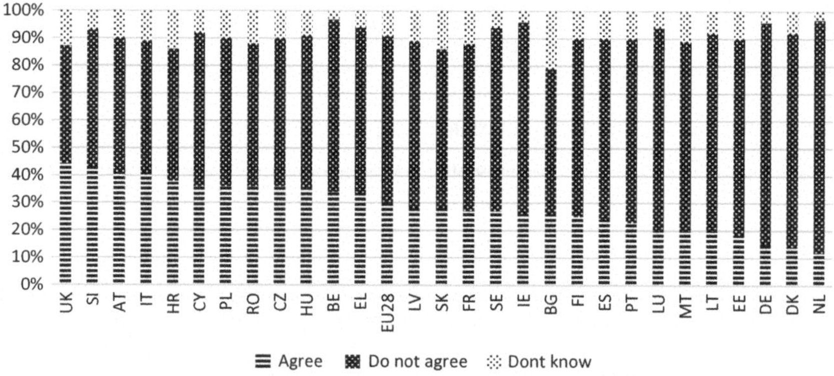

Fig. 5.7 Would your country have a better future outside the EU? (2018) (Source: Eurobarometer)

It is also true that the number of migrants from elsewhere in the Union has increased very significantly in the UK. Figure 5.8 shows the trend in this regard in the UK and in certain other countries. The number of migrants in the UK from elsewhere in the Union has increased very rapidly, in both absolute and relative terms.

The fact is, however, that scepticism towards migration is far more widespread in several other member states. When asked whether or not they would feel comfortable having an immigrant as a friend, only about 10 per cent replied 'completely comfortable' in Bulgaria and Hungary, as compared with 77 per cent in the UK (European Commission 2018). At the same time, the freedom to migrate is likely much more important for Bulgarians and Hungarians than it is for Britons. However, a powerful resistance to immigration has clearly made itself felt in relation to immigration by persons from outside Europe. During the recent refugee crisis

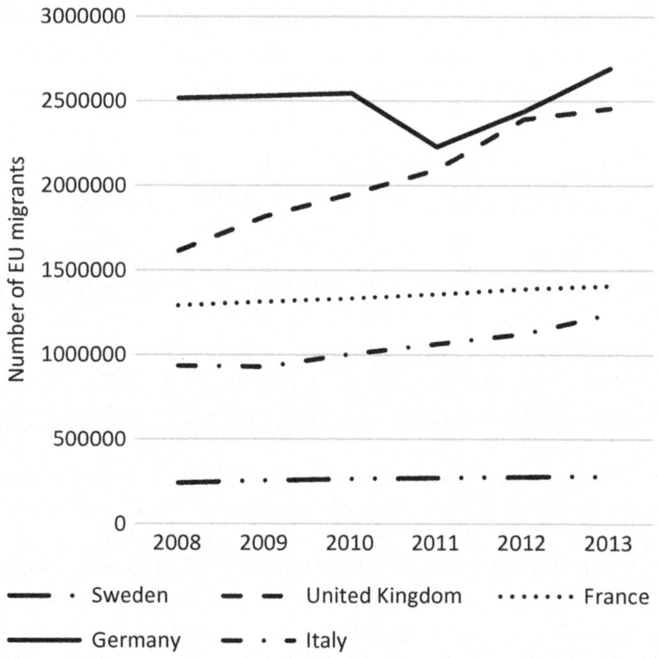

Fig. 5.8 Number of EU migrants 2008–2013 (Source: Eurostat Statistical Database 2019)

in connection with the Syrian war, a number of countries simply closed their borders.

The upsurge of nationalism in the EU today has a regional character in many cases, and one of the clearest examples can be seen in Catalonia (see Bremberg in this volume.) In view of the theory of optimal state size, this seems natural to some extent. For a region within a nation-state, the benefits of participation in the latter diminish under current conditions. The benefits afforded by the nation-state's integrated national market lose their significance when the Union's single market is operating, and economies of scale in the area of defence are dwarfed by the Union's increasing commitments in that field. Of course, this presupposes that regional independence can be achieved within the framework of the common market—which is far from obvious, since the nation-state concerned may have a strong incentive to block such a solution. At the same time, it is natural for successful regions to strengthen their position vis-à-vis their nation-state as their relevant market becomes more European and less national. A trend of this kind can also strengthen the Union vis-à-vis its member states. We can therefore expect that, over the long run, the current nation-states of the EU will become less important and the regions more so.

Conclusions: How Should Brexit Be Handled in Order to Ensure the EU's Survival?

Brexit represents a new chapter in the history of the EU, which could be interpreted as the return of the nation-state. But although there are new elements in Brexit, this chapter has shown that tensions within the EU are of long standing. In the Union's annual attitude surveys—the Eurobarometer—the citizens of the UK stand out. Only during a few years in the late 1980s and early 1990s did a majority of them say that their country had gained by joining the Union. During all the other years between 1983 and 2011, the majority judged their country to have lost by its membership. Why, then, is Brexit happening now? It is difficult to overlook the role played here by large migration flows within the EU, as well as into the Union from without. These have served as a trigger for nationalist currents. Moreover, the financial crisis that broke out in 2008 brought economic hardship to many member states, and approximately one million workers from other EU countries moved to the UK during the 2008–2013 period. In many cases, these new workers competed with people who had lost out from globalization, at least in relative terms: that is, low-skilled workers outside the big cities. Furthermore, expectations over the impact of an exit have likely been important for the stance on that issue which different citizens have taken. Uncertainty on this matter has been very great, because no exit from the Union has ever taken place before. In the lead-up to the referendum, a great variety of views on that score were aired in the British debate.

The EU's insistence on the indivisibility of the four freedoms, and its reluctance to countenance à la carte solutions for the UK, has turned out to be considerably stronger than many in the UK likely expected. Perhaps the UK's success as a member state in negotiating various special solutions for itself has contributed to the expectation that the Union would take a softer line and be more accommodating in negotiations over Brexit. As such expectations have come to grief, the perceived cost of withdrawal may be expected to have risen correspondingly, which may be a major reason why support for Brexit has weakened. Similarly, Brexit sends an important signal regarding the EU's attitude towards possible future attempts at exit. EU leaders have managed to maintain a united front, and they have continued to insist that exit means that market access will be limited. Scarcely any of the countries that lie closest to an exit in terms of their public opinion possess bargaining power anywhere near the UK's, and they would also have a lot more to lose from an exit. As Brexit has developed, then, it is reasonable to suppose that the risk of further exits has diminished, and that the process has also reduced the prospects for obtaining benefits by threatening to leave the Union.

At the time of writing, there is considerable uncertainty over what the conditions for Brexit will be, or whether an agreement will even be reached. Our discussion above on how the negotiations can be analysed in game-theoretical terms highlights some of the strategic challenges, and issues in a number of policy recommendations: (1) It is best to negotiate first over the difficult stumbling blocks—the issues over which the interests of the parties are most sharply opposed—and to take up the question of market access later. Doing so will benefit both the UK and the EU. (2) While the Union has an interest in deterring further attempts at exit, both sides will lose out if the EU tries above and beyond to punish the UK for leaving. (3) Finally, the EU has an interest in claiming that the four freedoms are indivisible regardless of its real preferences. However, if the UK mistakenly bets that the EU's real preferences on this score are soft, negotiations could end badly for both parties. The UK can accordingly reduce the risk for a poor outcome by assuming that the Union is firmly committed to linking free trade and freedom of movement for labour.

As it has become clear that the outcome for Britain will be significantly less favourable than the Leave side predicted prior to the referendum, popular support for Brexit has declined and demands have been raised for a new vote. The Union would be sensible to support such an opening. After all, the outcome of the referendum ought in itself to inspire some responsiveness on the EU's part, as well as a degree of humility as regards its ability to satisfy the interests of its citizens. Any steps towards cancelling Brexit should therefore be met with signals of a willingness to discuss conditions for continued membership and flexibility regarding the timetable. From this standpoint, the statement of the EU budget commissioner, Günter Oettiger, that Britain will likely lose its rebate if it remains a member was unfortunate (Stone 2018).

How might the EU be altered as a result of Brexit? Several of Europe's core countries, with France in the forefront, favour giving the Union more power. However, such a move towards greater federalism would risk repelling certain member states, such as some of the former EFTA countries. Another solution is a 'two-speed Europe', whereby some member states would deepen their cooperation (see, e.g. Stegmann McCallion in this volume). This has already happened to some extent, inasmuch as only some of the Union's member states use the euro as their currency. Finally, it cannot be ignored that freedom of movement within the Union is one of the most explosive aspects of the common market. It is not unlikely that rules in this area will be tightened in some fashion.

Has the EU become too big, then, so that it risks being torn apart? We do not believe so. However, the Union has expanded greatly and become far more heterogeneous, which means that it must balance rights and obligations in such a manner that all of its member states see clear benefits from membership. The UK, for example, has been an extremely valuable member—not just for the large and extremely well-developed national market it has offered but also for the major contribution it has made to the EU budget. At the same time, other member states have acted more recently in an unsolidaristic fashion vis-à-vis the Union, and behaved politically in ways contrary to its core democratic values or at odds with central commitments in the monetary union. Some of these states, furthermore, are large net recipients of aid from the Union. Just as heterogeneity within a nation tends to limit the degree of redistribution undertaken within it, the same may apply to the EU. Alternatively, movement in a more federal direction may limit the ability of member states to neglect common commitments.

References

Acemoglu, D., Johnson, S., & Robinson, J. (2005). The Rise of Europe: Atlantic Trade, Institutional Change, and Economic Growth. *American Economic Review, 95*(3), 546–579.

Alesina, A., & Spolaore, E. (1997). On the Number and Size of Nations. *The Quarterly Journal of Economics, 112*(4), 1027–1056.

Baldwin, R. (1999). A Domino Theory of Regionalism. In J. Bhagwati, P. Krishna, & A. Panagariya (Eds.), *Trading Blocs: Alternative Approaches to Analyzing Preferential Trade Agreements* (pp. 479–502). Cambridge: MIT Press.

Becker, S. O., Fetzer, T., & Novy, D. (2017). Who Voted for Brexit? A Comprehensive District-Level Analysis. *Economic Policy, 32*(92), 601–650.

Besley, T., & Persson, T. (2009). The Origins of State Capacity: Property Rights, Taxation, and Politics. *American Economic Review, 99*(4), 1218–1244.

Bolton, P., & Roland, G. (1997). The Breakup of Nations: A Political Economy Analysis. *The Quarterly Journal of Economics, 112*(4), 1057–1090.

Bolton, P., Roland, G., & Spolaore, E. (1996). Economic Theories of the Break-Up and Integration of Nations. *European Economic Review, 40*(3–5), 697–705.

Brewer, J. (1989). *The Sinews of Power: War, Money and the English State, 1688–1783.* London: Unwin Hyman Ltd..

Churchill, W. (1946, September). Speech. University of Zurich. Retrieved September 9, 2019, from https://rm.coe.int/16806981f3.

Cramér, P. (2019). Brexit, Trumpism and the Structure of the International Trade Regime. In A. Bakardjieva Engelbrekt, N. Bremberg, A. Michalski, & L. Oxelheim (Eds.), *The European Union in a Changing World Order* (pp. 47–80). Basingstoke: Palgrave Macmillan.

Dal Bó, E., Finan, F., Folke, O., Persson T., & Rickne, J. (2018). *Economic Losers and Political Winners: Sweden's Radical Right.* Retrieved September 9, 2019, from http://perseus.iies.su.se/~tpers/papers/CompleteDraft190301.pdf.

De Vries, C. E. (2017). Benchmarking Brexit: How the British Decision to Leave Shapes EU Public Opinion. *Journal of Common Market Studies, 55*(9), 38–53.

De Vries, C. E. (2018). *Euroscepticism and the Future of European Integration.* Oxford: Oxford University Press.

Dhingra, S., Ottaviano, G., Sampson, T., & Van Reenen, J. (2016), *The consequences of Brexit for UK trade and living standards.* Centre for Economic Performance Brexit Analysis 2 (CEPBREXIT02). London: London School of Economics and Political Science, CEP. Retrieved September 9, 2019, from http://eprints.lse.ac.uk/66144/.

European Commission. (2018). October 2017 Special Eurobarometer Survey 469 on Integration of Immigrants in the European Union. https://doi.org/10.2837/918822.

European Commission. (2019). The Standard Eurobarometer Database 1974–2019. Retrieved August 1, 2019, from https://ec.europa.eu/commfrontoffice/publicopinion/index.cfm/Survey/index#p=1&instruments=STANDARD.

Eurostat Statistical Database. (2019). Retrieved June 1, 2019, from https://ec.europa.eu/eurostat/data/database.

Forslid, R., & Nyberg, S. (2017). *Brexit – Balancing Trade and Migration.* CEPR Discussion Paper No. DP12370. London: Centre for Economic Policy Research. Retrieved September 9, 2019, from https://ssrn.com/abstract=3053898.

Gancia, G., Ponzetto, G., & Ventura, J. (2016). *Globalization and Political Structure.* NBER Working Paper No. 22046. Retrieved September 8, 2019, from https://www.nber.org/papers/w22046.pdf.

Herszenhorn D. M. (2018, May 17). Macron Declares 'Decision Time' for Europe. *Politico.* Retrieved September 8, 2019, from https://www.politico.eu/article/emmanuel-macron-france-germany-italy-banking-unions-eurozone-emu-declares-decision-time-for-europe/.

Krugman, P. (1979). Increasing Returns, Monopolistic Competition and International Trade. *Journal of International Economics, 9*(4), 469–480.

Krugman, P. (1980). Scale Economies, Product Differentiation, and the Pattern of Trade. *American Economic Review, 70*(5), 950–959.

Mayda, A. M. (2008). Why Are People More Pro-trade than Pro-migration? *Economics Letters, 101*(3), 160–163.

Putnam, R. D. (1988). Diplomacy and Domestic Politics: The Logic of Two-Level Games. *International Organization, 42*(3), 427–460.

Stone, J. (2018, October 12). UK Would Still Lose EU Budget Rebate if It Decided to Cancel Brexit, Brussels Budget Chief Says. *The Independent.* Retrieved September 9, 2019, from https://www.independent.co.uk/news/uk/politics/brexit-eu-budget-rebate-gunther-oetinger-second-referendum-remain-a8580616.html.

CHAPTER 6

EU Tax Law and the Return of the Nation-State

Cécile Brokelind

Introduction

Populism is often described as a threat to the existence of the European Union (EU). Several of the chapters in this volume focus precisely on this issue and suggest solutions that the Union should adopt to address the populist threat, especially in respect of migration and of the erosion of the rule of law in Poland and Hungary. The development of tax law, on the other hand, has looked very different. Instead of fighting the populist and nationalist tendencies in the member states, the EU seems to be advocating the protection of the national welfare state, which is financed by taxes. This is done by allowing member states to combat tax competition within the EU to secure their own tax bases, with the aim of protecting the state's tax sovereignty. At the outset, this protectionist trend seems to run counter the EU's basic principles of free movement and fair competition on the internal market. How has this development been possible?

This chapter explains the paradigm shift from liberalization of and free access to the internal market to tougher regulation that member states

C. Brokelind (✉)
Lund University, Lund, Sweden
e-mail: cecile.brokelind@har.lu.se

A. Bakardjieva Engelbrekt et al. (eds.), *The European Union and the Return of the Nation State*,
https://doi.org/10.1007/978-3-030-35005-5_6

adopt to protect their tax sovereignty against tax base erosion, a type of return of the nation-state. The Apple and Starbucks cases on corporate income tax (CIT), arisen from the LuxLeaks scandal, substantiate this development. Furthermore, the recent Anti-Tax Avoidance Directive (ATAD) limiting aggressive tax planning on corporate income tax (Council directive (EU) 2016/1164) also illustrates this trend. Previously, EU-level legislation on corporate income tax and aggressive tax planning had been virtually non-existent. Why did member states suddenly agree for the EU to legislate in this field of law? How did the member states agree to allow the EU to legislate to limit what they consider to be harmful tax competition? What are the implications for EU member states on a global scale? Given the member states' invocation of national sovereignty in other fields of law, is the evolution of EU tax law towards tax sovereignty also a sign that nationalism is affecting political and economic development in the EU?

The next eight sections try to provide an answer to these questions. The first one explains how the historical development of the EU tax competition policy has led to the present (July 2019) situation. The next section introduces the tax law concepts that are central in the Apple and Starbucks cases, such as 'tax base erosion'. The third one explains how international tax law traditionally addresses taxation of multinational enterprises' (hereafter MNEs) profits. These sections are needed to understand the next section on the pending EU state aid cases with Apple, Starbucks and other MNEs, which obtained favourable tax deals with some member states' tax authorities. In addition to these state aid cases, member states' tax sovereignty is expressed in other rules, such as the Anti-Tax Avoidance Directive, which will be dealt with in the following section. Finally, the last sections investigate in whose interest this development of EU tax law occurs and assess the digital tax proposal as one of the ways put forward in the EU to maintain national tax sovereignty.

What Happened Before the LuxLeaks Scandal?

In November 2014, 600 tax deals were unveiled in Luxembourg, a disclosure that received exceptional media attention, also known as the LuxLeaks scandal. It revealed that MNEs through agreements with some of the member state's tax authorities where they elected tax residence had the opportunity to negotiate very low taxes on their global profits. These companies included Amazon, Fiat and the energy company ENGIE. Belgium, Ireland and the Netherlands were also questioned for having applied the same type of tax arrangements for Apple and IKEA, among others. The whistle-blower in the LuxLeaks scandal considered the deals to be unethical and asserted that he undertook the disclosure to the press 'for the sake of the public' rather than for legal reasons (see Jaeger 2015).

The European Commission (Commission) responded by initiating proceedings against Luxembourg, Ireland, Belgium and the Netherlands for infringement of EU state aid prohibition (Article 107.1 Treaty of the Functioning of the EU, TFEU). These EU rules disallow member states to use selective tax incentives to attract foreign investment, since they distort competition on the internal market. The Commission therefore decided that the attractive tax agreements fell under the ban. The Commission's decisions were appealed by the member states concerned to the General Court. Neither the General Court nor the European Court of Justice has rendered their ruling in August 2019,[1] but should the member states be convicted, the companies in question would be required to pay additional tax. For example, for Apple, the total bill could amount to €13 billion, while ENGIE would have to pay €120 million and Amazon €250 million, excluding interest.

These multinational enterprises have exploited the effects of globalization to move their profits to the state where the corporate income tax is lowest. The fact that member states have been able to have different tax rates depends to a large extent on the member states' sovereign right to decide on tax policy and tax law, and consequently on the level of taxes levied on corporate income. Despite a clear difference between EU member states especially, research shows that corporate tax statutory rates have generally fallen since the 1990s, and at the same time, that most states have introduced tax incentives to attract mobile capital (European Commission 2019a).

Historically, the EU was unable to deal with this as member states have failed to reach a political agreement on the coordination of corporate income taxes. In 1997, however, EU member states tried to prevent harmful tax competition by presenting a Code of Conduct drafted under the EU's mandate. Under this Code of Conduct, member states were not allowed to use tax measures with a significantly lower effective level of taxation than the domestic standard, in a view to attract foreign investments. The Code of Conduct intended, among other things, to minimize

[1] The exception is the Belgian Excess Profit case with a favourable outcome for Belgium at the first stage of proceedings, see *Belgium v. Commission*, the General Court (2019).

distortions of competition in the internal market, to prevent tax evasion and to direct member states' tax structures towards an employment-friendly orientation. Anette Bruzelius analysed the Code of Conduct already in 2004. As Bruzelius pointed out, unregulated tax competition between member states could threaten the financing of the welfare state and ultimately affect citizens, hence justifying a common action at the EU level such as the Code of Conduct (Bruzelius 2004).

Despite the Code of Conduct, tax competition increased not only within the EU, but also at the global level. Today, 15 years later, the debate has shifted from defining the negative effects of tax competition to limiting MNEs' corporate tax planning, considered now as a kind of tax avoidance. This has led to EU member states jointly drafting and adopting in 2016 binding legislation on aggressive tax planning that neutralizes attractive tax incentives within and outside the EU, the so-called Anti-Tax Avoidance Directive (ATAD). This directive is a far-reaching stop-rule also applying to third states' investors. This type of regulation does not take place in isolation, but reflects a similar global trend in the G20 (featuring 19 states plus the EU) and the Organisation for Economic Co-operation and Development (OECD). These two organizations have agreed on the so-called BEPS project, which stands for 'Base Erosion and Profit Shifting' (BEPS) which aims to discourage MNEs from choosing to be taxed in low-tax jurisdictions, whether they operate there or not (OECD 2019).

These protectionist measures against tax competition at the EU level are aimed at safeguarding national tax bases and preventing public finances from being eroded, and hence protecting welfare and benefitting the individual. However, the decrease of tax competition leads to increased control over the domestic use of resources, to counteract that capital instead leaves the country to avoid taxation. This tendency is an expression of a broader and more profound phenomenon that has characterized the development of the EU, namely the contradiction between liberalization (i.e. liberalization and free movement) and social protection. EU cooperation has long been based on the liberalization of trade in goods, capital and services to implement the internal market.[2] In recent decades, however, political measures have increasingly focused on protecting citizens from the negative effects of liberalization.

[2] See TFEU Articles 26 (internal market), 49 to 55 (establishment), 56 to 62 (services), 45 to 48 (workers), 63 to 66 (capital).

In this context, the nation-state is understood from an economic perspective as the national welfare state. The welfare state aims to, inter alia, provide a social insurance system, financed by tax revenue. There are several benefits to having a public social insurance system and therefore it is well worth defending. The welfare state has been kept away from the EU's area of competence, which means that member states have always considered their taxing power to be an expression of their sovereignty. However, member states' taxing powers are limited by EU law on the internal market providing for free access of all EU member states, under the control of the Court of Justice of the European Union (CJEU). Here a conflict arises between, on the one hand, the sovereignty of the member states and, on the other, the primacy of EU law over national law. This conflict raises questions about compliance with EU law as member states take measures to protect their national sovereignty by invoking the need to protect the welfare state and potentially breaching the fundamental freedoms of movement within the internal market.

Tax Base Erosion, a Polarizing Phenomenon

Globalization has made it possible for businesses to establish themselves all over the world and thus better meet global demand and increase their profits. It also means that they can benefit from other states' tax systems and engage in tax planning, which can further increase their after-tax profits. Tax planning can be defined as a way for the taxpayer to optimize its tax costs in a way that is consistent with the purpose of the legislation, while tax avoidance instead means that the taxpayer with a legally valid transaction achieves a tax benefit by following the letter, but not the purpose of the law. What is described in the EU Anti-Tax Avoidance Directive as aggressive tax planning is a mix of these concepts. Tax evasion, which is not covered by this directive, refers to a criminal activity where taxpayers intentionally enter fictitious and illegal transactions.

MNEs with high-level knowledge on comparative tax rules such as low tax rates, tax incentives and intra-group pricing methods have been able to pay less corporate income tax globally than they would if they had only been operating home. They also use differences in legislation, for example, when income is not classified in the same way in two states and therefore remains untaxed in both. The problem is that domestic tax judges do not always have in the law an exact definition of what constitutes permissible or unlawful arrangement. The conflicts ending at court remain, however, under the control of the CJEU in respect of cross-border transactions on which the EU freedoms of movement apply. In its case law, the CJEU has always allowed taxpayers to organize a business in such way that the tax burden is reduced legally by strategically locating profits to the states where the tax is lowest, under the premise that allocation rules of taxing powers between states allow it (see the case *Cadbury Schweppes,* Court of Justice of the European Union 2006).

In international tax law, states have long ago agreed to allocate taxing powers among themselves. This has been done through double tax treaties (DTT) based on a model, drafted by the OECD (2017a). The model provides that the state of residence, that is where companies have registered their head office, as a rule, has priority over taxing the taxpayers' worldwide profits. In exceptional cases, where the business is carried out abroad through a permanent place from which the business is wholly or partly carried on (permanent establishment, PE), this other state (the source state) may tax the part of the company's profits that arise there. In other words, profits should be attributed to the state in which they originate. DTT usually solve problems of double taxation that can occur when both the source state and the resident state claim to tax the company for the same income.

Digitalization and new business models have made it difficult for states to apply the conditions for taxing income at source and hence to tax foreign companies which are able to make profits of access to their markets. For example, commercialization of products through a digital platform cannot be considered a permanent place of sale according to the OECD model. This means that the state in which the sale is made loses the opportunity to tax the company's income there, because of the lack of physical presence in this territory. The consequence of this is that the MNEs' tax planning can ultimately lead to zero source taxation, when being able to sell without any physical presence anywhere.

The newspapers and other media have raised this problem and pointed out that, because of these allocation rules, the BRIC (Brazil, Russia, India and China) states, as well as large EU states, have lost tax bases to the benefit of smaller states with attractive tax systems. In these states, such as the Netherlands, Belgium, Ireland and Luxembourg, MNEs establish their residence, thereby avoiding paying taxes on sales in the BRIC states and the major EU states which should (but do not succeed) tax income at source. The battle for tax bases between the state where the company is resident and the state where it has its market is thus an effect of globalization.

The OECD, followed by the EU, has, since 2012, through its project against tax base erosion and profit shifting (BEPS) tried to change the existing allocation rules since the 1920s, granting larger taxing power to the source states. In the past, the threshold was very high for the source states to tax MNEs because the rules required the companies to conduct full business operations from a permanent location. Moreover, the right to tax companies required that their income had a real and substantial connection to the source state. The more recent rules have lowered these requirements and indicate that companies' access to the source state's market is now sufficient for them to become taxable there. The permanent place of business as the prerequisite for taxation disappeared in the reform.

The problem with corporate income tax, which is a direct tax, is that it is based on companies' ability to pay taxes, which does not consist solely of its sales and market access possibilities. From a tax policy perspective, the state of residence has traditionally been considered best suited to assess the companies' ability to pay taxes, since companies file their tax return in that residence state. However, when the exchange of information between states does not work, the state of residence cannot control the company's income in the other state, and tax evasion can take place whereby taxpayers intentionally refrain from declaring their foreign income. Nevertheless, tax planning is not based on this kind of illegal behaviour, but on the exploitation of differences in the regulatory systems and the possibility of avoiding taxation of operations in the source state.

The OECD reform aims to allocating taxing powers by priority to the source state, and to tax MNEs profits at least once somewhere. In this way, the OECD, followed by the EU, expects to eliminate tax base erosion that occurs due to tax planning. The problem, however, is that all EU member states do not share the same view of the need to regulate or what method should be applied. Some states, such as the Netherlands, apply a liberal economic policy where tax competition and tax planning are a strength, while other states apply more interventionist methods, including France. Until now, the EU has not expressed any preference for either one or the other of the member states' views on how economic policy should be conducted. However, the criticism of 'tax avoidance' and 'tax base erosion' within and outside the EU has been highlighted by the media in respect of the ongoing reform of EU tax rules. In response to the criticism, the EU and its member states have started discussing which method should be applied in the joint efforts to secure tax revenue to the welfare states.

Tax Fairness, Ethics and Sustainability Paving the Way for a Reform of Tax Systems?

The academic scholarship assesses tax systems' fairness based on their horizontal and vertical equity (Kaufman 2001). The former is expressed through the 'ability to pay', according to which the residence state is given the right to tax the worldwide income of a company. Vertical equity is on the other hand based on the 'private-benefit principle', according to which the right to tax is given to the source state, the country which supplied the company with the resources to conduct its business. Both principles are applied in parallel in all tax systems. According to one of the fathers of the field of tax policies, Richard Musgrave, a balanced tax system takes into account both principles in a transparent manner (Musgrave 1959).

There are currently academic discussions as to which of these models a well-functioning tax system should be based on, as the present system visibly cannot be adapted to the effects of globalization, and hence is unable to cater to the citizens' needs for legitimacy. According to several researchers (see below), legitimacy is a concept that encompasses the citizens' conviction that the governance system is legitimate. Thus, a fair tax system is based on the willingness of the taxpayer to contribute to the tax system. If the taxpayer believes that other interests, such as that of large corporations, are being taken into account to a larger extent than theirs, it may lose confidence in the tax system. This may negatively affect the morals of the taxpayer and essentially lead to the de-legitimization of the tax system.

Some measures may be taken to avoid this scenario and limit taxpayers' cherry picking of the most beneficial way or state to invest in. This idea is based on the 'private-benefit principle' and has been promoted by, among others, Knut Wicksell (1954).[3] The OECD and other international organizations, such as the EU, have clearly shifted preferences from horizontal to vertical justice (private-benefit principle, or utility principle) in order to protect the source states and consequently restore the citizens' faith in the government as well as the resilience of the tax systems. This shift is notably expressed through the BEPS project.

[3] On Wicksell's influence, see Berggren (2012), Avi-Yonah (2000) and Piketty (2020).

Proponents of the private-benefit principle build their argument for the legitimacy of the tax system based on ethics and tax morality. They believe that tax planning and tax evasion are two phenomena that negatively affect society as the redistribution of tax bases takes place from the bottom upwards. They mean that middle- and low-income earners bear the economic costs of welfare and allowing high-income earners to become even wealthier, according to Hilling and Ostas (2018). Certain political measures are in other words justified for ensuring the welfare and economic success of states, consequently restoring the citizens' belief in the national tax system. Discussions taking place outside the field of legal research, such as those within the field of corporate social responsibility (CSR), also suggest that ethics and morals form the basis for paying taxes in addition to legal requirements. For instance, Gribnau and Jallai (2017) argue that the corporate law requirement to maximize profit leads to aggressive tax planning, while obedience to the rule of law requires self-restraint. According to this reasoning, avoiding the tax burden to maximize profit becomes unethical as it can threaten the very structure of a society.

Current discussions on EU tax policies are strongly influenced by this debate on legitimacy. Member states need to increase the credibility of their tax systems vis-à-vis citizens through taking control of tax base erosion. This type of control is considered to represent a fairer tax system, where tax is payable at least in one country. This so-called single tax principle forms the basis of the new EU rules, which is another indication that the EU indeed seems to have a strong preference for the utility principle expressed through vertical equity.

However, demanding that large MNEs pay more tax than they do today may not always be supported by strict legal analysis (Person Österman 2019). In cross-border situations involving tax planning, two legal rules in two states apply simultaneously. Companies can avoid being taxed by using either a legal loophole between the two rules or use the difference in standards to avoid being taxed on their foreign profits. The OECD has begun to address these loopholes through the BEPS project by proposing to include a provision in future tax treaties which give the right to at least one state to tax a company that uses loopholes. To explain the concept of loopholes, it is now appropriate to explain which state holds the right to tax corporate profit, and how MNEs allocate their profits in an international context.

How Is Income Allocated Within MNEs?

MNEs such as Apple and Starbucks are established globally, but incorporate a company in each country they are present according to the national rules. Each company is taxed separately according to its own tax ability, which consequently means that the group is not taxed as a single, cohesive unit. Despite the lack of a universal corporate tax rule, the pricing of transactions between the different affiliated companies is regulated according to the arm's length principle. According to this principle, the price of a transaction should be set as if the companies had been independent from each other. In other words, the pricing should be consistent with the market price. The United Nations (UN) and the OECD have both issued recommendations on rules aiming at upholding the arm's length principle. At the national level, states have introduced arm's length rules in their domestic law and in double tax treaties. They also allow MNEs to apply for advance pricing agreements (APA), which is a type of agreement with the tax authority of the country in which the company operates to set the level of taxation for their internal transactions.

Unlike companies operating only on a domestic market, MNEs can split the businesses' function, assets and risks between the various companies and states in which they operate. Hence, price setting of internal transactions can be freely set in such a way that it reduces the group's taxable profits. As a matter of a practical example, if a group of companies holds subsidiaries in two states of which one has a significantly higher tax rate, the group can produce a good in the country with the lower tax rate and sell the product to an exceedingly high price (compared to the market price) to the sister company in the state with the higher tax rate. The company purchases the goods at a price which may seem justified according to financial calculations and deducts the cost from its high tax bill. At the same time, the selling company receives a high price which increases its income, taxed at a lower rate than in the other state. This way, the group can minimize the costs generated globally by tax payments through this type of internal pricing.

Setting a higher or lower price than what is required by the arm's length principle may trigger tax authorities auditing the companies' tax returns and reassessing their taxable income. Disputes can also occur, resulting in the allocation of a larger portion of the income to the state which initiates the correction, for instance when the functions, risks and assets of a member of the group are not reflected in the internal transfer prices. Expressed differently, the arm's length principle may justify states initiating legal proceedings when the tax base of a country is eroded due to incorrect pricing.

The recently observed global intergovernmental tax competition consists of attracting MNEs by allocating company profits with support of internal pricing rules. Practically speaking, the residence state may allocate the income of a company to the source state, and the enterprise consequently avoids paying tax in any of the two states (double non-taxation). In the LuxLeaks case, where the Commission initiated proceedings against member states infringing state aid rules, states applied the internal pricing rule differently than they were intended to. In fact, they used the internal pricing rule as a tax incentive to reduce the domestic effective tax rate and to attract foreign investors. In these cases, which will be further discussed below, the MNEs negotiate with the residence state to allocate the taxable income to the source state, in which they are not taxed either because of for instance tax incentives or very low internal pricing. The OECD regulations have historically speaking not included any rules forcing the source state to tax the part of the income that the residence state loses due to this phenomenon. The doctrine speaks of stateless income, or more ironically, 'Atlantis income', as neither of the two states has the right to tax income that disappears 'into the ocean'.

The Cases in a Nutshell

The OECD (2017b) Transfer Pricing Guidelines for Multinational Enterprises and Tax Administrations, which are not binding either in Sweden or in any other EU member state, provide for guidance on how to set the price of internal group transactions and how to attribute profits in respect of functions, risks and assets allocated within the group.

The rules recommend five different methods for calculating prices of goods and services, and thereby the taxable profits. These five methods are in turn divided into two general categories, namely the direct and indirect pricing methods. Setting prices according to the direct price level means that an enterprise sets their prices in the same way as their market competitors. However, there are numerous situations where there are no competitors to compare with, for example, when a company holds a monopoly over a technology through a patent. The price will then be determined by methods that indirectly refer to the market. These indirect methods include the resale price method, which reflects the risks put on manufacturers in the production chain as they produce the goods. In many countries, prices are set in advance pricing agreements with local tax authorities. Enterprises should in any case document objective profit allocation methods and be able to prove that they did not get an over advantageous pricing method, a so-called sweetheart deal with the state's tax authorities.

Until the autumn of 2018, the Commission had launched nine in-depth investigations on breaches of state aid rules in five member states. Their tax authorities were suspected of having agreed to 'sweet heart deals' through, inter alia, advance pricing agreements with the MNEs in question. In certain cases, the Commission also made decisions on/condemned member states to be in breach of state aid rules, which were subsequently appealed to the General Court. The situation is summarized in Table 6.1 (first decision and then investigations in chronological order, most recent cases listed first).

Member states are prohibited by EU law to give any form of state aid which distorts or threatens to distort competition by favouring certain

Table 6.1 The European Commission's investigations regarding breaches of state aid rules

Member state	*MNE's taxation*	*Date of decision (D) or investigation (I)*	*Motivation*
United Kingdom	CFC rules	02.04.2019 (D)	CFC rules non-applicable to MNEs
Luxembourg	Huhtamäki	07.03.2019 (I)	Interest-free loans
The Netherlands	Nike	10.01.2019 (I)	Royalty tax rulings
Luxembourg	McDonalds	19.09.2018 (D)	Favourable rulings on transfer pricing
Luxembourg	ENGIE	20.06.2018 (D)	Tax rulings on internal financing
The Netherlands	Ikea	18.12.2017(I)	Intellectual property rights valuation
Luxembourg	Amazon	04.10.2017 (D)	Tax rulings on royalty pricing
Ireland	Apple	30.08.2016 (D)	Tax rulings on tax residence and pricing
Belgium	Excess profit exemption	11.01.2016(D)	Attractive tax regime for non-residents
The Netherlands and Luxembourg	Starbucks/Fiat	21.01.2015 (D)	Transfer pricing methods not in line with OECD

Source: European Commission (2019b)

undertakings or the production of certain goods, in so far as it affects trade between member states. Selective benefits for certain enterprises prevent the market from rewarding the most competitive enterprises. The question thus arises whether these rules also forbid tax competition between states through attractive tax measures and lower tax rates. The case law of the CJEU on this issue is not clear. A 'general' measure, such as reducing tax rates, is allowed under the Treaties as it does not benefit specifically some companies, but is widely and generally applied. According to the CJEU case law, however, a lower tax rate which deviates from the general system could be considered as state aid as it may give selective benefits. As a matter of a practical example, a corporate tax law applied favourably only to foreign companies may be considered a selective measure and may thus be prohibited. This was ruled by the CJEU in the Gibraltar case (Court of Justice of the European Union 2011), in which the United Kingdom sought to attract financial multinational enterprises through changing the corporate tax base for foreign companies which chose to establish in Gibraltar. The CJEU ruled that this deviation from the regular corporate income tax base was sufficient to prove selectivity.

Going back to the recent cases mentioned at the beginning of this chapter, Apple, Starbucks, ENGIE and Amazon all received individual advance pricing agreements with a very favourable level of taxation on their global income from the tax authorities in Luxembourg, the Netherlands and Ireland. The Commission criticized these APA as it took the view that the method applied differed from the standard rule on the arm's length principle. Indeed, the MNEs in question could base their prices on an indirect pricing method. According to the Commission, only direct price comparisons can fully reflect the standard rule of the arm's length principle. What is of interest here is the differing view of the Commission to that of the OECD; the latter interprets both indirect and direct price comparisons to be consistent with the arm's length principle. What most bothers the Commission seems to be the fact that this income was not taxed in the other states in which the enterprise operated (United States).

The Apple case is perhaps the case which raises the most interesting and relevant questions. Through a cost-sharing agreement, which is an indirect pricing method, between Apple USA and its two Irish subsidiaries within the Apple group, Apple Sales International (ASI) and Apple Operations Europe (AOE), these subsidiaries could use Apple's intellectual property (IP) rights to manufacture and sell Apple products outside the United States. ASI, and to a lesser extent AOE, made large annual payments to Apple for research and development taking place in the United States. These payments were deductible in Ireland. ASI purchased Apple products from independent manufacturers to sell them in Europe, the Middle East, Africa and India. Regardless of where the consumers were based and whether they bought their products online or in a store, the sales agreements were signed with ASI. All sales and profits from these sales were thus registered in Ireland. The goods were never shipped via Ireland, but were shipped directly to the customer from the manufacturing site.

Neither ASI nor AOE had their tax residence in Ireland according to Irish law, since they were both controlled from the United States. However, since neither of the two enterprises was incorporated in the United States, they could not have their tax residence established there according to US tax law. Consequently, neither ASI nor AOE were taxed for their global profits in the United States, except for the payments relating to the use of patents which they received from Ireland. Indeed, almost all profits which were realized by the two companies were allocated internally to a 'head office' in the United States with eight employees. According to the Commission's estimates, this 'head office' existed only on paper and could thus impossibly have generated such profits. As a result of the allocation method which was accepted in the advance pricing agreements by the Irish tax authorities, Apple paid an actual corporate tax of 1% on its profits made in ASI in 2003. This rate decreased to 0.005% in 2014. The Commission further criticized that the United States did not tax these profits, either, and moreover, considered that the Apple group received an advantage in Ireland which no other Irish company could get.

In other words, all taxable income in both the European Union and in the United States disappeared. The Commission claimed that it would not have criticized Irish if Apple's profits had been taxed either in the United States or where the actual sales took place. Some academic writers, on the other hand, submit that the Commission erroneously uses state aid rules to solve the problem of tax base erosion (see, e.g. Wattel 2016). Instead, they argue that global disparity between the laws of different states causes the issue. The provision of a specific tax advantage to a specific taxpayer in itself cannot be problematic. State aid controls are not intended to be used to stop the exploitation of differences in national rules by member states. It is moreover difficult to determine to whom Ireland has lost tax. Additionally, the overall purpose of the structure of internal pricing in the Apple case was to avoid taxation in other jurisdictions, not in Ireland specifically. Therefore, there may be reasons to speculate that the General Court and the CJEU may reject the Commission's decision in the Apple case on this ground.

The Commission's motivation for applying state aid rules to reach the Apple group is unclear. The number of infringement procedures under state aid is normally quite low, as the Commission usually only takes legal action against a member state once it is certain that it will win the case. Why did the Commission then choose to proceed on this relatively thin ice, since state aid rules are not meant to regulate the differences between the tax rates in different states?

Some argue that the Commission seems to have acted on the request of the member states to limit American enterprises selling their products on the European market, without the member states being able to tax the enterprises. In other words, member states seem to be willing to protect their sovereignty at any cost (Mason 2017). Sovereignty in this context is understood as securing taxes to the welfare state, through taxing multinational enterprises. The Commission has, according to this reasoning, encouraged the reforms such as the proposal of a directive on digital transactions as well as the Apple and Starbucks state aid cases. These measures thus seek to limit tax base erosion in source states carried out by the MNEs, such as Apple, to generate the highest profit possible. It should also be noted that this case exacerbates the current political tension between the United States and the European Union.

Others instead argue that it is not the role of the Commission to ensure that member states correctly apply or enforce tax rules (Lyal 2015). Furthermore, it is doubtful whether state aid rules would be a suitable tool for dealing with the BEPS project, such as in the Apple case. State aid rules are not meant to capture the exploitation of differing national rules, since the former require that the state aid is provided by one single member state, and not several, such as in the Apple case.

The US Department of the Treasury blames the Commission for acting beyond its competences within the competition and state aid law. However, this argument proves to be quite weak, as both competition law and state aid rules are two exclusive EU competences. Transactions with third states, such as the United States, also fall under these exclusive competences. Advance pricing agreements regarding internal pricing may thus very well fall under state aid rules if the Commission proves that this competitive advantage is being used to attract a certain type of activity to a territory and distort competition, such as in the Gibraltar case.

Protection Against Tax Base Erosion: From Weak to Strong EU Governance

This section explores the hypothesis that member states, by acting at the EU level, successfully defended their self-interest to protect their tax bases on the pretext of protecting the welfare state. In other words, the role of the EU has shifted from weak governance in the field of direct taxation to the member states authorizing the EU to take a more active political role.

One can easily draw a parallel between, on the one hand, the state aid infringement procedures explained above and, on the other hand, the Anti-Tax Avoidance Directive. The directive was adopted unanimously in 2016. Its objective was to limit tax base erosion within the EU and between the EU and third states. The directive successfully unified member states around the common objectives of protecting their own tax bases and of obtaining taxing rights over MNEs worldwide income within the EU.

Aggressive tax planning leading to tax base erosion has recently been put on equal footing with tax avoidance, which I myself commented when the directive was adopted. The directive provides the EU and its member states with tools to deal with zero taxation arising from the lack of harmonized rules, as shown in previous sections. The directive also introduces a new principle, the so-called 'single tax principle', according to which MNEs must pay corporate income tax at least once and this tax should preferably be paid in an EU member state. This taxation model takes inspiration from how federal states tax companies, where a state within the federation is allocated the responsibility to tax. However, the EU is not a federation and the power to tax remains within the legislative competence of the member states. The directive was criticized for this very reason (Brokelind 2016, 2017, 2019). In conclusion, the EU used the opportunity to control 'aggressive tax planning' to acquire the power to allocate taxes to and within the EU and to legislate concerning direct taxes.

It should moreover be noted that the directive cites the OECD and G20 reports on BEPS. The preamble to the directive states that the current political priorities in the field of international taxation highlight the need to ensure that taxes are paid where profits and added value are created. One of the essential objectives of the directive is to improve the resilience of the EU internal market to cross-border tax avoidance methods. Member states cannot achieve this to a sufficient extent when they act alone; action must instead be taken at the EU level.

Thus, the directive introduces a new principle on the distribution of tax bases, which also affects third states. An amendment to the original directive of 2016 suggested that the income emanating from an EU member state should be allocated to the member state in question, in cases where the residence state in a third country did not tax the same income in 'mismatch situations'. This occurs when neither the EU member state nor the third country tax the revenue due to different definitions of what is taxable. The directive thus covers all forms of double deductions and other ways to use loopholes in the tax systems because of institutional differences, including those with third states. Sweden and Malta both expressed doubts concerning this issue during the legislative process. The Swedish and Maltese parliaments carried out subsidiarity tests of the draft legislative proposal. Their criticism concerned the fact that some of the rules in the directive would also cover internal transactions and even those dealing with stand-alone companies. The fact that these transactions would also be regulated by the EU was not explained by the Commission and could fall outside of the EU's competences.

The ATAD has been assessed as very ambitious and far-reaching (Smit 2018). Firstly, the question is whether the allocation of tax bases, regulated by the directive, falls within the EU's shared competence on the internal market. The CJEU never allowed differences in legislation to justify protectionist measures, whether in tax or other fields of law, in its case law on the freedom of establishment. On the contrary, the Court has considered that institutional competition between EU member states is a sound precondition for the effective functioning of the internal market. In addition, coordinating the laws of member states falls outside the jurisdiction of the Court, which is why it has avoided taking a position on such issues. The Court has nevertheless allowed EU member states to control situations of abuse, while however using a very narrow definition of abuse. According to the case law of the Court, wholly artificial transactions constitute a form of abuse and can therefore justify that states take protectionist measures.[4] By contrast, a much broader definition of abuse is used in the ATAD as it covers all types of zero taxation, irrespective of economic substance. This has been disputed, as double taxation is not considered to fall within the EU's competences. Why, then, would zero taxation, or double non-taxation, fall within the competences of the EU?

[4] See, for example, the case *Cadbury Schweppes* (European Court of Justice 2006: para 67).

Going back to the failed reform on harmful tax competition under the initiative of the OECD during 1997–2004, which in the end took the form of a Code of Conduct, it now appears that member states are in favour of these measures. The difference today, 20 years later, is that the EU initiates reforms, rather than the OECD. However, it is hardly surprising that the EU adapts to the preference and needs of its member states. In the field of political science, the EU is sometimes described as a paradoxical organization, whose development in economic policies has shifted between market-friendly measures, on the one hand, and supra-nationalism and interventionism on the other. Against this background, it is possible to argue that the support given to the member states to limit tax base erosion arising from unregulated market access falls within the latter category.

What on the other hand is peculiar in this case is that member states successfully agreed on legislation against abuse, tax competition and the allocation of tax bases, while they could not come to an agreement on alternative tax models in the EU that could regulate the market by harmonizing taxes instead of reinforcing their tax borders. In 2011, a project aiming to address the latter problem was launched by the EU, called the Common Corporate Tax base (CCTB) and the Common Consolidated Corporate Tax Base (CCCTB) (see European Commission 2016). The main idea of the CCCTB was to establish a common corporate tax base in the EU for multinational companies. Companies would pay taxes where their economic activities took place and where they made their profits due to large markets, instead of being taxed in their residence state which is the case today. The project was abandoned, as member states failed to find a political agreement, but was re-launched in 2017 as a follow-up of the LuxLeaks scandal. Many smaller member states with smaller domestic markets, such as Sweden, opposed the project. The reason behind their opposition is that the project would not benefit the tax bases of smaller economies, since (Swedish) companies mainly operate in other large markets. The current state of research suggests that the success of the CCCTB project is uncertain, to say the least, as it does not address the institutional differences between the member states. This could, instead, possibly be resolved through a harmonized tax system.

Who Benefits from the Development of EU Tax Law?

The EU member states chose to protect their own tax bases through granting priority of taxation to the source, which they notably did in the state aid cases and in the case of the ATAD. It is highly likely that member states with large domestic markets will be the winners of the reform, which limits tax competition. Smaller member states with smaller markets (e.g. the Netherlands, Luxembourg and Sweden among others) will be the losers of the reform, as they previously used tax competition to attract foreign investors, which will no longer be possible.

One of the main contested issues of the reform concerns the approximation of the tax base erosion. Academics disagree over the methods used to calculate the erosion and some even question whether tax base erosion is really occurring. In Sweden, for instance, the standard corporate tax rate has been progressively reduced from 28% to 20.6% (2021) while corporate tax revenues have remained largely stable, apart from the disparities which have been caused by cyclical fluctuations. Indeed, tax revenues from enterprises have remained at around 3% of GDP (Andersson 2013).

Other researchers, however, show that Swedish multinational enterprises with cross-border activities pay less tax than enterprises operating only on the domestic market (Hansson et al. 2018). The Swedish government carried out an impact assessment on tax base erosion, whose results indicated that Sweden could benefit from the adoption of the BEPS project. The impact assessment was, however, never officially released. This could be linked to the fact that Sweden adopted certain measures to attract some of the activities that, were the BEPS project to be adopted, would be taxed in another country where the value is created (Andersson 2016). The OECD tried to measure the impact of global tax base erosion within the framework of the BEPS project and estimated that 4–10% of corporate tax revenues are lost due to tax planning. This corresponds to 100–240 billion USD per year. According to the OECD, the biggest losers of this phenomenon are the United States and developing states, while the losses within industrialized states such as the EU member states are much more limited, as their state finances are based on indirect taxes rather than corporate taxes.

Regardless of the conclusions of economic research, the risk that the corporate tax that is currently paid in the EU is further reduced is very high if it is moved to states where 'value' is created. Demanding evidence for the 'value creation' of an investment entails that those transactions reducing the enterprise's tax burden, are classified as aggressive tax planning and thus equated to tax avoidance not to say evasion. Without the tax incentives used to attract multinational corporations, enterprises might move their staff and investments to larger markets in large states.

Introducing a new variable of moralizing the problematic effects of tax competition is meant to help solving the problem of tax base erosion. In that way, the new legislation presumes that tax planning is abusive. This assumption has cleared the path for far-reaching corrective measures and a radical change concerning the allocation rules for tax bases. In fact, all cases of double non-taxation due to institutional differences are considered by the legislator as abusive. This type of far-reaching legislation may result in MNEs, mainly US enterprises such as Apple and Starbucks, leaving the EU and moving their business to their domestic market. Thus, they do not have to prove that they did not abuse differences between the tax systems. This could consequently result in less trade and reduced capital flows, possibly leading states to increasingly introducing protectionist measures to incentivize enterprises to produce goods on the domestic market. The states would thus secure tax bases on income which would otherwise have been taxed in other states. By extension, this sort of protectionism could pose a serious threat to the internal market and possibly also to the EU itself.

However, finding an alternative to the BEPS project that would be accepted at the global level seems increasingly difficult. The success of the BEPS project is based on voluntary participation to tackle free tax competition, the emergence of tax havens and tax avoidance, including the type of tax incentive that certain (smaller) states apply to attract MNEs. The BEPS project entails a certain level of harmonization, as it is based on minimum standards which the OECD states together with the G20 states have vowed to implement. These minimum standards can be partially found in the EU's Anti-Tax Avoidance Directive, which indicates the large impact of the BEPS project, especially in comparison with the previously failed attempts to coordinate tax bases and minimize institutional differences between tax systems of states, as discussed in the beginning of this chapter.

However, Mason (2017) and Wattel (2016) consider the BEPS project to be an attempt at reaching the big American high-tech enterprises. These enterprises can manage to avoid paying taxes in the United States due to American tax law which exempts foreign subsidiaries from tax, as long as their income is not distributed in form of dividends to the United States. Accordingly, it seems that the American high-tech enterprises only invest abroad (such as the EU) if they receive tax incentives there achieving double non-taxation, which the BEPS project aims to put an end to. The Trump administration has, however, expressed concern about the BEPS project as it considers that the project can hamper global tax competition. It has therefore come with a reform of its own, which provides the United States with protective measures against tax base erosion. From the perspective of tax policies, the BEPS project can therefore potentially aggravate the current trade war between the EU and the United States and not least allowing member states to discourage third states' enterprises to invest in the EU through protectionist measures.

Is Digital Taxation an Option for the EU?

Some states attempting to link the tax to their territory have already introduced a new type of corporate income tax departing from the OECD principles on source and residence taxation. The United Kingdom, Australia and India have introduced a diverted profit tax which aims to capture tax bases which have previously been lost due to the recent digitalization of business models. The French and Hungarian 'click/Starbucks/ad tax'[5] instead attempt to avoid this problem by introducing a tax targeting access to market by MNEs through digital means.

Against this background, the EU also attempts to reform the digital economy. The digital economy creates value through a combination of algorithms, user data, sales methods and knowledge. For instance, a user may contribute to creating value through sharing its preferences, such as by liking a page on social media. These data are stored and used by the enterprises to make profits through targeted ads. According to the Commission, this profit is not necessarily taxed in the state where the user sees the ad, but rather where the commercial algorithms used in targeted advertising were developed. In consequence, the added value created by the user cannot be taken into account when and where the enterprise is taxed. This phenomenon creates tax base erosion. The legislative proposal presented by the Commission on a digital tax for certain enterprises, on which member states failed to reach an agreement in March 2019 and was consequently abandoned, but may appear again, introduced two new components. Firstly, the Commission proposed to change the corporate tax system in the EU by reforming the rules concerning where profits are taxed. The proposed changes entailed that profits would be registered and taxed where enterprises significantly interact with users through digital

[5] See, for example, the case *Hungary v Commission*, General Court of the European Union (2017).

channels. Secondly, the Commission also proposed, as requested by several member states, an interim tax covering the most significant digital activities currently not covered by any tax in the EU.

Much like in the case of the BEPS project, there have been two strands of research as regards the reform (see, e.g. Schön 2018). Those in favour of the reform consider that the access to new customers that companies gain through internet platforms increases their ability to pay tax. This, in turn, justifies that profit is taxed in the source state, rather than in the residence state. As was previously discussed, the requirement of a fixed place of business is no longer sufficient to trigger source taxation. Defining the access to new customers' market through internet platform as a value creation forms a link which justifies taxation in the source state. Other researchers question the existence of a link between the customer and the created value which is being taxed. For instance, a tool based on artificial intelligence which uses algorithms to calculate the potential clientele to a certain good or service may be considered as a similar analysis of a substantial creation of value for the production. This does not mean that the mere existence of the market suffices to trigger source taxation, as the artificial intelligence is not exclusively related to the source state, either.

Corporate income tax is assessed on companies' worldwide income reflecting their ability to pay taxes. It does not seek to tax the sales' opportunities of an online market, that is, the 'value creation' which was previously discussed. Creating value remains only a small part of the tax ability of an enterprise. Thus, taxing *solely* value creation is incompatible with the current model of corporate income tax, as this model presumes that the enterprise is taxed only when its costs (such as risks, functions and assets) have been taken into account. Consequently, the BEPS project and a digital tax may have the potential to erase the current model of corporate income taxation.

The Commission's proposal on a digital tax was called 'fair taxation', thus justifying the competence of the EU to legislate in the area of direct taxation due to political reasons for saving the welfare state. While member states undoubtedly need to protect the welfare of the nation-state, taxes need to be regulated through laws which should be applied objectively. There are reasons to believe that the proposed reform is based on philosophical criteria, such as fairness or justice that are inadequate to justify the measures proposed by the Commission. The fact that the EU refers to these criteria could be interpreted as a sign of the return of the nation-state, as the member states manage to get their interests through.

The investors' trust in the EU may be challenged if a new system of taxation based on vague claims of fairness and justice is adopted and move their investments to other states with clearer rules, making it easier for businesses to access new markets and increase their profits.

Premises for Tax Fairness

This chapter has demonstrated that the developments within the field of EU tax law towards increased protection of the sovereign state may be a sign that nationalism affects political and economic development within Europe. Nationalism, in this context, means that states have a tendency to cater to their own needs at the expense of the global context. The BEPS project and the ATAD both suggest that member states increasingly expect international organizations to solve the problem of disappearing tax bases which threaten the existence of the national welfare state.

The EU is acting as a guarantor of protectionist methods, which are designed to protect the national welfare state, expressed through the ATAD and other initiatives. The member states express a sort of nationalism through their willingness to close their national borders in order to secure their tax bases in the name of fairness, instead of keeping them open for free competition. Following years of cautious projects and measures within the field of tax law, previously unthinkable initiatives suddenly appear to be appealing to member states in order to protect their tax bases. From a legal and political perspective, the fact that member states are now required to tax the increased value produced on their territory if other states do not tax it remains controversial.

If this is the intention, member states should perhaps instead agree on a common fiscal policy which would reflect the need to fully protect the internal market instead of only protecting the states' own welfare and their national tax sovereignty. There is a significant risk that populist movements, which are fiercely opposing globalization and advocating the protection of the national tax sovereignty and the national welfare state, consider the BEPS project and the possible new EU tax policies to be consistent with their views.

The EU is currently facing huge challenges, such as a surge in populism such as the Brexit case, as well as increased migration and terrorism. In this context, EU member states should refrain from advocating tax justice and instead try to reach an agreement on the opportunities offered by an integrated internal market with a single currency. The EU needs to first and foremost respond to the populist argument that the integrated EU trade area symbolizes the loss of tax sovereignty (Vanistendael 2018).

In order to counter such arguments, which seek to undermine the legitimacy of the EU, research needs to focus on analysing why non-taxation is occurring in integrated economic areas such as the EU, and which enterprises or EU member states benefit from it. It is highly unlikely that invoking ethics and morals is sufficient to cover loopholes in the system caused by the lack of coordination between the tax systems of member states. Moreover, although the member states already have agreed to adopt a directive to fight aggressive tax planning, the main issue of tax competition remains. Tax sovereignty acts as a barrier to counteract the tax avoidance which affects everyone. Thinking constructively and adopting a common tax base for cross-border transactions seems to be the only way forward.

References

Andersson, K. (2013). Base Erosion Profit Shifting—A New World Tax Order. *Svenskt Skattetidning, 2013*(9), 659–687. Retrieved September 1, 2019, from https://www.svensktnaringsliv.se/migration_catalog/artikeln-i-svensk-skattetidning_579085.html/BINARY/Artikeln%20i%20Svensk%20Skattetidning.

Andersson, K. (2016). Vad är BEPS och vad innebär det för Sverige? *Skattenytt, 2016*(9), 639–654.

Avi-Yonah, R. S. (2000). Commentary. In New York University School of Law (Ed.), *The Tillinghast Lecture, 1996–2005* (pp. 117–125). New York: NYU School of Law. Retrieved September 1, 2019, from https://repository.law.umich.edu/cgi/viewcontent.cgi?referer=http://www.law.umich.edu/library/home/pubsfaculty/facultypages/Pages/avi-yonah_reuven.aspx&httpsredir=1&article=1064&context=book_chapters.

Berggren, N. (2012). The Calculus of Consent: Some Swedish Connections. *Public Choice, 152*(3–4), 313–321.

Brokelind, C. (2016). Anti-Directive Shopping on Outbound Dividends in Light of the Pending Decision in Holcim France (Case C-6/16). *European Taxation, September*, 395–399.

Brokelind, C. (2017). Interactive Law Building and EU Tax Law. In D. Weber (Ed.), *EU Law and the Building of Global Supranational Tax Law: EU BEPS and State Aid* (pp. 1–16). Amsterdam: IBFD.

Brokelind, C. (2019). The Anti-Tax Avoidance Directive Under Scrutiny: A Matter of Competence? In J. Monsenego & J. Bjuvberg (Eds.), *International*

Taxation in a Changing Landscape, Liber Amicorum in Honour of Bertil Wiman (pp. 45–57). Alphen aan den Rijn: Kluwer.

Bruzelius, A. (2004). Skattekonkurrens – hinder eller förutsättning för en nationell välfärdsstat? In S. Gustavsson, L. Oxelheim, & N. Wahl (Eds.), *Europaperspektiv EU, skatterna och välfärden* (pp. 111–136). Stockholm: Santérus.

Court of Justice of the European Union. (2006). *Cadbury Schweppes*, C-196/04. EU:C:2006:544.

Court of Justice of the European Union. (2011). *Commission v. Gibraltar*, C-106/09 P and C-107/09 P. EU:C:2011:732.

European Commission. (2016, October 25). Commission Proposes Major Corporate Tax Reform for the EU (Common Consolidated Corporate Tax Base (CCCTB)). Press release IP-16-3471. Retrieved September 1, 2019, from https://europa.eu/rapid/press-release_IP-16-3471_en.htm.

European Commission. (2019a). Taxation Trends in the European Union. Retrieved September 1, 2019, from https://ec.europa.eu/taxation_customs/business/economic-analysis-taxation/taxation-trends-eu-union_en.

European Commission. (2019b). On State Aid and Tax Rulings. Retrieved September 1, 2019, from https://ec.europa.eu/competition/state_aid/register/.

General Court. (2019). *Belgium v. Commission*, T-131/16 and T-263/16, EU:T:2019:91.

Gribnau, H. J., & Jallai, A. G. (2017). Good Tax Governance: A Matter of Moral Responsibility and Transparency. *Nordic Tax Journal, 2017*(1), 70–88.

Hansson, Å., Olofsdotter, K., & Thede, S. (2018). Do Swedish Multinationals Pay Less in Taxes Than Domestic Firms? *The World Economy, 41*(2), 393–413.

Hilling, A., & Ostas, D. T. (2018). Corporate Income Taxation, CSR and the UN's 2030 Agenda for Sustainable Development. *Kluwer International Tax Blog*. Retrieved September 1, 2019, from http://kluwertaxblog.com/2018/05/14/corporate-income-taxation-csr-uns-2030-agenda-sustainable-development/.

Jaeger, T. (2015). From Santander to LuxLeaks – And Back. *European State Aid Law Quarterly, 14*(3), 345–357.

Kaufman, N. H. (2001). Equity Considerations in International Taxation. *Brooklyn Journal of International Law, 26*(4), 1465–1470.

Lyal, R. (2015). Transfer Pricing Rules and State Aid. *Fordham International Law Journal, 38*(4), 1017–1044.

Mason, R. (2017). Special Report on State Aid—Part 3: Apple. *Tax Notes, 154*; Virginia Law and Economics Research Paper No. 2017–18.

Musgrave, R. A. (1959). *Theory of Public Finance; A Study in Public Economy*. New York: McGraw-Hill.

OECD. (2017a). *Model Tax Convention on Income and on Capital: Condensed Version 2017.* Paris: OECD Publishing. https://doi.org/10.1787/mtc_cond-2017-en.

OECD. (2017b). *OECD Transfer Pricing Guidelines for Multinational Enterprises and Tax Administrations 2017.* Paris: OECD Publishing. https://doi.org/10.1787/tpg-2017-en.

OECD. (2019). Inclusive Framework on BEPS (Base Erosion and Profit Shifting). Retrieved September 1, 2019, from https://www.oecd.org/tax/beps/.

Österman, R. P. (2019). Perspectives on Corporate Taxation from a Sustainable Business Perspective. In S. Arvidsson (Ed.), *Challenges in Managing Sustainable Business: Reporting, Taxation, Ethics and Governance* (pp. 371–397). Cham: Springer.

Piketty, T. (2020). *Capital and Ideology.* Cambridge: Harvard University Press.

Schön, W. (2018). Debate: Facilitating Entry by Facilitating Exit: New Paths in EU Tax Legislation. *Intertax, 46*(4), 339–341.

Smit, D. (2018). The Anti-Tax-Avoidance Directive. In P. J. Wattel & B. Terra (Eds.), *European Tax Law Volume I General Topics and Direct Taxation* (pp. 553–571). Wolters Kluwer: Deventer.

Vanistendael, F. (2018). Debate: Democratic Taxation: Necessity or Utopia for Euroland? *Intertax, 46*(4), 342–351.

Wattel, P. J. (2016). Stateless Income, State Aid and the (Which?) Arm's Length Principle. *Intertax, 44*(11), 791–801.

Wicksell, K. (1954). *Value, Capital and Rent.* London: Allen & Unwin.

CHAPTER 7

The Euro and the Nation-State That Never Disappeared: Would Europe Benefit from the Return of National Currencies?

Fredrik N. G. Andersson

Introduction

On the first of January 1999, 11 countries abandoned their national currencies and adopted the euro. Eight countries have joined since, making the euro area the second largest economy in the world behind the United States. An evaluation of the euro-project, so far, has to conclude that it has been successful in many ways. Inflation has been low and stable, and Europe has avoided the recurring currency crises that characterized the 1980s and the early 1990s. However, the euro is not a complete success story. The euro area has stumbled from crisis to crisis for more than a decade. On occasions, the very existence of the euro has been threatened.

One of the euro area's core problems is the strength of the individual member states in relation to the European Union (EU). It is easy to highlight instances when a euro country has acted in its own national interest against the common good. Germany's reluctance to accept a fully fledged

F. N. G. Andersson (✉)
Lund University, Lund, Sweden
e-mail: fredrik_n_g.andersson@nek.lu.se

A. Bakardjieva Engelbrekt et al. (eds.), *The European Union and the Return of the Nation State*,
https://doi.org/10.1007/978-3-030-35005-5_7

banking union and a strong fiscal union is one example. Italian budget fights with the European Commission and its threat to introduce a new parallel currency to rival the euro is another. The theme of this book is the return of the nation-state. The problem for the currency union is not so much the return of the nation-state as the fact that the member states' powers were never curtailed. Complete monetary integration was never followed by equal levels of economic and political integration. The euro area thus lacks sufficient common policy tools to properly govern the euro area economy. As a consequence, large and growing economic imbalances have been left unresolved causing political conflicts within and between member states.

The understanding that a monetary union requires complementary economic and political unions is not new. Germany's former chancellor, and one of the architects behind the euro, Helmut Kohl labelled the idea of a monetary union without economic and political unions as 'absurd'. However, while the euro countries were willing to fully surrender power over monetary policy, they were never equally willing to reduce their influence over other policy fields such as taxation, labour market regulations and welfare systems. Here, member states have retained a large amount of influence causing national variations in policies that in effect prevent the free flow of labour, capital and services. Without common policy tools and without high levels of mobility, the euro area countries began to diverge economically, which in turn caused social and political imbalances that threaten the existence of the euro. The Commission has suggested deeper economic and political integration to strengthen the euro. Steps have been taken along this road, but progress has been slow. Member states remain reluctant to hand over more powers to the EU.

The European situation with a currency union requiring more economic and political integration and member states that cling on to their powers raises a few questions. First, if the Commission's reform programme is implemented in full, is it enough to avoid future euro crises? Second, is it realistic to expect member states to be willing to further integrate in the near future to protect the euro? Third, if countries are not willing to integrate more, would it be better to dismantle the euro area and reintroduce national currencies?

Drawing on data and previous research, I will address these questions. I demonstrate how the individual member states, acting in their own national interest, have contributed to the growing economic and social imbalances in the euro area. I then turn to the Commission's proposed reform programme to strengthen the economic and political unions. Here

I come to the conclusion that the programme is backward-looking and focusing on preventing the financial crisis of 2008/09 and the following euro debt crisis from occurring, after they have occurred. Forward-looking proposals that take clear steps towards more integration are few and vague. The shortcomings of the Commission's proposals are easy to understand in the context of heterogeneous member states with slightly different economic models and with different economic interests. Countries are unwilling to fully integrate because their economic and political interests vary. I conclude that the euro has a future, but it requires that some countries leave the currency union. A smaller euro area has the opportunity to integrate and prosper. Countries that reintroduce their national currencies are given a chance to solve the economic imbalances and recover economically. Reintroducing a national currency is not a silver bullet, but it is likely to be one key component in any realistic programme to solve the euro area imbalances. In addition, a smaller euro area would likely benefit the European project as a whole Economic and social tensions within the euro area are threatening not just the euro but the entire EU. A smaller euro area would help to reduce these tensions and benefit Europe as a whole.

Why a Common Currency?

There is a long-standing debate on the merits of a system of flexible exchange rates versus a system of fixed exchange rates. Both systems have their costs and benefits and no system is optimal for all countries and all times. In history, countries have moved from one regime to another as the economic and political circumstances have changed. A currency union with a common currency and a common monetary policy is the strictest form of a fixed exchange rate system with irrevocable exchange rates between the members of the union (Andersson and Jonung 2019). Another kind of fixed exchange rate system is pegged rates, where countries maintain their national currencies but peg the value of the respective currencies against each other. The values of the currencies remain fixed until a country either voluntarily decides to change the peg or is forced to do so by the exchange rate markets. The pegged rate system is thus a less strict system of fixed exchange rates compared to a currency union. As an illustration, the predecessor to the euro was the European Exchange Rate Mechanism (ERM) with pegged but adjustable rates. Between 1979 and 1998, there were 18 instances of exchange rate realignments before the possibility of devaluations was removed with the introduction of the euro.

A key benefit that comes with a system of fixed exchange rates is that it reduces transaction costs and encourages foreign trade, which in turn promotes economic specialization and economic development. Countries with a poor history of economic management and high inflation may also benefit from a common monetary policy that ensures price stability. The main cost is the lack of the exchange rate as a policy tool to solve economic imbalances and help countries adjust to economic shocks. Without adjustable exchange rates, countries have to rely on labour and capital mobility as well as price and wage flexibility to adjust to country-specific, so-called asymmetric, economic shocks. Common economic shocks are solved using common policy tools, such as the common monetary policy.

Whether the benefits of a common currency exceed the costs is an empirical question. To test if countries would benefit from forming a currency union, Mundell (1961) pioneered a theory of optimal currency areas. Others have contributed to the theory over time, for example, McKinnon (1963) and Kenen (1969), among others (see e.g. De Grauwe 2005). Simply put, for the benefits of a currency union to exceed the costs, the following five criteria should be met by each country that considers joining the union:

1. A high degree of labour and capital mobility. Without an adjustable exchange rate, countries must rely on the mobility of capital and labour to correct for economic imbalances that may occur within the currency union due to country-specific shocks.
2. A high degree of price and wage flexibility. Price and wage flexibility is an alternative/complement to labour and capital mobility to correct for economic imbalances within the currency union.
3. A fiscal union. Fiscal transfers across the union are necessary to assist weaker countries economically when they adjust to economic shocks. A common fiscal policy also increases the number of common policy tools the union has at its disposal to respond to common shocks.
4. A harmonized business cycle. Countries' business cycles should be highly correlated to ensure that a common stabilization policy is suitable for all countries. Monetary policy may otherwise become destabilizing rather than stabilizing.
5. Similar policy preferences. A common monetary policy requires similar preferences in terms of output and inflation stabilization. In addition, labour and capital mobility require harmonization of

labour market regulations, banking regulation, taxation and welfare systems. Such harmonization requires similar political preferences and a strong political union to implement the common rule book.

The simple message from the theory is that a monetary union requires flexible economies and a high degree of economic and political integration. Economic integration is essential to ensure the free flow of goods and services, and labour and capital. Political integration is necessary to harmonize national legislation to ensure that goods and services, and labour and capital can flow freely across national borders, not just in theory but also in practice.

Clearly, the benefits of a common currency do not always exceed the costs, especially when the economic and political unions are underdeveloped. National currencies are preferable when countries are relatively different economically and politically. Nevertheless, a system of flexible exchange rates is not perfect and a flexible rate does not always reflect the underlying state of the economy (Dellas and Tavlas 2009; Andersson 2014). No system is perfect.

The European Currency Union

The euro is the third step in the Economic and Monetary Union (EMU). The first and second steps were preparatory steps for the introduction of the euro. They liberalized capital markets, increased monetary policy co-operation, established the European Central Bank (ECB), and aimed to foster greater economic convergence. The EMU in turn is part of a larger economic and political integration project that also includes, for example, the Single Market.

Monetary integration within the euro area is complete with a single currency and a common monetary policy. The ECB sets interest rates based on the state of the euro-wide economy without national considerations. However, monetary policy is indirectly more adjusted to economic conditions in larger economies because they account for a larger share of the euro-wide economy. Consequently, it is more important for smaller economies to be flexible enough to deal with asymmetric shocks without the support of monetary policy than it is for larger economies.

The level of economic and political integration has increased over time; however, the individual member states are still relatively powerful. There are common rules and guidelines restricting the member states' powers.

Nevertheless, differences in terms of labour market regulations, taxation systems and welfare models, to name just three policy areas, still exist. Policy differences create implicit barriers preventing the free flow of labour, capital and certain services. In other words, the economic and political unions have become stronger over time but are still less developed compared to the monetary union.

There is no formal fiscal union, although there is economic support for economically weaker economies through the European Structural and Investment funds. The Growth and Stability Pact (GSP) puts restrictions on national fiscal policy to ensure sustainable public finances. Budget deficits are not allowed to exceed 3 per cent of Gross Domestic Product (GDP) per year, in normal times, and the government debt ratio should be below 60 per cent of GDP. Several countries, including France and Germany, broke the GSP rules during the early years of the euro resulting in weak public finances that threatened the stability of the euro during the international financial crisis. Steps have been taken since to strengthen GSP. For example, the Commission's powers to supervise and advise countries have grown to ensure compliance with the rules. The Commission has also been given a greater role in supervising macroeconomic developments to ensure that macroeconomic imbalances are corrected in time before they may threaten the stability of the euro. European Planning Semesters were introduced in 2010 to ensure that the common European interest is reflected in the national policymaking processes and that economic policies are co-ordinated for the common good.

In relation to the five criteria for an optimal currency area, the euro area fails to fully satisfy several of them. The main problem is the weakness of the economic union and the political union. The euro area thus lacks sufficient policy tools to solve economic imbalances that may occur among the member states. As we shall see, this has become a major problem for the currency union.

Table 7.1 illustrates the economic developments in the euro area since the introduction of the euro for three representative northern European countries (France, Germany and the Netherlands) and three representative southern European countries (Greece, Italy and Spain). The table also includes Sweden (an EU country with its own currency) and the United States as a comparison. Average incomes (GDP/capita) in purchasing power adjusted real US dollars (2010 prices), the unemployment rate and the government debt ratio are shown for 3 years: the year before the euro

Table 7.1 Economic indicators for the euro area, Sweden and the United States 1998, 2008 and 2017

	Northern Europe				*Southern Europe*			*Euro area*	*USA*
	DEU	*NED*	*FRA*	*SWE*	*ITA*	*SPA*	*GRE*	*EA*	*USA*
			GDP/capita (thousand USD)						
1998	34.3	39.4	32.0	32.7	33.6	27.0	23.5	31.4	42.2
2008	40.5	46.1	36.7	42.2	36.5	33.6	31.3	37.1	49.3
2017	43.9	47.4	37.6	45.5	34.1	33.7	23.7	38.3	53.1
			Unemployment (per cent)						
1998	9.4	4.2	10.3	8.2	11.3	16.4	12.0	---	4.5
2008	7.4	3.7	7.4	6.2	6.7	11.3	7.8	7.6	5.8
2017	3.8	4.9	9.4	6.7	11.2	17.2	21.5	9.1	4.4
			Government debt ratio (per cent of GDP)						
1998	59.4	58.4	61.3	66.8	110.8	62.5	98.9	71.9	63.3
2008	65.2	54.7	68.8	37.8	102.4	39.5	109.4	68.7	67.7
2017	64.1	56.7	97.0	40.6	131.8	98.3	178.6	86.7	105.4

Note: GDP/capita is in constant 2010 prices and adjusted to the cost of living in each country (i.e. purchasing power adjusted)

Source: Eurostat 2019a, 2019b, 2019c; OECD 2019c

was introduced (1998), the year the international financial crisis broke out (2008), and the last year with available data (2017).

Southern Europe tends to be poorer compared to northern Europe and the United States. In 1998, average Greek incomes were 30 per cent below the German level and Spanish incomes were 20 per cent below. Italy was the exception, with income levels comparable to German incomes at the time. There were some economic convergence and some divergence until 2008. Thereafter follows a decade of clear economic divergence. In 2017, the income gap between Greece and Germany had grown to 50 per cent. For Italy and Spain the gaps had grown to 25 per cent. In fact, average incomes in Italy and Greece were as high in 2017 as in 1998. Both France and the Netherlands grew at a modest past from 1998 to 2017, below the Germany growth rate. The only countries that have kept up with Germany in terms of growth are the United States and the non-euro (but EU) member Sweden.

The euro area economies are diverging. This is a relatively new phenomenon as the gap between the countries tended to become smaller from the 1960s until the late 1990s when the euro was introduced. Does this mean that the euro is to blame for the divergence? The answer to that question is both yes and no. The euro is not the single factor causing divergence, but it contributes to it. To understand why the member states are diverging economically and the role of the euro, let us consider four important factors: (1) an asymmetric euro-boom that turned into a major bust in southern Europe and Ireland following the introduction of the euro; (2) an internal German devaluation during the early 2000s; (3) a long-run economic and technological stagnation in southern Europe; and (4) poor European crisis management during the international financial crisis and the European debt crisis. The first, second and fourth factors are directly related to the construction of the euro and the weakness of the economic and political unions. The third factor is not the fault of the common currency, but its construction enforces the economic and social problems it causes. Let us consider each factor in turn.

The euro-boom. One benefit of a common currency is that it can boost the international confidence in a country that has a history of economic mismanagement. With the introduction of the euro, Ireland and countries in southern Europe did gain in economic credibility. As a result, long-term interest rates fell rapidly by between two and four percentage points. In the northern European countries, that already enjoyed a high level of trust, there was no decline in the already relatively low rates. The decline in interest rates became an asymmetric shock and credit flooded from northern Europe to southern Europe. Economic growth was boosted and unemployment fell (see Table 7.1). In Ireland and Spain credit fuelled a property boom, with rapidly rising property prices and household debt levels. Germany and France were at the same time stuck in a prolonged recession until 2005. In other words, one part of the euro area was booming while another was in a recession. The euro area broke against the fourth criterion of an optimal currency union: a harmonized business cycle. Monetary policy became too expansionary for the booming economies and too contractionary for the economies in a recession.

With monetary policy paralysed, the responsibility to cool off the credit-fuelled boom fell to fiscal policy in the respective countries. As is evident from Table 7.1, fiscal policy was relatively contractionary in the booming economies. Debt ratios fell by 30 percentage points in Spain (and by a similar amount in Ireland) and by roughly ten percentage points in Italy between 1998 and 2008. However, it was insufficient to stop the boom from spiralling out of control. History shows that it is difficult to stop credit-fuelled booms using fiscal policy without the assistance of monetary policy (Dell'Ariccia et al. 2014). The lack of policy tools to effectively deal with the situation contributed to the severity of the economic crisis when the boom went bust in 2008.

The German internal devaluation. The German economy had stagnated in the early 2000s with stubbornly high unemployment and had become known as the 'sick man of Europe'. The epitaph was somewhat misleading as unemployment was at comparable levels in many other countries as Table 7.1 illustrates; however, the economic performance was below the historical track record for Germany. The German response was to reform the labour market and to reduce wage growth (see e.g. Stockhammer 2011; Dustmann et al. 2014). The result was an internal devaluation (i.e. a reduction in production costs through lower wages and prices) that reduced the cost of production compared to other countries and boosted growth.

The size of the German internal devaluation is illustrated in Table 7.2. The top quarter of the table shows nominal wage growth for the same euro area countries as depicted in Table 7.1. Sweden is also included in the table. Swedish wages are transformed from Swedish krona to euros to make them comparable with the other countries. The second quarter of

Table 7.2 Wages, productivity and international competitiveness 1998–2008 and 2011–2017

	Northern Europe				*Southern Europe*		
	DEU	*NED*	*SWE*	*FRA*	*ITA*	*ESP*	*GRE*
	(1) Nominal wage growth in EUR						
1999–08	1.2	3.1	2.7	3.0	2.9	3.8	5.4
2011–17	2.7	1.4	2.3	1.4	0.6	0.5	−3.1
	(2) Productivity growth						
1999–08	0.9	1.2	1.9	1.0	0.0	0.1	2.3
2011–17	0.7	0.8	0.8	0.6	−0.3	0.9	−0.9
	Change in production costs in EUR = (1)–(2)						
1999–08	0.3	1.9	0.8	2.0	2.9	3.6	3.1
2011–17	1.9	0.5	1.5	0.8	0.9	−0.4	−2.2
	Competitiveness compared to Germany (1998 = 1)						
1998	1.000	1.000	1.000	1.000	1.000	1.000	1.000
2008	1.000	1.177	1.043	1.185	1.289	1.389	1.361
2017	1.000	1.065	0.981	1.097	1.189	1.082	1.250

Note: (a) Labour productivity is measured output per employee; (b) 2009 and 2010 are excluded due to the effects of the international financial crisis

Source: OECD 2013, 2019a, b

the Table illustrates labour productivity growth. A country's competitiveness depends on production costs. These are calculated as nominal wage growth less productivity growth. The countries forming the euro area have agreed on an inflation target of 'below but close' to 2 per cent, whereby costs should grow by roughly 2 per cent per year on average. As is evident from Table 7.2, German wage increases were too low compared to its productivity growth, causing an average yearly increase in production costs of only 0.3 per cent per year between 1999 and 2008. Production costs in France and the Netherlands were in line with the common inflation target, while costs increased too much in southern Europe, partially due to the euro-boom. As a result, all countries lost competitiveness compared to Germany (see the bottom of Table 7.2). In northern Europe, the loss of competitiveness was approximately 20 per cent and in southern Europe 30–40 per cent. A back-of-the-envelope calculation shows that roughly two-thirds of the loss of competitiveness in southern Europe was due to low wage increases in Germany and one-third was due to too high wage increases in these countries. In other words, a large share of the competitiveness problem southern Europe experiences is not the cause of their own actions. It is the cause of Germany pursuing a policy that was right for Germany but wrong for Europe. Rather than finding a German solution to the economic stagnation, there should have been a common European solution to what was a common European problem. The euro area broke the fifth criterion of an optimal currency union: common policymaking. Sweden with its own currency did not suffer a similar loss of competitiveness as other northern European countries despite costs growing at almost 2 per cent per year when measured in Swedish krona. The reason for this is a depreciating exchange rate, which reduced the cost increase in euros to levels comparable to those in Germany. In other words, the flexible exchange rate was key for Sweden to maintain its international competitiveness.

Long-run economic stagnation. Average economic growth rates have declined in most developed countries since the 1970s. The downward trajectory is especially strong in southern Europe, most notably in Italy. While productivity growth in northern Europe averaged between 1 and 2 per cent per year between 1998 and 2008, it was roughly zero in Spain and Italy during the same time period, see Table 7.2. A key reason for lower growth in southern Europe is a lack of investments in new technology such as Information and Communication Technologies (ICT) (Andersson 2017). A lack of ICT investments is not the fault of the euro or the common monetary policy. However, the construction of the euro area, with weak economic and political unions and no proper fiscal union, enhances the economic problem that declining growth rates cause. With economic stagnation follows rising social and political tensions as unemployment grows and wages decline. One way of reducing the negative effects of economic stagnation is through adjustments of exchange rates. In currency union when that is not possible, the alternative is for capital and labour to flow from countries in decline to the prosperous and growing areas of the currency union. However, persistent national barriers, such as differences in, for example, welfare systems and taxation, prevent such movement of labour at a larger scale. Consequently, stagnation is allowed to cause economic, social and political tensions without effective policy tools to reduce the pressures. Again, the lack of a strong economic and political union causes imbalances within the euro area.

Poor European crisis management. The ECB acted as swiftly as other central banks during the financial crisis of 2008/09 to support the banking system and the real economy. Emergency credit was supplied and interest rates reduced. However, monetary policy alone cannot solve a financial crisis. A wide set of policy tools are needed. The effects of the crisis were aggravated in the euro area due to its decentralized policymaking with strong individual member states. The responsibility to refinance a bankrupt banking system was a national responsibility. Small countries with a banking sector that had become too large during the euro-boom, struggled to pay the bills. Government debt ratios exploded. Financial markets became concerned about ballooning government debt ratios and lack of a strong coherent European-wide response to the crisis and interest rates increased (Eichengreen 2015; Tooze 2018). Countries' ability to service their debt was put into question. In the end, some countries (Ireland, Greece and Portugal) had to be bailed out by the International Monetary Fund (IMF) and the EU. Countries that did not experience a major banking crisis were also hit by higher interest rates. An example is Italy. Italian debt levels were high before the crisis, but they had declined by 10 percentage points leading up to the financial crisis at a time when French and German debts were increasing. While Italy could maintain its high debt ratio before the crisis, it became a problem when growth declined in the crisis and interest rates increased. They became the victims of a slow common European response to the financial crisis.

Greece also suffered from higher interest rates. Greece had clearly mismanaged their public finances before the crisis. A fiscal crisis was inevitable at some point. That was not the case for the other countries where the fiscal situation before the crisis was either healthy or moving in the right direction. Again, Europe struggled to respond to the Greek situation, leading to a further loss of confidence in Europe and higher interest rates in the weaker economies. Speculations grew that some countries may be forced to leave the euro area to devalue their currency and deal with their debt levels. It was not until 2012 when the ECB stepped in and began to purchase large amounts of government bonds to lower interest rates that the situation was stabilized.

The lack of proper common policy tools to deal with the crisis aggravated the crisis and made it deeper. Without a proper fiscal union, there was no mechanism at the time to support fiscally weak countries during the crisis. Slow response allowed markets to lose confidence in the euro area. In the end, policymakers did respond with bailout packages and the European Financial Stability Facility and the European Stability Mechanism. However, it took a long time, causing major economic harm, not least to the already vulnerable southern European economies (Eichengreen 2015; Moody 2018; Tooze 2018). A crisis that could have been contained was allowed to grow due to an inefficient immediate policy response.

The four factors we have highlighted in this section are not the only factors contributing to economic imbalances in the euro area, but they are important. They illustrate how a complete monetary integration with irrevocable exchange rates coupled with weak economic and political unions is fraught with danger. The concern for the euro area is not the return of the nation-state but that the member states remain strong in relation to the EU.

Reforming the Euro Area

The weakness of the euro has initiated a debate about possible reforms to strengthen the currency. Some suggestions are narrow and focus on one specific proposal: for example, on the creation of a fiscal union. Other proposals are broader and aim to address several weaknesses. One of the most comprehensive and concrete proposals is the Commission's reform programme to increase the level of economic and political integration in key areas. Work on the proposal began after the debt crisis in 2012 and was completed in 2017, when the Commission submitted a Reflection Paper (see European Commission 2017) on deeper economic and monetary integration to all EMU countries including the non-euro countries. Some of the proposals were completely new; others had already been implemented or were in the process of being implemented.

According to the proposal, the euro area's weaknesses can be summarized as follows: uneven economic growth across the member states; weak public finances; poor crisis management during the financial and debt crisis; and too little common supervision of the financial system and sharing of financial risks. In many ways, these weaknesses relate to the four factors behind the economic imbalances discussed in the previous section. The Commission's solution is to increase co-operation and harmonization within three new or existing unions: a financial union; a fiscal union; and an economic union.

A financial union. The Commission proposes two set of reforms. First, tearing down national barriers that prevent the full free movement of capital across the euro area. Further financial integration will improve the allocation of capital and spread risks across the currency union. Second, a banking union with common rules and supervision and common deposit insurance. Again, the aim is to spread risks across all member states to avoid a future Ireland, which went bankrupt trying to save their own banking sector during the financial crisis. A common rule book will enhance financial integration and avoid regulatory competition among the member states. Such competition is perceived to have aggravated the credit boom during the 2000s.

A fiscal union. The purpose of the fiscal union is to enhance fiscal discipline among the member states and to improve fiscal co-ordination. The original GSP has proven insufficient to guarantee fiscal sustainability. In the proposal, the Commission is given powers to oversee annual national budgets and to recommend changes. Their ability to issue fines to countries that do not follow the common rules increases. Unsustainable fiscal policies, such as in Greece, are to be avoided through supervision, early warning signals and fines. The Commission also proposes that the EU is given additional resources to temporarily assist countries facing economic difficulties. Support for weaker economies already exists through European Structural and Investment funds. The suggestion is to increase the available support. A common ministry of finance at the EU level is proposed to administrate the increased role of the Commission in co-ordinating and shaping national fiscal policies. It is important to note that the Commission does not propose full fiscal integration. Fiscal policy remains primarily a national competence. The euro area fiscal union, if fully implemented, will remain substantially weaker compared, for example, to the fiscal union in the United States.

An economic union. The EU already has an economic union with a single market. However, there are regulatory differences among the countries that prevent full economic integration in vital sectors. To improve integration, the Commission suggests reforms primarily within the energy sector and digital services, two sectors where interaction across national borders is relatively weak. The financial union is, of course, another step towards more economic integration within the financial sector. They also suggest greater co-ordination of national economic policies through a strengthening of the European Planning Semesters. The Commission suggests that they become multiannual to ensure that the common European interest is properly represented in the national decision-making processes. A system of macroeconomic indicators is constructed through the Macroeconomic Imbalance Procedure to provide early warning signals if dangerous macroeconomic imbalances are building up that may threaten the stability of the euro. A country that fails to deal with the imbalances may face fines. A major property bubble or a dramatic loss of competitiveness should not be able to occur in the future. The key to all these proposals is that the Commission does not propose taking powers away from the member states. Instead, they propose more co-ordination or what the ECB calls a process of 'coordinating their sovereignty' (ECB 2016).

Is the Commission's proposal sufficient to secure the euro for the future? My view is that it probably is not. The proposals are steps in the right direction, but not enough. There are at least three key shortcomings. First, most of the reform programme is backward-looking and not forward-looking. The aim is to prevent the financial crisis and the debt crisis from occurring, after they have occurred. All crises are different and trying to prevent a similar crisis from occurring in the future does not mean that another kind of crisis cannot occur. Second, the forward-looking proposals are few and vague. A currency union requires a high level of economic and political integration. 'Coordinated sovereignty' is not enough to strengthen the euro. The currency union will remain weak and will struggle to deal with a future major economic crisis. In addition, at present the burden to solve the economic and social imbalances the euro area suffers from falls mostly on the weaker economies (De Grauwe and Ji 2015) irrespective of whether they have caused the problems themselves or not. Little of what the Commission proposes will change that.

The political tensions among the member states will persist and possibly continue to grow.

Third, and perhaps most importantly, none of the proposals will actually solve any of the major economic and social imbalances that have already occurred. As an illustration, let us consider two of the four factors we previously discussed: southern Europe's competitiveness problem and their long-run economic stagnation.

Competitiveness. Southern Europe lost 30–40 per cent of their competitiveness compared to Germany between 1999 and 2008, partially caused by the German internal devaluation. There are primarily three ways in which they can regain their competitiveness. First, Germany can reflate its economy. However, the German industry is not willing to give up its economic advantage. The German interest continues to be put before the common European interest despite having part in causing southern Europe's loss of competitiveness. Second, southern Europe can follow Germany's example and perform their own internal devaluation. That process is already under way as is evident from the moderate wage increases after 2011, illustrated in Table 7.2. However, it is a slow process. As long as costs increase by 2 per cent in Germany per year, and southern Europe wishes to avoid deflation, they can only regain 2 per cent of their loss per year. It will thus take 20-plus years to restore competitiveness, or more or less a generation. An internal devaluation is carried out by restricting domestic demand and increasing unemployment. An international devaluation is, in other words, economically costly. Enforcing such costs during an entire generation causes political upheaval and conflicts. It is unlikely that this process is going to be successful. But it will—and has already—come with large economic, social and political costs.

Third, southern Europe can regain its competitiveness by increasing its productivity. Rapid productivity growth coupled with low wage growth will restore competitiveness levels. One problem, however, is that productivity growth has largely stalled due to lack of investments, for example, in ICT. The Commission hopes that so-called structural reforms (deregulation of labour markets, changes in taxation laws and changes to welfare systems) will boost economic growth. Such reforms are in all probability necessary if southern Europe is to prosper in the future. However, they are unlikely to cause a major boost to the economy. Firstly, southern Europe underwent a major reform programme in the 1980s and 1990s in preparation for the Single Market and the euro. It did not prevent trend growth from declining (Andersson 2015). An idea that influences most of the

Commission's policies is the belief in long-term economic convergence. Income data in Table 7.1 show that the opposite has happened. Moreover, economic research on regional growth in developed countries shows that regional divergence has been more common than convergence since the 1970s (see e.g. Henning et al. 2011; Ganong and Shoag 2017). Being a country with one labour market and more or less the same economic policies throughout the entire country is insufficient to guarantee economic convergence.

Let us take the United States as an example. The US states have the same currency and the economic and political unions are strong. There are variations in policies across states but the differences are relatively small compared to Europe. Nevertheless, the United States suffers from similar trends of economic divergence as the euro area. Some states have observed strong growth, such as the ICT-intensive states of California and Washington. Old industrial states, such as Michigan and Ohio, have struggled to keep up. Why certain regions struggle to grow in the present economic environment is a puzzle without clear answers, but variations in ICT investments, and the new human capital-intensive economy benefits from forming small clusters rather than being spread out over a larger area are often cited as important factors.

Given the global trends of regional divergence, it is unlikely that structural reforms are sufficient to solve the southern European growth and competitiveness problems. Rather than designing policies for convergence that may never happen, policies should be designed to reduce the economic, social and political tensions economic stagnation and divergence causes. In the United States, labour migration and a strong fiscal union reduce the negative effects of uneven economic development among the states. Labour moves from states in economic decline to growing states. In fact, labour mobility in the United States is substantially higher compared to Europe (Åslund 2006). Consequently, there is little variation in unemployment rates across the states. In 2018, Hawaii had the lowest unemployment rate at 2 per cent and Alaska the highest at 6 per cent. In the euro area, unemployment varies between 4 per cent in Germany and 20 per cent in Greece. Another major problem of economic stagnation is flat-lining or declining tax revenues. In the US fiscal union, some states pay or receive up to 10 per cent of their GDP through the fiscal union. The average support through the EU budget, on average, is one-sixth as large (D'Apice 2015).

The lesson from the United States is that it is important to form well-functioning economic and political unions to complement the currency union to reduce economic and social tensions caused by economic divergence. The euro area should focus on tearing down barriers that prevent migration—for example, differences in labour market regulations, taxation and welfare systems—in order to promote the mechanism needed to deal with economic stagnation in certain parts of the union. That will require economic and political integration by far more than the Commission is proposing.

Why is the Commission not more ambitious in calling for deeper economic and political integration? Why are they still suggesting a middle road between politically independent member states and federalism? The answer to these questions is likely found in the member states' unwillingness to hand over more powers to the EU. For a political union to work, countries forming the union must share political preferences (the fifth criterion for an optimal currency area). The good news for the euro area is that, according to Alesina et al. (2017), there are common policy preferences in Europe. However, political integration is hindered by strong national identities and a weak European identity. Voters are willing to accept political compromises with other voters within a country but less so with voters in other countries. Consider, for example, Germany: voters are generally against a European fiscal union, with economic transfers from the richer Germany to the poorer southern Europe. However, they are willing to accept a welfare state that transfers resources among people within Germany. Without a common identity, Alesina et al. (2017) conclude, deeper political integration is not possible. Consequently, the Commission, faced with this reality, is forced to continue to argue for a middle road between federalism and sovereign nation-states (see Bergman and Blomgren in this volume). Unfortunately, it is likely to be insufficient to strengthen the euro in the long run.

Large and unresolved economic and social imbalances, growing political tensions and the lack of political will to truly solve the problems raise the question of whether maintaining the euro area in its present form is the best solution or is a partial breakup of the euro area the preferred option?

Would Europe Benefit from a Partial Breakup of the Euro Area?

There are two main alternatives to the euro: a return to national currencies or the introduction of parallel national currencies to circulate alongside the euro. As I will argue later, the option of parallel currencies is probably the worst option as it would cause new problems and solve few of the existing ones. Consequently, the prime alternative to the euro is the reintroduction of national currencies. However, a complete breakup of the euro area is both costly and unnecessary. There are countries that have benefitted from the euro membership (Puzzello and Gomis-Porqueras 2018; Gasparotti and Kullas 2019). These countries are also sufficiently similar to integrate further in the future. Thus, the question is not whether the euro should be abandoned altogether, but whether some countries should leave the currency union. At the top of the list are Italy and Greece.

The return to a national currency is not a silver bullet that solves all problems. But there are clear benefits from having a national currency. First, it is the prerequisite for an external devaluation, that is, reduction in the value of the national currency in relation to other currencies. An external devaluation is quick and immediately restores a country's international competitiveness. An internal devaluation lasting many years, with major economic, social and political costs, is avoided. Restored competitiveness increases growth and reduces unemployment. Higher growth makes it easier to return to sound public finances. It also increases optimism, leading to more firm investments and higher long-term growth. Despite higher growth, southern Europe is still likely to grow at a lower rate compared to northern Europe. Additional reforms are needed to strengthen the weaker economies to boost their growth rates. But, the lesson from the 1980s and the 1990s is that exchange rate realignments are necessary, although not sufficient, to restore and maintain economic balance in Europe (Höpner and Spielbau 2018).

Second, improved economic and social conditions reduce political tensions. Economic stagnation is a key factor behind growing populism and nationalism (Eichengreen 2018). Higher growth makes it easier to form responsible governments that can undertake necessary economic and fiscal reforms. Collaborations between the member states and the EU would also be made easier (Moody 2018; Stiglitz 2018).

Third, with national currencies as a regulator, the need for deep political and economic integration subsides. Countries can maintain some policy differences. The exchange rate would partially compensate for differences in policy.

Fourth, the exchange rate and the interest rate will regain their role as economic indicators of the state of the economy. The euro and the ECB's euro rescue-mission after 2012 have partially eliminated the link between economic management and these two important indicators. Countries with weak policies have enjoyed the same stable currency and relatively low interest rates. A return to a national currency would change that. With the link restored, countries with poor policies would face a choice: either they change policies or suffer the cost of a depreciating currency and higher interest rates. The choice is theirs and not imposed by the EU or another euro area member. Shifting the ownership of reforms from outside actors to the domestic policymaking process is key to increasing the likelihood that the reforms are successful. Reforms designed by domestic policymakers are often better designed, face less political resistance and last longer compared to externally imposed reforms (Andersson 2016; Manasse and Katsikas 2017).

Of course, there are also potential economic and political costs associated with a return to national currencies, not least in the short run (see e.g. Eichengreen 2010; Krugman 2013). The financial risks with a breakup of the euro are probably the gravest of them all. Consider a southern European country that announces it will leave the euro. Such an announcement would immediate cause a bank run, with people withdrawing their euro deposits from the banks to protect the value of their savings. If they let the money stay in the bank, they are transformed into the new national currency, which is likely to lose value in relation to the euro. Without liquidity support from the ECB, the bank run would quickly turn into a fully fledged banking crisis.

Another problem for the southern banking sector is that most of their assets are domestic, while a substantial part of their debt is to lenders in northern Europe. The banks would face large losses if their assets are redenominated into a national currency that is devalued at the same time as their debts remain largely euro-denominated. Large losses may very well lead to a banking crisis. To protect the banking sector from such losses, an alternative is to let all existing assets and debts to remain in euros. However, that will not fully solve the problem, as households' future incomes are in the devalued national currency. Lower incomes with the same debt increase the debt ratio and decrease the households' ability to repay their loans. As has been the case in most historical currency reforms, both assets and debts have to be converted into the new currency simultaneously.

Most studies of a euro breakup assume that the breakup either is forced upon a country by financial markets or is a unilateral decision against the will of the other euro countries. This is a key assumption as it implies that there is no mechanism to limit the potential costs of the breakup. Stiglitz (2018) takes a different approach: He asks the question, what would happen if there is a friendly divorce where countries co-operate to limit the costs? His conclusion is that there would be small economic costs in the short run, but it would be manageable. Furthermore, he argues that the costs are small compared to the benefit of reducing the present political tension among the euro members.

The risks with the return to a national currency have caused some to argue for parallel currencies, that is, national currencies circulating alongside the euro (see e.g. Goodhart and Tsomocos 2010). The idea was first outlined during the debt crisis in 2010, only to be returned to in the spring of 2019 by the Italian Conte government. The idea is quite simple. Only the ECB can issue money by law. However, national governments can issue non-interest-bearing bonds that can circulate as, in effect, banknotes. Depending on the construction, they would have value either by law or because they can be used to pay taxes. The benefit of a parallel currency is that the country can maintain its membership in the euro area while at the same time performing at least a partial external devaluation, and this will give the government some space to increase borrowing and spending.

Despite these benefits, a parallel currency is probably the worst solution compared to keeping the euro or leaving the euro area all together. Two currencies would be expensive to administrate and increase transaction costs. It would split the economy into two parts: the euro economy and the national currency economy. People in the euro economy would benefit in relation to the national currency economy, thus creating social tensions. In terms of fiscal policy, part of tax revenues would be in the national currency while most of the debt would be in euros. A depreciating national currency would reduce revenues in relation to the debt, making servicing the debt more difficult.

The ability of member states to issue their own currency increases their power vis-à-vis the EU and the other member states. They would be in the position to ignore any common economic policy decision they disagree with. Rules would be broken and political tensions among the euro countries would further increase. It is telling that recent proponents for a parallel currency, for example, Stiglitz (2019), see it as a first step towards a complete exit from the euro area. A parallel currency system is not a long-term solution.

Joining the euro area turned out to be an economic cost for many countries. Estimates show that economic growth has been lower in many countries due to the euro area membership (Puzzello and Gomis-Porqueras 2018; Gasparotti and Kullas 2019). EU countries outside the euro area have not suffered economically from having their own currencies (Gyoerk 2017; Olsson 2019). In fact, growth has on average tended to be higher among these countries compared to many euro area countries.

Leaving the euro area is also potentially costly. The question thus becomes, which is the least costly solution? No one can provide a definite answer to that question. There are too many unknowns. In my opinion, a friendly divorce between the euro area and some of the southern European countries is probably the least costly solution. I base this judgement on three key observations. First, the structural weakness of the euro and the member states' unwillingness to integrate sufficiently to strengthen the currency union and solve the structural problems. Second, the growing political tensions among the member states as a result of the economic imbalances, which may break the euro area in the future. Third, the historical record of devaluations as a needed policy tool to restore economic balance in Europe. Eighteen exchange rates realignments between 1979 and 1998 is a powerful argument against a common currency. Fourth, markets may in the future cause a breakup of the euro area. It almost happened in 2011/12 with rapidly rising bond yields in southern Europe. A disorganized breakup is associated with a huge economic and political cost for the entire European economy. It is better to prepare a friendly divorce that minimizes the potential costs of a breakup.

Time to Prepare for a Friendly Divorce

For a time after the ECB's emergency decision to save the euro in 2012, it appeared as if the euro area was moving towards safer waters. Political parties that had toyed with the idea of leaving the currency union, such as Rassemblement National in France and the League in Italy, began to tone down their opposition to the common currency. The election of the populist Conte government in Italy in 2018 changed the dynamics. The consequences of the economic imbalances in the euro area that remain unsolved were again laid bare. The idea of Italy introducing a parallel currency popped up on the agenda again. The Commission's integration agenda has largely stalled. Partially because opposition to more integration is growing not just in the south but also in the north. The Dutch Prime Minister Rutte, and the leader of the German Christian Democrats, Annegret Kramp-Karrenbauer, have both spoken out against further integration (Rutte 2018; Kramp-Karrenbauer 2019). Nevertheless, that a country would voluntarily leave the euro area appears unlikely during the fall of 2019.

In my opinion, that is a grave mistake. It is highly unlikely the euro countries can find a realistic common solution to the imbalances in the euro area. The countries are too different and too different political agendas. Researchers such as Hall (2012) and Hassel (2014) divide Europe into between two and five different economic models. They are all capitalistic market-based economies, but there are important differences in, for example, the role of the state, how labour markets are organized, and in the construction of the welfare systems. Each model has evolved over time, based on the respective countries' economic, social and political history. Merging these different models into one common model is unlikely to succeed. At the same time, integrating them into one model is essential to solve the imbalances in the euro area. It is possible that these differences may disappear over time, but it will be a slow process. As discussed by Opper and Andersson (2018), history casts a long shadow and differences across regions tend to persist over centuries despite relatively high levels of migration and economic interactions. There are euro countries that are sufficiently similar to enjoy the benefits of a common currency, but not the present 19 member states.

The partial dismantling of the euro area is just the beginning of a process to return economic and social balance to Europe. More reforms are needed. The sole purpose of reintroducing a few national currencies is to provide Europe with a safety valve that will reduce some of the present tensions the euro area suffers from. The EU is more than the euro. A reduction of tensions is in the long run beneficial for the EU as it makes it easier to collaborate on other important issues, such as security, trade and climate change. The entire EU would suffer irredeemable damage if a country were to be forced out of the euro during a major economic crisis. Although no country would voluntarily leave the euro in the fall of 2019, it is high time to at least prepare a friendly divorce to be prepared for a future euro crisis. Brexit illustrates that being prepared for the unexpected is not a bad idea.

References

Alesina, A., Tabellini, G., & Trebbi, F. (2017). Is Europe an Optimal Political Area? *Brookings Papers on Economic Activity*, 169–213.

Andersson, F. N. G. (2014). Exchange Rates Dynamics Revisited: A Panel Data Test of the Fractional Integration Order. *Empirical Economics, 47*(2), 389–409.

Andersson, F. N. G. (2015). Comments on Finland and Sweden in a Cross-Country Comparison. In T. M. Andersen, U. M. Bergman, & S. E. Hougaard Jensen (Eds.), *Reform Capacity and Macroeconomic Performance in the Nordic Countries* (pp. 306–309). Oxford: Oxford University Press.

Andersson, F. N. G. (2016). A Blessing in Disguise? Banking Crises and Institutional Change. *World Development, 83*, 135–147.

Andersson, F. N. G. (2017). Sekulär stagnation–vad är det, finns det och hur påverkar det penningpolitiken? *Ekonomisk Debatt, 45*(4), 13–25.

Andersson, F. N. G., & Jonung, L. (2019). Iceland Should Replace Its Central Bank with a Currency Board. In R. Z. Aliber & G. Zoega (Eds.), *The 2008 Global Financial Crisis in Retrospect. Causes of the Crisis and National Regulatory Responses* (pp. 349–369). Cham: Palgrave Macmillan.

Åslund, O. (2006). Är EU en gränslös arbetsmarknad? In S. Gustavsso, L. Oxelheim, & N. Wahl (Eds.), *En Gränslös Europeisk Arbetsmarknad? Europaperspektiv* (pp. 71–96). Stockholm, Sverige: Santérus Förlag.

D'Apice, P. (2015, December). Cross-Border Flows Operated Through the EU Budget: An Overview. *European Commission Discussion Paper.* 019.

De Grauwe, P. (2005). *Economics of Monetary Union* (2nd ed.). New York: Oxford University Press.

De Grauwe, P., & Ji, Y. (2015). Has the Eurozone Become Less Fragile? Some Empirical Tests. *Journal of Policy Modeling, 37*(3), 404–414.

Dell'Ariccia, G., Igan, D., Laeven, L., & Tong, H. (2014). Policies for Macro-Financial Stability: Dealing with Credit Booms and Busts. In S. Claessens, A. M. Kose, L. Laeven, & F. Valencia (Eds.), *Financial Crises. Causes, Consequences, and Policy Responses* (pp. 325–364). Washington: United States: International Monetary Fund.

Dellas, H., & Tavlas, G. S. (2009). An Optimum-Currency-Area Odyssey. *Journal of International Money and Finance, 28*(7), 1117–1137.

Dustmann, C., Fitzenberger, B., Schönberg, U., & Spitz-Oener, A. (2014). From Sick Man of Europe to Economic Superstar: Germany's Resurgent Economy. *Journal of Economic Perspectives, 28*(1), 167–188.

ECB. (2016, May). Safeguarding the Euro as a Currency Beyond the State. *ECB Occasional Paper Series* 173.

Eichengreen, B. (2010). The Breakup of the Euro Area. In A. Alesina & F. Giavazzi (Eds.), *Europe and the Euro* (pp. 11–56). Chicago: The University of Chicago Press.

Eichengreen, B. (2015). *Hall of Mirrors. The Great Depression, the Great Recession and the Uses – And Misuses – Of History.* Oxford: Oxford University Press.

Eichengreen, B. (2018). *The Populist Temptation. Economic Grievances and Political Reaction in the Modern Era.* Oxford: Oxford University Press.

European Commission. (2017). *Reflection Paper on the Deepening of the Economic and Monetary Union.* Brussels: European Commission.

Eurostat. (2019a). Unemployment Rate – Annual Data. Retrieved June 1, 2019, from https://ec.europa.eu/eurostat/en/web/products-datasets/-/TIPSUN20.

Eurostat. (2019b). Harmonised Indices of Consumer Prices (HICP). Retrieved June 1, 2019, from https://ec.europa.eu/eurostat/web/hicp/data/database.

Eurostat. (2019c). Government Deficit/Surplus, Debt and Associated Data. Retrieved June 1, 2019, from http://appsso.eurostat.ec.europa.eu/nui/show.do?dataset=gov_10dd_edpt1&lang=en.

Ganong, P., & Shoag, D. (2017). Why Has Regional Income Convergence in the US Declined? *Journal of Urban Economics, 102*, 76–90.

Gasparotti, A., & Kullas, M. (2019). 20 Years of the Euro: Winners and Losers. *Centre for European Policy (CEP) Study February 2019*. Retrieved September 1, 2019, from https://www.cep.eu/fileadmin/user_upload/cep.eu/Studien/20_Jahre_Euro_-_Gewinner_und_Verlierer/cepStudy_20_years_Euro_-_Winners_and_Losers.pdf.

Goodhart, C. & Tsomocos, D. (2010). The Californian Solution for the Club Med. *Financial Times*, January 24. Retrieved September 1, 2019, from https://www.ft.com/content/5ef30d32-0925-11df-ba88-00144feabdc0.

Gyoerk, E. (2017). Economic Costs and Benefits of EMU Membership from the Perspective of a Non-member. *Open Economies Review, 28*(5), 893–921.

Hall, P. A. (2012). The Economics and Politics of the Euro Crisis. *German Politics, 21*(4), 355–371.

Hassel, A. (2014). Adjustments in the Eurozone: Varieties of Capitalism and the Crisis in Southern Europe. *LSE Europe in Question Discussion Paper Series*, 76.

Henning, M., Enflo, K., & Andersson, F. N. G. (2011). Trends and Cycles in Regional Economic Growth: How Spatial Differences Shaped the Swedish Growth Experience from 1860–2009. *Explorations in Economic History, 48*(4), 538–555.

Höpner, M., & Spielau, A. (2018). Better Than the Euro? The European Monetary System (1979–1998). *New Political Economy, 23*(2), 160–173.

Kenen, P. B. (1969). The Theory of Optimum Currency Areas: An Eclectic View. In R. Mundell & A. K. Swoboda (Eds.), *Monetary Problems of the International Economy*. Chicago: University of Chicago Press.

Kramp-Karrenbauer, A. (2019, March 10). Europa jetzt richtig machen. Welt am Sonntag.

Krugman, P. (2013). Revenge of the Optimum Currency Area. In D. Acemogly, J. Parker, & M. Woodford (Eds.), *NBER Macroeconomics Annual, 27*(1) (pp. 439–448). Chicago: University of Chicago Press.

Manasse, P., & Katsikas, D. (Eds.). (2017). *Economic Crisis and Structural Reforms in Southern Europe: Policy Lessons*. New York: Routledge.

McKinnon, R. I. (1963). Optimum Currency Areas. *The American Economic Review, 53*(4), 717–725.

Moody, A. (2018). *Euro Tragedy. A Drama in Nine Acts.* Oxford: Oxford University Press.

Mundell, R. A. (1961). A Theory of Optimum Currency Areas. *The American Economic Review, 51*(4), 657–665.

OECD. (2013). Labour Productivity Levels in the Total Economy. Retrieved June 1, 2019, from https://stats.oecd.org/Index.aspx?DataSetCode=LEVEL.

OECD. (2019a). GDP Per Capita and Productivity Levels. *OECD Productivity Statistics* (database). Retrieved June 1, 2019, from https://doi.org/10.1787/data-00686-en.

OECD. (2019b). Average Annual Wages. Retrieved June 1, 2019, from https://stats.oecd.org/Index.aspx?DataSetCode=AV_AN_WAGE.

OECD. (2019c). United States, Selected Indicators. Retrieved June 1, 2019, from https://data.oecd.org/united-states.htm.

Olsson, B. (2019). Sverige med euron: rikare eller fattigare? Forthcoming in *Ekonomisk Debatt.*

Opper, S., & Andersson, F. N. G. (2018). Are Entrepreneurial Cultures Stable Over Time? Historical Evidence from China. *Asia Pacific Journal of Management*, 1–28.

Puzzello, L., & Gomis-Porqueras, P. (2018). Winners and Losers from the Euro. *European Economic Review, 108*, 129–152.

Rutte, M. (2018, March 2). *Underpromise and Overdeliver: Fulfilling the Promise of Europe.* Speech at Bertelsmann Stiftung, Berlin, Germany.

Stiglitz, J. (2018). *The euro. How a Common Currency Threatens the Future of Europe.* New York: Norton Paperbacks.

Stiglitz, J. (2019, April 19). How to Exit the Eurozone. Italy Is Right to Consider Leaving the EU's Common Currency Area. *Politico Global Policy Lab.* Retrieved September 1, 2019, from https://www.politico.eu/article/opinion-italy-germany-how-to-exit-the-eurozone-euro-reform/.

Stockhammer, E. (2011). Peripheral Europe's Debt and German Wages: The Role of Wage Policy in the Euro Area. *International Journal of Public Policy, 7*(1–3), 83–96.

Tooze, A. (2018). *Crashed: How a Decade of Financial Crisis Changed the World.* London: Allen Lane.

CHAPTER 8

Sanctions Against Individuals and the Rule of Law: Can the Member States Let the EU Decide?

Jane Reichel

Introduction

One of the fundamental differences between a nation-state and an international organization lies in the relationship of the two to the exercise of public power. Within a nation-state, this power is exercised by a cohesive executive which ultimately relies on its monopoly on the use of force to carry out its will. In a democratic constitutional state, public power is presumed to be exercised in accordance with the rule of law: that is, it must be limited, it must be applied in a law-bound and predictable manner, and must be exercised within a framework of constitutional rules which ensure

The author would like to express her gratitude to Gustaf Sjöberg and Antonina Bakardjieva Engelbrekt of the Faculty of Law, Stockholm University, and to Aron Szugalski Verständig, Finansinspektionen, for valuable input on this chapter. Many thanks also to Peter Mayers for translation.

J. Reichel (✉)
Faculty of Law, Stockholm University, Stockholm, Sweden
e-mail: jane.reichel@juridicum.su.se

A. Bakardjieva Engelbrekt et al. (eds.), *The European Union and the Return of the Nation State*,
https://doi.org/10.1007/978-3-030-35005-5_8

the protection of fundamental rights.[1] In this sense, the rule of law serves the dual purpose of making accountability possible and of providing citizens and others within the state's jurisdiction with guarantees against the arbitrary or improper exercise of power (Macchia 2016: 261). For example, administrative decision limiting fundamental rights of individuals must be based on law[2] and procedures for setting out safeguards for individual rights are to be enacted.[3] Within the sphere of international law, by contrast, a cohesive executive power with a monopoly on the use of force is absent; instead, the enforcement of agreed-upon rules is dependent on the sincere cooperation of the adhering parties. The rule of law must therefore work differently at the international level (Macchia 2016: 268).

The European Union (EU) is not a traditional international organization; instead, it has acquired ever more supranational features over the years. Cooperation within the Union has not gone so far that said organization has taken over the monopoly on the use of force from its member states; nevertheless, the EU has adopted legal provisions that can serve as the basis for decisions that encumber individuals, such as criminal or administrative sanctions. In cases of this kind, limits on the exercise of public power are particularly important (Reichel 2019: 78).

The question of the application of the rule of law and the protection of fundamental rights within the scope of EU law is among the most debated issues in European constitutional doctrine (Bernitz 2012; Dougan 2015; Moberg in this volume). At the national level, EU law enjoys primacy and has a direct effect. It has been necessary, therefore, to devise a system for safeguarding fundamental rights to be applied both by the Union and by its member states.[4] One crucial question is, thus, what constitutes the scope of EU law (Lenaerts 2000; Eeckhout 2002; Dougan 2015).

The chapter analyses two situations where Union law is relevant when sanctions against individuals are decided: first, when encumbering

[1] Harlow (2006: 212) refers to 'the twin ideals of democracy and rule of law' as the legitimating principles of any Western system of administrative law. See also The European Commission for Democracy Through Law (Venice Commission) (2011: 41).

[2] Compare the ECHR and the EU Charter, which both require exceptions to the rights they lay down. In the case of the ECHR, this is done in each exemptible article, as in Article 8.2. In the case of EU Charter, it is done in Article 52.1.

[3] See, for example, Article 6 ECHR and Article 41 and 47 EU Charter.

[4] When member states act within the scope of Union law. See, for example, the cases *Internationale Handelsgesellschaft*, *Hauer*, and *Cipriani* (CJEU 1970, 1979, 2002).

decisions are taken by national courts and authorities in a cross-border situation; and, second, when EU law sets out rules on how sanctions against individuals are to be applied within a member state. It is in connection with the first situation that member states have expressed some reservations in recent years, not least with regard to the European Arrest Warrant[5] (EAW). In recent years, namely, it has happened that a court in a prospective sending state has called the rule of law in a requesting state into question in connection with the treatment of extradited persons. As will be discussed, examples include the refusal of courts in some member states to extradite suspected criminals to Hungary and Poland, due to the lack of protection afforded to fundamental rights in those countries; as well as the strict scrutiny applied by the Higher Regional Court of the German state of Schleswig-Holstein to the conditions for extraditing the former regional premier of Catalonia, Carles Puigdemont, to Spain. Similar situations have occurred in relation to asylum law.

Regarding the second situation—decisions on sanctions against individuals taken within a member state or directed at individuals within a member state by an EU body—the corresponding criticism has generally been absent. Situations of that kind have no cross-border element; instead, the rule of law at the national level competes with that at the level of the Union. The *Åkerberg Fransson* case (Court of Justice of the European Union 2013a) that has attracted attention in Sweden concerns the application, in cases examined under the EU's value-added tax (VAT) directives, of the prohibition on double jeopardy featured in the EU Charter of Fundamental Rights, 'the EU Charter'. As long as the courts and members of the public see the principles of Union law as enhancing protection for individuals at the national level, the trend in this area can be seen as positive in many cases, in the sense of strengthening the rule of law and protection for fundamental rights. In two additional cases, discussed below—in relation to penalties for violations of EU rules which have been introduced by the new General Data Protection Regulation 2016/679 (GDPR) and penalties in the form of fines imposed under the direct supervision of the European Securities and Markets Authority (ESMA)—the question of limits on the exercise of public power has hardly been discussed at all.

[5] Council Framework Decision 2002/584/JHA.

In the first situation, one might get the impression at first glance that the matter concerns the return of the nation-state. A trend is now evident in cases where a member state must decide whether to extradite an individual to another member state where that person's fundamental rights are at risk. These states are not prepared to make their own citizens, or others under their protection, pay a personal price for the sake of giving effect to a provision of Union law. However, this situation does not primarily have to do with any conflict between the Union and the member states in question. The organs of the Union, including the Court of Justice of the European Union (CJEU), namely share the view of the refusing states that reciprocity and trust in each other's legal systems can no longer be maintained in these situations. In the second case, the situation is not as clear. The vulnerability of the individual in question—which in these cases is often a company—is not as palpable, as there is no clear alternative with which to compare. On the contrary, the idea generally is that individuals should be treated equally, regardless of the member state in which they find themselves. The task of Union law is to guarantee the uniform and effective implementation of EU legislation, while at the same time guaranteeing a high level of protection for all, on equal terms. As discussed below, however, there may be reason to ask whether the necessary conditions are really present for upholding the rule of law in the exercise of public power in such situations. Perhaps the question here is rather whether the member states should demand power back? The overarching question discussed in this chapter is the following: who—the EU or its member states—ultimately guarantees the rule of law and the protection of fundamental rights when decisions are made on sanctions against individuals within the scope of EU law?

This chapter is arranged as follows. In the next section, I discuss the application of rules for ensuring the rule of law and safeguarding fundamental rights within the scope of EU law at the national level. I then analyse sanctions based on EU law against individuals in cross-border situations. In the subsequent section, I examine the application of penalties based on EU law in an internal situation, that is, within a member state. In the next-to-last section, I ask whether the impact of the EU's rule-of-law principle is uniform across cases or whether instead it is best described as variable. In the concluding section, I review problems with the current order and sketch a tentative way forward.

The Rule of Law Within the Scope of EU Law

As mentioned above, the application of the rule of law and the protection of fundamental rights have been among the most debated issues in European constitutional law in recent decades. Since the end of the 1980s, the Court has held that the member states are required to apply the general principles of EU law when acting within 'the scope of Union law'. These principles derive in turn from the common constitutional traditions of the member states and from international conventions, in the first instance the ECHR (see *Wachauf* CJEU 1989 and *ERT*, CJEU 1991). Article 51(1) of the EU Charter, which codifies the principles elaborated by the CJEU, states that the provisions of the Charter are addressed to the member states 'only when they are implementing Union law'. The question of the scope of the EU's principles here can be divided into two parts: First, how should the area referred to as the 'scope of EU law' be demarcated? Second, what effect should the EU's principles have in this area? In other words, to what extent are the member states obliged to apply the Union's principles and to what extent can national protections for these values still be applied instead.

As regards the first question—on the scope of EU law—the area can be divided in accordance with situations of two main types: situations in the non-harmonized area, where the member states utilize a permitted exception from the principle of freedom of movement (what Michael Dougan calls 'derogation'); and situations in the harmonized area, where the Union legislator has enacted secondary legislation regulating a specific policy area ('implementation') (Dougan 2015: 1210). This distinction corresponds to that between, on the one hand, the competence which the member states have allocated to the Union in the Treaties, that is, the competence to establish a common market based on free competition in which barriers may not be erected to the free movement of goods, services, capital, and labour, and, on the other, the more specific competences which the member states have granted the Union to enact secondary legislation in a number of areas.[6] What makes drawing this line difficult is the fact that legislative competence is often shared between the member states and the Union. The catalogue of competences in the Treaty of Lisbon divides the EU's competences into three broad types: exclusive

[6] See, for example, Article 26 Treaty of the Functioning of the European Union (TFEU) on the internal market and Article 16 TFEU on data protection.

competence; shared competence; and supportive, coordinative, or supplementary competence.[7] Thus, even if a matter falls within the scope of EU law, that does not preclude it from being governed by national law as well. The scope of EU law thus overlaps with that of national legislation in many areas, including legislation which has been enacted wholly independently of Union law.

One central question in this chapter is whether these nationally enacted rules fall within the scope of EU law, and what in that case this means. The CJEU has answered the first question in the affirmative: even if a legal area is regulated only in part by EU law, it nonetheless falls within the scope of EU law. In the *Åkerberg Fransson* case, which concerned the imposition of Swedish penal and administrative sanctions in relation to the violation of rules on VAT (i.e., in connection with tax evasion and tax surcharges), the Court seems to say that the question is in fact quite simple:

> Since the fundamental rights guaranteed by the Charter must therefore be complied with where national legislation falls within the scope of European Union law, situations cannot exist which are covered in that way by European Union law without those fundamental rights being applicable. The applicability of European Union law entails applicability of the fundamental rights guaranteed by the Charter. (Åkerberg Fransson, CJEU 2013a: 21)

The second question identified at the beginning of this chapter—concerning the effect which the EU's principles regarding the rule of law and the protection of fundamental rights should have at the national level—is to be examined next. Article 51 of the EU Charter states that the member states must 'respect the rights, observe the principles and promote the application thereof'. In view of the Court's case law in this area, we may conclude that the meaning of this requirement will vary, depending partly on whether any Union bodies are involved in the implementation of EU law at the national level, and partly on the intensity of Union regulation within the policy area in question.

Put schematically, EU law is implemented in accordance with three different models of administration: direct, indirect, and shared (Harlow 2011: 443; Hofmann et al. 2011: 259). Direct administration is that which the Commission, an EU authority, or other Union body carries out.

[7] Articles 2–6 TFEU.

Indirect administration refers to the implementation of Union law by the member states. Shared administration, finally, is when the member states cooperate with EU organs to implement Union law. When direct administration by EU bodies vis-à-vis individuals in a member state is in question, the principles here considered—the rule of law and protection for fundamental rights—are quite straightforward in their implications. The task of EU organs in that case is simply to apply the principles of Union law fully. Direct administration as such is unusual, as are decisions by central EU bodies' to impose sanctions on individuals. As mentioned at the outset, the Commission has the competence to decide—within the scope of EU competition law—on penalties in the form of fines against individual companies (which can come to very large amounts). The CJEU has produced abundant case law on the safeguards for legal certainty and due process which the Commission must uphold in its decision-making, and developed a far-reaching juridical doctrine as well (Hofmann et al. 2011; Galetta et al. 2015). These issues will not be discussed further here.

The indirect model proceeds on the traditional assumption: that is, that the member states implement EU law independently of the Union. The forms for implementing Union law can thus vary considerably between the states. This model is most common nowadays in policy areas with less intensive EU regulation, where the member states have retained a large share of regulatory competence. The aforementioned case, *Åkerberg Fransson*, was concerned with tax law. In that area, the EU has only adopted secondary legislation bearing on limited parts of national tax law, namely VAT. Åkerberg Fransson had been the subject of both administrative proceedings on tax surcharges and criminal proceedings on tax evasion—for the same tax offence. The question in the case thus concerned whether the Swedish system of penalties for violating Swedish tax law, including those parts based on the EU's VAT directives, was compatible with the prohibition against *ne bis in idem*—the ban on double jeopardy. This prohibition is found both in Article 50 of the EU Charter and in Article 4 of Protocol 7 to the ECHR. As we have seen, the Court found that the EU Charter was applicable here, because the link between the sanctions and the VAT directives meant that the matter fell within the scope of EU law. The CJEU left it to the national court to determine whether the ban on double jeopardy had been violated in the specific case; however, it also provided some instructions on how such proceedings ought to be conducted. The Court stated:

> That said, where a court of a Member State is called upon to review whether fundamental rights are complied with by a national provision or measure which, in a situation where action of the Member States is not entirely determined by European Union law, implements the latter for the purposes of Article 51(1) of the Charter, national authorities and courts remain free to apply national standards of protection of fundamental rights, provided that the level of protection provided for by the Charter, as interpreted by the Court, and the primacy, unity and effectiveness of European Union law are not thereby compromised. (Åkerberg Fransson, CJEU 2013a: 29)

Thus, in areas where the measures undertaken by the member states are not fully harmonized through EU law, national courts and authorities retain the competence to apply national standards for the protection of fundamental rights, as long as the minimum demands of EU law are satisfied and Union law is not compromised. In the area of taxation, the application of the Union's general principles may be relevant in the non-harmonized part of EU law as well, in the event that tax rules have been so designed as to impede trade between member states in an inadmissible manner. In this situation too, penalties for possible infringements are regulated by national law. In this way, fundamental rights in the indirect administrative area are handled in a way similar to how they are handled in the cross-border situation discussed above. Member states may uphold their own traditions, as long as the EU's interpretation of the rule of law and of the protection of fundamental rights is not compromised. As the *Åkerberg Fransson* case makes clear, the application of EU principles can nonetheless have significant consequences for national law. Said case has been the basis for a shift on an issue of tax law that has been discussed in Sweden since the 1970s—namely, whether it is appropriate that two penalties be imposed for the same violation (i.e., Fast 2014).

The model of indirect administration as well has become increasingly unusual, especially in policy areas that are regulated more or less fully by EU law. Various forms of shared administration have instead become the main rule (Chiti 2005). Today, for example, a far-reaching legal framework governs how authorities work with each other in connection with data protection, financial markets, and the EU's structural and agricultural funds. There are minimum rules for how such cases are to be handled. Within the framework of this model, a dense form of administrative cooperation—sometimes termed composite or integrated administration—has developed. Integrated administration is characterized by close cooperation between authorities of equal hierarchical standing within a specific policy area, where the forms of cooperation vary widely between the areas (Hofmann et al. 2011). Thus, the effect at the national level of the EU principles considered here—the rule of law and protection for fundamental rights—becomes complicated and hard to foresee. In the section below, the application of these principles in two types of situation is analysed: first, the transfer of individuals in connection with EU asylum and criminal law; and second, when administrative penalties based on EU law are imposed within an individual member state. The first situation is a case of indirect administration, where the member states implement Union law independently of EU bodies; the second is one of shared administration, where EU agencies and national organs are jointly responsible for implementation.

Sanctions and Encumbering Decisions in Cross-Border Situations

The first type of situation analysed in this chapter concerns decisions by national courts and authorities to impose sanctions on individuals in cross-border situations. EU provisions in both asylum and criminal law call upon member states to transfer individuals to other member states in some cases. The operative principle here is closely linked to the EU law that prohibits member states from engaging in self-help enforcement, that is, from taking steps to remedy deficiencies in the legal systems of other member states. This prohibition was enshrined in the *Hedley Lomas* case. The United Kingdom had taken measures to stop the export of live sheep to Spain, as the British authorities lacked confidence in the compliance of Spanish authorities with EU rules on animal welfare. The CJEU ruled that, by taking matters into its own hands, Britain had acted in violation of EU law: 'A Member State may not unilaterally adopt, on its own authority, corrective or protective measures designed to obviate any breach by another Member State of rules of Community law' (*Hedley Lomas*, CJEU 1996: 20). Mutual trust should thus apply in relation to the legal systems of the member states, among other things in connection with the rule of law and protection for fundamental rights.

In recent years, however, the Court has allowed for the possibility of exceptions to the ban on self-help. It has thereby conceded that individual member states may refrain from complying with EU law on the grounds that another member state's legal arrangements do not measure up. In the case of *N.S. v. Secretary of State for the Home Department*, the issue was whether British and Irish courts and migration authorities could transfer asylum-seekers to Greece in accordance with the Dublin III Regulation and the concept of the first country of asylum (CJEU 2011). The background was that the conditions in Greece for the reception of refugees were so poor that the European Court of Human Rights had found in a previous case—*M.S S. v. Belgium and Greece*—that Belgium, by transferring an asylum-seeker back to Greece, had violated Article 3 of the ECHR and the ban on torture and inhuman or degrading treatment or punishment (ECtHR 2011: 358, 360, and 367).

The violation consisted of exposing asylum-seekers to risk, among other things, because the asylum conditions in Greece were so bad as to constitute degrading treatment. In examining the refusal of the Irish and British courts to execute the transfer, the Court interpreted the corresponding rule on the prohibition of torture and degrading treatment set out in Article 4 of the EU Charter. The Court began by stating that not every kind of infringement of a fundamental right which the responsible member state has committed affects the obligation of the other member states to comply with applicable Union law. Nevertheless, the Court found, there was cause in the current situation to reach a different conclusion. In the event there are 'substantial grounds for believing that there are systemic flaws in the asylum procedure and reception conditions for asylum applicants in the member state responsible, resulting in inhuman or degrading treatment, within the meaning of Article 4 of the Charter, of asylum seekers transferred to the territory of that member state, the transfer would be incompatible with that provision'. In such a situation, member states may refuse to transfer asylum-seekers (CJEU 2011: 82, 86.) In a subsequent case, *C. K. et al. V. Republika Slovenija*, the Court found that a violation of Article 4 of the EU Charter may also occur if there is a real and proven risk that the person concerned will suffer inhuman or degrading treatment—even if, that is, the host country's organization for the reception of refugees displays no systemic flaws (CJEU 2017: 96). The question in this case concerned the transfer of a woman who had recently given birth and who showed severe depressive and suicidal tendencies.

Union criminal law too provides for the transfer of individuals from one member state to another, through the EAW. The issue of the member states' trust in each other's judicial systems has been extensively debated in the doctrine, and a common view seems to be that the EAW challenges the ability of national legal systems to maintain their own version of the rule of law (i.e. Souminen 2011; Efrat 2019). To be sure, the preamble to the framework decision on the EAW states that a national court or authority may refuse to execute the EAW in the event that a member state seriously and persistently violates the principles set out in Article 2 of the Treaty on European Union (TEU) on respect for human rights, democracy, and the rule of law.[8] No such decision has ever been taken. However, as Moberg discusses in this volume, an Article 7 case is currently underway against Poland. The question will be discussed further shortly.

In the widely noted *Melloni* case, the question arose of which standard of fundamental rights was to apply: the EU Charter, the constitutional rules of Spain, or the framework decision on the EAW. The case concerned an Italian man living in Spain who had long evaded a criminal investigation into financial crime. He had then been sentenced *in absentia* to ten years in prison in Italy, and Italian authorities requested his extradition. The Spanish court found that such a procedure violated the requirement of the Spanish constitution for a fair trial, as well as violating the corresponding provisions of the EU Charter—Articles 47 and 48—which also guarantee a fair trial. But the CJEU did not concur, ruling instead that the procedure was compatible with applicable Union law (CJEU 2013b: 53). Against this background, the restriction enjoined by the Spanish constitution could not be upheld either. Such an interpretation, according to the Court, would namely violate the primacy of Union law, since a member state could thereby refrain—citing its own national law—from applying EU legislation, even though said legislation had been found to be compatible with Union law and the EU Charter (ibid., 63).

Since 2016, the CJEU has allowed in two cases for member states' refusal to execute an EAW due to deficiencies in the protection of fundamental rights in the issuing state, under the proviso that the matter concerns a violation of the EU Charter and not just of national law. The issue in the first instance—the joined cases *Aranyosi and Căldăraru* (CJEU

[8] See Article 7(2) TEU (Recital 10 Council Framework Decision 2002/584/JHA).

2016)—concerned arrest warrants issued by Hungarian courts against two persons residing in Germany who were suspected of burglary and of driving without a licence, respectively. The persons in question claimed that a transfer to Hungarian detention risked violating Article 3 of the ECHR and Article 4 of the EU Charter, that is, the ban on torture and other inhuman or degrading treatment. In a manner recalling that seen in the above-mentioned case of *N.S. v. Secretary of State for the Home Department,* the CJEU had previously found that conditions in Hungarian prisons were such that Article 3 of the ECHR could be said to have been violated (*Varga and Others v. Hungary,* ECtHR 2015). Article 3 of the ECHR, the Court noted, corresponds to Article 4 of the EU Charter, which sets forth the fundamental values of the Union and its member states (CJEU 2016: 86–87). The principles of mutual recognition and mutual trust between member states may be restricted 'in exceptional circumstances':

> [T]he executing judicial authority must determine, specifically and precisely, whether there are substantial grounds to believe that individual concerned by a European arrest warrant, issued for the purposes of conducting a criminal prosecution or executing a custodial sentence, will be exposed, because of the conditions for his detention in the issuing Member State, to a real risk of inhuman or degrading treatment, within the meaning of Article 4 of the Charter, in the event of his surrender to that Member State. (ibid., 82, 88)

If such grounds are found to obtain, the member state in question may refrain from executing the EAW.

In the summer of 2018, in the *LM* case, the Court took another step in the same direction. The case concerned a man suspected of drug offences in Poland, whose extradition was requested in accordance with arrest warrants from three Polish courts. The person in question claimed that, due to recent legislative reforms in Poland, he was deprived of his right to a fair trial, and that said reforms jeopardized the basis for mutual trust between the member states. Unlike the situation in the cases discussed above, there was no verdict here from the CJEU to the effect that the right to a fair trial under Article 6 of the ECHR—corresponding to Article 47 of the EU Charter—had been violated. However, the Court cited the ongoing proceedings under Article 7 TEU, in which the Commission has submitted a reasoned proposal to the Council (CJEU

2018: 61). Against this background, the CJEU found that the executing authority, an Irish court, could make its own determination in the case. Thus it fell to the national court, the CJEU ruled, to judge whether it had information 'indicating that there is a real risk of breach of the fundamental right to a fair trial guaranteed by the second paragraph of Article 47 of the Charter', and whether substantial grounds obtained for believing the person in question would run such a risk were he surrendered to the Polish authorities (ibid., 79).

A further example of the challenges posed in relation to the EAW by the member states' differing interpretations of the rule of law can be seen in the case mentioned at the outset: that of Carles Puigdemont, former regional premier of Catalonia. The issue was whether Puigdemont could be extradited to Spain. After Spanish law-enforcement agencies had launched an investigation that could lead to very long prison sentences for Catalan leaders who had organized a referendum on Catalonia's independence from Spain, the former regional premier chose to leave the country and to make his way to other member states. A Spanish court then issued a warrant for his arrest, partly on suspicion of having committed high treason or engaged in sedition, and partly on suspicion of having misused public funds. This put the other member states in a tricky situation. At last the matter came to trial before the Higher Regional Court of the German state of Schleswig-Holstein. Said court found that extradition for the accusation of embezzlement of public funds was admissible, but that extradition for the accusation of rebellion was not (Oberlandesgericht for the State of Schleswig-Holstein 2018). As a result of this ruling, the Spanish court could not consider the question of high treason. According to media reports, the Spanish court then withdrew the arrest warrant, and the matter never came up for consideration by a higher court (The Guardian 2018).

Sanctions and Encumbering Decisions Within a Member State

The second type of situation analysed here concerns cases where Union law sets out rules on sanctions against individuals which are to be applied when Union law is implemented within a member state. In these cases, the European legal dimension takes on a different character. Sanctions and other encumbering decisions typically serve as a means for exerting pressure for the effective implementation of EU law, and they are widely employed in the various policy areas of the Union. In addition to the provisions on data protection and financial markets discussed here, competition and environmental laws can be cited as examples (Halila et al. 2018: 59). The question is how the ever denser Union regulation in the area of administrative sanctions affects the implementation of safeguards for the rule of law and fundamental rights.

As stated above, the traditional assumption has been that the member states follow their own procedures for imposing sanctions, even when the case in question falls within the scope of EU law. However, the leeway that member states enjoy to apply their own procedures depends to a great extent on how detailed the regulation by Union law is within a given area. When decisions on sanctions and other encumbering decisions are made in a context of integrated administration—that is, where responsibility is shared between the Union and the member states—the EU's principles regarding the rule of law and the protection of fundamental rights may function differently than under the more traditional arrangement of indirect administration. Instead of applying minimum rules, national courts, and authorities in a system of shared administration can be expected to apply the general principles of the Union fully.

An example of this can be seen in the reimbursement of EU funds paid out to individuals in the member states. This is an area where shared administration applies. If an individual—generally a company—has received assistance from the Union's structural or agricultural funds, and if for some reason the aid must be repaid, the issue then is which principles shall govern the determination: those of the Union, or those of the member state in question? The revocation of positive administrative decisions is a well-known concept in the internal administrative law of all member states; however, the way in which different member states handle the question of legal certainty for the individual varies (*Algera*, CJEU 1957). In applying the concept to matters of Union law in a context of indirect administration, the CJEU has upheld the traditional premise that each member state applies its own internal administrative and procedural arrangements, provided that the principles of equivalence and effectiveness are observed (Kühne and Heitz, CJEU 2004).

But when shared administration is in question, as in the recovery of EU monies, the Court has taken a different position in the last decade. EU legislation on financial support generally contains express rules on the circumstances under which wrongly paid-out monies are to be recovered. Since national law does not apply to the procedure, the Court has deemed in these situations that reimbursement of the aid should be assessed solely on the basis of the Union's principles of legal certainty and legitimate expectation (Vereniging Nationaal Overlegorgaan Sociale Werkvoorziening, CJEU 2008: 53; Agroferm, CJEU 2013c: 49; Wall 2014: 311). The Supreme Administrative Court of Sweden (2016) has, for example, incorporated this case law. How far the conclusions of this case law are to be applied is unclear at present. Do they apply, for instance, to the implementation of secondary legislation through integrated decision-making on administrative sanctions, which is becoming more common (Wenander 2017: 648)?

As mentioned at the beginning of this chapter, the GDPR sets out rules on sanctions for violating EU rules on data protection. The legal consequences arising when these rules are broken fall into three categories: those spelled out in Article 82, which concerns the right to compensation in case of infringement (i.e., damages); those specified in Article 83, which addresses the imposition of administrative fines; and those set out in Article 84, which requires member states to establish rules for other penalties (which according to the preamble should be criminal). The GDPR does not provide much in the way of instructions to member states regarding the grounds for compensation in the form of damages, and very little regarding the other (preferably criminal) penalties; by contrast, it set outs a good many rules governing the imposition of administrative fines (Chamberlain and Reichel 2019). Article 83 sets out the basic criteria for determining which administrative fines are to be levied, when they are to be paid, and how they are to be calculated; the assumption, however, is that the criteria hereof will be made more comprehensive and complete at the national level. Before the GDPR entered into force, the diversity of national laws—which had not been harmonized at that point—had resulted in a high degree of variation in the regulation of sanctions (Giurgiu & Larsen 2016: 344). Nowadays, however, the guidelines adopted by the Article 29 Data Protection Working Party (2017)—the predecessor of the European Data Protection Board—indicate how the rules are to be applied. Furthermore, the GDPR preamble states that the consistency mechanism introduced through the GDPR should be fit for purpose in decisions on sanctions (Recital 150). All in all, there is relatively dense regulation of how the GDPR's rules on sanctions are to be applied in the member states (Hijmans 2016).

The GDPR gives somewhat contradictory indications on which rule-of-law principle and what rules for the protection of fundamental rights are to apply to administrative sanctions in the member states. The preamble states: 'The imposition of penalties including administrative fines should be subject to appropriate procedural safeguards in accordance with the general principles of Union law and the Charter, including effective judicial protection and due process' (Recital 148). Similarly, where criminal penalties are concerned, it states: 'However, the imposition of criminal penalties for infringements of such national rules and of administrative penalties should not lead to a breach of the principle of *ne bis in idem*, as interpreted by the Court of Justice (Recital 149).' Thus, only the Union's interpretation of the relevant general principles of law is included. Article 58(4) GDPR, which sets out the powers of the data protection authorities, reads as follows: '[T]he powers conferred on the supervisory authority pursuant to this Article shall be subject to appropriate safeguards, including effective judicial remedy and due process, set out in Union and member state law in accordance with the Charter.' Member state law thus rates a mention, but it is to be interpreted in accordance with EU law (i.e., the Charter). Lastly, in Article 83(8) GDPR—which regulates the imposition of administrative fines—reference is made to EU law and to national law as two independent sources:

> The exercise by the supervisory authority of its powers under this Article shall be subject to appropriate procedural safeguards in accordance with Union and Member State law, including effective judicial remedy and due process.

What this means in the concrete case is not altogether easy to ascertain. The question has not particularly drawn attention in the legal doctrine or in the general debate, which may be due to the fact that the GDPR is a vast piece of legislation with a plethora of application problems for individuals, companies, and authorities.[9] This certainly does not make the lack of clarity surrounding the legal consequences of violations less worrisome.

Further examples of an integrated regulation of administrative sanctions can be found in Union law on financial markets. Following the advent of

[9] De Hert (2017: 160) compares GDPR with the writings of Haruki Murakami's in 'riddles are left unsolved, story lines and plots are not always fully developed and some of the strange imaginary lacks clear, rational or empirical coherent meaning'.

the financial crisis in 2008, EU regulation in the area has significantly expanded. This has included the establishment of three agencies, charged with the regulation of banking, the insurance sector, and securities and markets, respectively: the European Banking Authority (EBA), the European Insurance and Occupational Pensions Authority (EIOPA), and the previously mentioned ESMA. The Credit Rating Agencies (CRA) Regulation grants ESMA powers to supervise certain financial actors directly, as well as to take measures such as withdrawing the registration of credit rating agencies and imposing fines for regulatory infringements.[10] As part of their investigations, moreover, ESMA officials may conduct site visits to an actor under supervision, and the competent authority of the member state in question may be invited to participate. ESMA may also request that said authorities carry out special inquiries on its behalf, in which case they must have the same powers as ESMA.[11] The procedure may thus be described as intermediate between direct and shared administration.

In 2017, the Commission proposed to the EP and the Council that the direct supervision of financial markets be increased further. An agreement was reached to that effect in the spring of 2019; the resulting legislation is expected to be finalized[12] in the fall of 2019. The purpose of the legislation is to strengthen direct supervision, to introduce more consistent supervisory practices, and to ensure that EU rules on financial services are followed (European Commission 2017: 3). What is noteworthy in this connection is that neither the Commission in the course of its investigation, nor the companies and other stakeholders who have submitted comments at earlier stages of the legislative process, seem to have regarded the issue as a problem from the standpoint of the rule of law. The Commission's account of the comments it has received shows that the concerns raised by some actors have turned mainly on matters of a practical nature: for example, that national authorities have the best knowledge of national markets, and that boundary difficulties may arise in relation to the remaining elements of national supervision (European Commission 2017: 11). For its part, the Commission takes up the EU Charter at one point, giving its assurance that the proposal shows due respect for rights and that it observes

[10] See Articles 20, 21 and 36 Regulation (EC) No 1060/2009.

[11] See Article 23 a, 23 b, 23 c Regulation (EC) No 1060/2009.

[12] Council, Note from the Presidency, Amended proposal for a Regulation of the European Parliament and of the Council amending Regulation (EU) No 1093/2010 establishing a European Supervisory Authority (European Banking Authority), etc. Brussels, 29 March 2019 (OR. en) Interinstitutional File: 2017/0230(COD), http://data.consilium.europa.eu/doc/document/ST-7940-2019-ADD-1/en/pdf.

the principles contained in the Charter (European Commission 2017: 16). The one item therein given particular attention is Article 37, which calls upon the Union and its member states to ensure a high level of environmental protection, in accordance with the principle of sustainable development (ibid.). To be sure, the environment is always crucial to consider. However, the reference to it here does not seem so relevant in relation to the matter at hand: that of putting limits—in a very complex context of administrative law—on the power of public authorities to impose sanctions on individuals.

A Variable Rule of Law?

As stated at the outset, the rule of law is understood here as the requirement that public power be exercised in law-bound and predictable manner, that is, within a framework of constitutional rules that set limits on the discretion of public organs and the respect of fundamental rights. Such rules can thus serve as a benchmark against which to hold public bodies accountable. Individuals must therefore be able to identify which rules are applicable, who has the 'last word', who can legitimately demand that public organs exercise their powers in a lawful way, and who can monitor the latter's performance in that regard.

The two types of situation analysed here—the one cross-border in character, the other set within the framework of a member state's administration—appear to work in different ways. In the first-mentioned situation, the level of protection afforded by one member state for fundamental rights and the rule of law is set against that afforded by another member state, and the question arises whether either state can be forced to take part in proceedings contrary to its understanding of the rule of law. In the second situation—that within the framework of a given member state's administration—there is no direct object of comparison in the form of another member state; instead the question has to do with the extent to which a member state can apply its own national interpretation of the rule of law on matters lying within the scope of EU law. Two factors, however, are common to the two situations. First, national measures may not be applied in such a way as to undermine the Union's protection for fundamental rights. As is evident from the cases of *N.S. v. Secretary of State for the Home Department*, *Aranyosi and Căldăraru*, *LM*, and *Åkerberg Fransson*, the Union may require its member states to maintain a minimum level of protection for fundamental rights and the rule of law when they act within the scope of EU law. Similarly, a member state may not maintain so high a level of protection as to undermine the supremacy and efficiency of Union law. As the *Melloni* case makes clear, the fact that an EU rule infringes the national constitution of a member state does not in itself mean that the latter may refuse to apply Union law. Union law thus constitutes both a floor and a ceiling for the application of the rule of law by the member states. The big difference lies in how much space the member states have to move between the floor and the ceiling—or in other words, how much leeway they enjoy to apply their own national interpretation of the rule of law within the scope of EU law.

The verdict of the CJEU in *Åkerberg Fransson* makes it clear that the leeway enjoyed by the member states depends on the degree to which national law has been harmonized, that is, on how intensively a jurisdiction is governed by Union law (CJEU 2013c: 29). Areas that are only partly regulated by Union law afford greater leeway to the member states. Thus, the application of sanctions and encumbering decisions in cross-border situations relating to EU asylum and criminal law as well as internal situation within indirect administration-situation follow the same principle, that is, member states can generally apply their own understanding of fundamental rights and the rule of law, as long as the level of protection does not fall below the requirements of Union law. The internal legal order is kept intact: within one and the same state, public power can be exercised the same way in similar situations, whether it be based on national or on EU regulations.

In cases where a member state provides weak protection, Union law can serve as an instrument for strengthening the rule of law. Further, in a cross-border situation, when a member state is faced with a decision on whether to transfer an individual to a member state with poor protection for the rule of law, the Court's recent case law concerning the EAW can be used as a tool for limiting the harsh regime of some member states. There is now a trend for states which identify themselves as champions of the rule of law to make use of the space supplied by Union law and the CJEU to push for greater respect for fundamental rights (Bovend'Eerdt 2016; Marguery 2018).

In a situation of intensive EU regulation, as within the integrated system of European administration, the situation is different. The scope for applying a national interpretation of fundamental rights and the rule of law is less extensive here, perhaps even non-existent. As is clear from the CJEU's case law on the recovery of EU aid, the starting point is that the exercise of public power must be assessed on the basis of the EU's interpretation of the rule of law, even if the individual affected by the decision has only had contact with a national authority (*Vereniging Nationaal Overlegorgaan Sociale Werkvoorziening* and *Agroferm*). Union law thus requires that national authorities apply principles other than those applied in purely national cases, or those applied in cases which fall within the scope of EU law but in less intensively regulated parts thereof. How far conclusions are to be drawn from this case law is currently unclear, but it does not seem unreasonable to assess integrated decision-making on administrative sanctions—as in connection with data protection and financial markets—on the basis of a uniform understanding of the rule of law across the Union. Different versions of the rule of law and of protection for fundamental rights may thus be applicable to similar decision-making processes within the same authority. Of course, the difference between European and national principles can vary between different areas within each member state, as well as between different member states. Thus, the application of the EU's rule-of-law principle can be described as variable in several respects. It risks becoming unpredictable. Conflicts within the Union's system of administration are likely to become more and more common (De Lucia 2012).

The Problems and the Way Forward: Wait and See, or Confront the Problem Head-On?

Two problems with the prevailing order can be identified. First, it can be questioned whether such a variable application of the rule-of-law principle is compatible with the principle of equal treatment, which requires that like cases be treated alike and unlike cases differently. If the entire Union strictly maintains the same version of the rule of law, the consequence thereof may be that the least common denominator sets the standard. This is hardly desirable. Even within a given member state, moreover, problems can arise if only one of two similar cases are considered to fall within the scope of EU law. The question, however, is which situations are to be regarded as alike: the application of similar rules in two adjacent jurisdictions within the same authority, or the application of the same rule by the competent authorities of different member states? It is a matter of perspective: is it most important that all national situations within a given area be treated alike, or that all European situations under a certain regulatory framework be treated alike (regardless of which member state the situation arises in)? If it is an area intensively regulated by Union law—such as agricultural aid, data protection, or financial-market supervision—it may be important that all cases in the policy area be treated alike, irrespective of country. However, if only part of the policy area is regulated by Union law (e.g., tax law), it may be more natural to treat all cases within the same member state alike. Persuasive arguments are not lacking, therefore, for applying the rule of law in like manner throughout an integrated system of European administration—when each legal area is considered in isolation. The problem is rather that the system risks becoming impenetrable and unpredictable for individual actors who briefly find themselves within a given area (Reichel 2014, 2019).

The rule of law as understood here presupposes that public power be exercised in accordance with law, that is, that it be based on constitutional rules that set limits on the power of public bodies to make decisions. If it is hard to figure out what the basic rules are, who finally determines their meaning, and who has the 'last word', there is a problem (von Bogdandy 2008: 412). National authorities can hardly be expected to know these things on the basis of intuition; it must be possible to get a concrete answer to apply in concrete situations. Uncertainty over where the limits to the exercise of public power go, and who is responsible for ascertaining these limits, poses a problem in itself for the rule of law. As Herwig Hofmann points out, ensuring 'compliance of administrative procedure law with higher ranking constitutional provisions is a formidable challenge in a unitary system, in which legislation, executive rule-making and final individualised decision-making are undertaken by the same body of law within the same legal person. Within the EU, the conditions are more complex' (Hofmann 2015: 4). Yet, they need not to be unsurmountable. A heightened awareness of the problems on the part of the EU legislator, and a continued development of case law on the part of the CJEU—in dialogue with the national courts—should make it possible to achieve greater clarity over time. This presupposes, however, that conflicts not be swept under the rug. As De Lucia puts it, 'it is important to abandon an idealised, peaceful vision of integrated administration in order to adhere to a more realistic vision which considers conflict between public interests as one of the founding elements of the European multilevel system' (De Lucia 2012: 76). Clear vision is lacking on these matters today, even on such fundamental issues as the rule of law. The legislative proposal from the Commission discussed above—on increased direct supervision over financial markets—hardly touches on fundamental rights or the rule of law at all, save with a reference to environmental protection and sustainable development which seems out of place in this context (European Commission 2017: 16).

The second problem that can be identified is the lack of respect for the rule of law as such which is evident in certain member states. Of the two types of situation examined here—those of a cross-border character and those where Union law is applied within one and the same member state—it is in connection with the first that this problem has come to ahead. In cross-border situations involving the transfer of asylum-seekers or suspected criminals, the failure of some member states to respect the rule of law may spill over to other member states. The latter may then see themselves as obliged to deviate from the Union's principles of mutual trust and mutual recognition. As an organization, the EU has undertaken to uphold a legal order based on the rule of law. It cannot be accepted, therefore, that individuals risk having their fundamental rights violated when Union rules are applied to the transfer of persons from one member state to another, due to deficiencies in the legal system of some member states. In particular instances, the negative consequences arising from the lack of respect for the rule of law shown by some member states have been remedied. The question, however, is whether the problem is larger than that. Within the area of shared administration, where decisions on administrative sanctions are made on an integrated basis, the expectation is higher that member states will uphold not just a national version of the rule of law, but a uniform European one as well.

But how are the EU legislator and the CJEU to develop a transparent and predictable system of integrated administration, when parts of the administration do not accept the basic foundations of the rule of law—that is, a law-governed exercise of public power based on constitutional rules putting limits on the discretion of public organs? In recent years, Poland and Hungary have come in for far-reaching criticism for shortcomings in this regard, as Andreas Moberg analyses in his contribution to this volume. Also, other member states may follow the same path. Will the Union be capable, over the long run, of maintaining its requirement that the member states uphold the rule of law within the integrated administration which some national constitutional organs are not willing or able to uphold at the national level?

As stated at the outset, the issue may seem to be about the return of the nation-state in cases where national courts, in a cross-border situation, have refused to hand over individuals to member states whose practises in connection with the rule of law have been thought unreliable. After all, in a democratic and law-governed state, it is the national constitutional organs—generally the courts—which are charged with ensuring that the rule of law is followed when sanctions are imposed on individuals within their jurisdiction. In this case, however, it is scarcely a question of the nation-state against the EU 'superstate'. As we have seen, the CJEU has not hesitated to accept deviations from the principle of mutual recognition in cases where obvious deficiencies have come to light in the legal system of one of the states involved in a conflict between two states over forms of protection. It bears stressing, rather, that there is a greater scope and need for national courts to safeguard the rule of law in the second type of situation discussed here—that is, when decisions on sanctions against individuals are decided within the framework of the integrated system of European administration. Challenges to the rule of law are more difficult to identify in such cases, and neither the EU legislator nor the Commission nor the CJEU has shown any greater understanding of the problems that thereby arise. Yet it is difficult for national courts to demand, in their dialogue with the CJEU, that transparent, balanced, and impartial decision-making processes be established in so complex an environment of administrative law as that which has emerged within the integrated system of European administration. The responsibility for addressing this must lie primarily with the EU legislator.

If the EU legislator cannot provide a clear answer to these questions, it is doubtful whether national courts will be prepared in the long run to accept what can hardly be anything but *ad hoc* solutions from the CJEU. Instead of taking a wait-and-see attitude, the EU legislator should confront the problem head-on and introduce legislation on the question of what restrictions on the exercise of public power shall be upheld within the scope of EU law. As noted above, there are good arguments for applying one and the same understanding of the rule of law in policy areas which are intensively regulated by Union law. However, it should be clarified which areas these are, and what specifically is required by the Union's understanding of the rule of law. In that case, the courts, both at Union level and within the member states, will have something against which to test the exercise of public power. Otherwise, it may be better for national courts to refuse to apply the Union's interpretation of the rule of law when deciding on sanctions against individuals and to apply their own instead.

References

Bernitz, U. (2012). *Europarättens genomslag*. Stockholm: Norstedts Juridik.

Bovend'Eerdt, K. (2016). The Joined Cases Aranyosi and Căldăraru: A New Limit to the Mutual Trust Presumption in the Area of Freedom, Security, and Justice? *Utrecht Journal of International and European Law, 32*(83), 112–121.

Chiti, E. (2005). The Relationship Between National Administrative Law and European Administrative Law in Administrative Procedures. *What's New in European Administrative Law*, EUI Working Paper Law, 10, 7–10.

Council, Note from the Presidency, Amended proposal for a a Regulation of the European Parliament and of the Council amending Regulation (EU) No 1093/2010 establishing a European Supervisory Authority (European Banking Authority), etc. Brussels, 29 March 2019 (OR. en) Interinstitutional File: 2017/0230(COD), http://data.consilium.europa.eu/doc/document/ST-7940-2019-ADD-1/en/pdf.

Court of Justice of the European Union. (1957). *Algera v. Common Assembly of the European Coal and Steel Community*, C-7/56 and C-3/57 to 7/57. ECLI:EU:C:1957:7.

Court of Justice of the European Union. (1970). *Internationale Handelsgesellschaft*, C-11/70. ECLI:EU:C:1970:114.

Court of Justice of the European Union. (1979). *Hauer v Land Rheinland-Pfalz*, C-44/79. ECLI:EU:C:1979:290.

Court of Justice of the European Union. (1989). *Wachauf v Bundesamt für Ernährung und Forstwirtschaft*, C-5/88. ECLI:EU:C:1989:321.

Court of Justice of the European Union. (1991). *Elliniki Radiophonia Tiléorassi (ERT) v Dimotiki Etairia Pliroforissis*, C-260/89. ECLI:EU:C:1991:254.

Court of Justice of the European Union. (1996). *The Queen v Ministry of Agriculture, Fisheries and Food, ex parte: Hedley Lomas (Ireland) Ltd*, C-5/94. ECLI:EU:C:1996:205.

Court of Justice of the European Union. (2002). *Cipriani v Ministero delle Finanze*, C-395/00. ECLI:EU:C:2002:751.

Court of Justice of the European Union. (2004). *Kühne & Heitz NV v. Produktschap voor Pluimvee en Eieren*, C-453/00. ECLI:EU:C:2004:17.

Court of Justice of the European Union. (2008). *Vereniging Nationaal Overlegorgaan Sociale Werkvoorziening*, C-383/06–385/06. ECLI:EU:C:2008:165.

Court of Justice of the European Union. (2011). *N. S. v. Secretary of State for the Home Department*, C-411/10 and C-493/10. ECLI:EU:C:2011:865.

Court of Justice of the European Union. (2013a). *Åkerberg Fransson*, C-617/10. ECLI:EU:C:2013:105.

Court of Justice of the European Union. (2013b). *Melloni v. Ministerio Fiscal*, C-399/11. ECLI:EU:C:2013:107.

Court of Justice of the European Union. (2013c). *Agroferm A/S v. Ministeriet for Fødevarer, Landbrug og Fiskeri*, C-568/11. ECLI:EU:C:2013:407.

Court of Justice of the European Union. (2016). *Pál Aranyosi and Robert Căldăraru*, C-404/15 and C-659/15 PPU. ECLI:EU:C:2016:198.

Court of Justice of the European Union. (2017). *C. K. et al. v. Republika Slovenija*, C-578/16 PPU. ECLI:EU:C:2017:127.

Court of Justice of the European Union. (2018). *LM*, C-216/18 PPU. ECLI:EU:C:2018:586.

Data Protection Working Party. (2017, October 3). Guidelines on the Application and Setting of Administrative Fines for the Purposes of the Regulation 2016/679 (WP 253). Retrieved July 4, 2019, from ec.europa.eu/newsroom/just/document.cfm?doc_id=47889.

De Hert, P. (2017). Data Protection as Bundles of Principles, General Rights, Concrete Subjective Rights and Rules: Piercing the Veil of Stability Surrounding the Principles of Data Protection. *European Data Protection Law Review, 3*, 160.

De Lucia, L. (2012). Conflict and Cooperation Within European Composite Administration (Between Philia and Eris). *Review of European Administrative Law, 5*(1), 49–88.

Dougan, M. (2015). Judicial Review of Member State Action Under the General Principles and the Charter: Defining the "Scope of Union Law". *Common Market Law Review, 52*(5), 1201–1245.

Eeckhout, P. (2002). The EU Charter of Fundamental Rights and the Federal Question. *Common Market Law Review, 39*(5), 945–994.

Efrat, A. (2019). Assessing Mutual Trust Among EU Members: Evidence from the European Arrest Warrant. *Journal of European Public Policy, 26*(5), 656–675.

European Commission. (2017). Commission Proposal, 2017/0230 (COD), 20 September 2017. COM(2017) 536 final.

European Court of Human Rights. (2011). *M. S. S. v. Belgium and Greece*, No 30696/09. ECLI:CE:ECHR:2011:0121JUD003069609.

European Court of Human Rights. (2015). *Varga and Others v. Hungary*, Nos 14097/12, 45135/12, 73712/12, 34001/13, 44055/13 and 64586/13. ECLI:CE:ECHR:2015:0310JUD001409712.

Fast, K. (2014). Tusen skäl att förekomma istället för att förekommas-en kommentar till dubbelbestraffningsfallen i EU-domstolen och Högsta domstolen 2013. *Juridisk Tidskrift, 1*, 24–44.

Galetta, D.-U., Hofmann, H. C. H., Puigpelat, O. M., & Ziller, J. (2015). The General Principals of EU Administrative Procedural Law. An In-Depth Analysis (RIDPC 2015/5). *Rivista Italiano di Diritto Pubblico Comunitario, Anno XXV, Fasc 5–2105, 25*, 1421–1437.

Giurgiu, A., & A Larsen, T. (2016). Roles and Powers of National Data Protection Authorities. *European Data Protection Law Review, 2*(3), 342–352.

Halila, L., Lankinen, V., & Nilsson, A. (2018). *Administrativa sanktionsavgifter: En nordisk komparativ studie*. Copenhagen: Nordic Council of Ministers.

Harlow, C. (2006). Global Administrative Law: The Quest for Principles and Values. *European Journal of International Law, 17*(1), 187–214.
Harlow, C. (2011). Three Phases in the Evolution of EU Administrative Law. In P. Craig & G. de Burca (Eds.), *The Evolution of EU Law* (pp. 439–464). Oxford: Oxford University Press.
Hijmans, H. (2016). The DPAs and Their Cooperation: How Far Are We in Making Enforcement of Data Protection Law More European. *European Data Protection Law Review, 2*, 362–372.
Hofmann, H. (2015). Current Debates in European Administrative Law–Background and Perspectives. In J.-B. Auby & T. Perroud (Eds.), *Droit de Procedure Administratif.* Brussels: Bruylandt.
Hofmann, H. C., Rowe, G. C., & Türk, A. H. (2011). *Administrative Law and Policy of the European Union.* Oxford: Oxford University Press.
Lenaerts, K. (2000). Respect for Fundamental Rights as a Constitutional Principle of the European Union. *Columbia Journal of European Law, 6*(1), 1–25.
Macchia, M. (2016). 12. The Rule of Law and Transparency in the Global Space. In S. Cassesse (Ed.), *Research Handbook on Global Administrative Law* (pp. 261–281). Cheltenham: Edward Elgar Publishers.
Marguery, T. P. (2018). Towards the End of Mutual Trust? Prison Conditions in the Context of the European Arrest Warrant and the Transfer of Prisoners Framework Decisions. *Maastricht Journal of European and Comparative Law, 25*(6), 704–717.
Oberlandesgericht for the State of Schleswig-Holstein. (2018). Matter Carles Puigdemont: The Extradition for the Accusation of Embezzlement of Public Funds Is Admissible; An Extradition for the Accusation of Rebellion Is Inadmissible. Carles Puigdemont Remains Free. Retrieved July 4, 2019, from https://www.schleswig-holstein.de/DE/Justiz/OLG/Presse/PI/201806Puigdemontenglisch.html.
Reichel, J. (2014). Communicating with the European Composite Administration. *German Law Journal, 15*(5), 883–906.
Reichel, J. (2019). The rule of law in the twilight zone: administrative sanctions within the European composite administration. In R. L. Weaver, D. Fairgrieve, & S. I. Friedland (Eds.), *Administrative Law, Administrative Structures, and Administrative Decisionmaking, Comparative Perspectives* (The Global Papers Series, Volume IX) (pp. 73–89). Durham: Carolina Academic Press.
Reichel, J., & Chamberlain, J. (2019, September 1). *The Relationship Between Damages and Administrative Fines in the EU General Data Protection Regulation.* Faculty of Law, Stockholm University Research Paper No. 72 (2019); Mississippi Law Journal, 2020. Available at SSRN: https://ssrn.com/abstract=3447854 or http://doi.org/10.2139/ssrn.3447854.
Suominen, A. (2011). *The Principle of Mutual Recognition in Cooperation in Criminal Matters: A Study of the Principle in Four Framework Decisions and in*

the Implementation Legislation in the Nordic Member States. Cambridge: Intersentia.

Supreme Administrative Court of Sweden (2016). HFD 2016 ref. 13.

The European Commission for Democracy Through Law (Venice Commission) (2011). Report on the Rule of Law, Study No. 512/2009 CDL-AD(2011)003rev.

The Guardian. (2018, 19 July). Spanish Court Drops International Warrant for Carles Puigdemont. Retrieved July 4, 2019, from https://www.theguardian.com/world/2018/jul/19/spanish-court-drops-international-warrant-puigdemont-catalan.

Von Bogdandy, A. (2008). Pluralism, Direct Effect, and the Ultimate Say: On the Relationship Between International and Domestic Constitutional Law. *International Journal of Constitutional Law, 6*(3–4), 397–413.

Wall, G. (2014). *Rättskraft och korrektiv: en förvaltningsrättslig studie.* Doctoral dissertation, Uppsala University: Department of Law.

Wenander, H. (2017). Skydd för berättigade förväntningar i svensk förvaltningsrätt?– Negativ rättskraft, EU-rätt och styrning av förvaltningen. *Förvaltningsrättslig tidskrift, 2017*(4), 637–649.

CHAPTER 9

Europeanisation and the Longevity of the Nation-State: Survival by Transformation?

Malin Stegmann McCallion

Introduction

The integration process of the European Union (EU) began in 1952 with the signing of the Treaty of Paris, which set up the European Coal and Steel Community, and the Rome Treaty setting up the European Economic Community in 1957. These treaties laid the foundations for economic and political collaboration between six European states under the guidance of common supranational institutions. Up until and including the 2010s this collaboration has expanded to include 28 member states and covers a diverse range of policy areas, although it seems very likely that the UK will leave during the second half of 2019, reducing the number of member states to 27. During this time period, the pendulum has swung several times, from emphasising the EU's intergovernmental features to the other

M. Stegmann McCallion (✉)
Department of Political, Historical, Religious and Cultural Studies, Karlstad University, Karlstad, Sweden
e-mail: malin.stegmann-mccallion@kau.se

A. Bakardjieva Engelbrekt et al. (eds.), *The European Union and the Return of the Nation State*,
https://doi.org/10.1007/978-3-030-35005-5_9

end of the swing emphasising the supranational features[1] of the collaboration.[2]

The starting point for this chapter is the following question: *how can Europeanisation processes be understood in a time when the pendulum is moving towards more intergovernmental features of the collaboration?* Europeanisation processes should not be seen as synonymous with the EU integration process.[3] In the literature, two perspectives of Europeanisation are highlighted: first, the top-down Europeanisation process, which also is the one that is easiest to identify. This process explores how member states change due to EU membership. Research into it focuses upon '*if* the EU has an effect upon politics in a broader understanding (*politics, policy,* and *polity*) at lower levels (national and subnational levels) and if so *which* adaptations or changes take place, and *how* and with what *effect*' (Johansson 2010: 635 emphasis in original). The second Europeanisation process is *bottom-up*: in this process, the member states or other political actors influence the EU level by uploading their political preferences to the EU's political system. But whether they focus on top-down or bottom-up processes, researchers agree that the member states are shaped in important ways by EU membership. They do not disappear or become powerless but they *do* evolve and become parts of a 'fused' continental polity that binds them vertically to the EU institutions and horizontally to each other (Wessels 1997).

Consequently, it is a mistake to view the EU as either intergovernmental or supranational: it is both, simultaneously. The member states retain control over the powers the EU has, and the rules that govern its working,

[1] Through membership in the European Union the member states have delegated part of their sovereignty to some of the institutions found at EU level, namely the European Commission, European Parliament, the Council of the European Union (Council of Ministers), and Court of Justice of the European Union. The EU institutions have the powers to make legislation which is applicable to all member states.

[2] Intergovernmentalism in this chapter is understood as when the decision-making powers are still with the member states, which can be contrasted to supranationalism, where the decision-making power has been placed with the EU institutions.

[3] European integration, in this chapter, is seen as the *process of the member states merging with each other*, thus it is the result or 'product' of co-operation within political, economic, social, and legal areas. Europeanisation, on the other hand, is seen as how *political decisions* at EU level influence the dimensions of policy, politics and policy in the member states. This chapter focuses solely upon EU member states and thus does not discuss how European integration and/or Europeanisation processes influence non-EU member states.

but they also are fundamentally altered by their participation in the integration process.

This chapter is divided into five sections. The first section explores Europeanisation through a top-down perspective. The second section focuses upon Europeanisation from a bottom-up perspective, that is, how member states have influenced politics at EU level. This is followed by the third section exploring member states' strategies to meet pressures to change placed on them by the EU. The penultimate section of the chapter analyses if and how the EU is moving towards a more differentiated integration process which enables member states to 'opt out' of certain EU measures, and the pros and cons of such a process. The final section explores if there is support from the citizens for increased supranational co-operation at the EU level and if the transformation of the nation-state via EU membership has led to its longevity.[4]

Europeanisation Through a Top-Down Perspective

Europeanisation processes can be understood from a top-down perspective as changes within the member states that can be traced back to the EU. Neill Nugent (1999: 471) succinctly describes the cost of EU membership: '[t]he most obvious price states pay for membership of the EU is a substantial loss of national decision-making powers'. It is here that the tension between intergovernmental and supranational co-operation becomes visible in the integration process. The member states have often been reluctant to transfer decision-making powers to the EU level in policy issues that are seen as politically sensitive and which touch upon core parts of the member states' sovereignty. These sensitive policy areas are more likely to be intergovernmental in their nature. However, they have also often realised the benefits of such competence, as in the case of the single currency. As a result, the EU has the authority to make policy—competence—in a range of issue areas, and to different degrees: the member states can give the EU, exclusive, shared, or supporting competence in an issue area. In other words—some polices are more Europeanised than others!

[4] This chapter explores the *political* aspects of Europeanisation and not the legal equivalents as there is only space for discussing the political aspects in this chapter, for a discussion on the legal effects see, for example, Alter (2003) and Snyder (2000).

The member states of the EU have chosen to co-operate within different policy areas, for example, within economic and monetary issues, energy, trade, fisheries and maritime issues, and the environment. It is thus a given that the EU will have an influence on the member states' policies within these areas. The degree of Europeanisation is dependent upon a member state's level of adaptation to the EU laws in question, which, in turn, can be either strictly binding or a looser suggestion or framework adaptation depending upon which legal act is stipulated in the decision-making process. The usual procedure is that the legal act originating at EU level shall be transposed into national legislation and then implemented. The level of adaptation by a member state is also dependent upon issues such as how successfully the member state in question uploaded their political preferences to the EU level during the legislative process (I will return to this in the next section of the chapter), it can also depend upon how well the member state in question choose to implement an EU policy.

Described below are some examples of different types of legislative acts and how these are transposed into national legislation and later implemented. This is thus an example of Europeanisation of *policy*, that is, the content of politics in the form of actual propositions which aim to solve societal problems/issues. The other two dimensions in which one can discern processes of Europeanisation are *polity* and *politics*. Polity is the rules of the political process, and the legal frameworks and the characteristics of the political system, whereas *politics* refers to actors' (relative) power and their strategies relating to political contestation.

The legal acts which are at the disposal of the EU are regulations, directives, decisions, recommendations, and opinions. These have formally different effects upon the member states, and the first three will be described in more detail. A regulation is a legal act that must be applied and implemented in the member states. It is binding for all member states (apart from member states that have opted out). An EU regulation is also directly incorporated into the national legislation of a member state thus no measures for the transmission of the regulation into the national legislative process are needed for the regulation to legally take effect. Regulations are most common in policy areas where the EU has exclusive competence, or where the EU and member states share competences. Also, regulations specify both policy substance and policy tools, that is, both what member states must do, and how they must do it.

Directives are another type of legislative act. Directives are not directly transposed into national legislation but have to go through the national legislative procedure to come into legal effect in the member states. When it comes to implementation of an EU directive the member states have a certain time period in which they can adapt or adjust their policies within the specific area. Another difference between regulations and directives is that a directive is only binding in relation to the political objective which it is set to achieve whereas the actual process to the reach the objective, that is, *how* the objective is being reached, is decided by the member state themselves. The third binding legal act at the EU level is *decisions*. A decision is binding to the member state or states to which it is addressed. A decision can also be addressed to one or several organisations and/or business which has their legal domicile in a named member state. Decisions are thus also a clear example of top-down Europeanisation.

With these examples of clear cases of top-down Europeanisation let us focus upon what this means for the member states' rules of the political game (i.e. constitutions and rule of law), that is, the national *polity*. Blomberg and Bergman (2005) describe member state polities as interconnected with the EU, whereas Jacobsson and Sundström (2006) describe this as meaning that the national polity is interwoven into the EU's political system. When a state becomes a member of the EU, another level is added to already existing levels in the national political system, that is, a supranational level. However, this new supranational level—the EU level—does not 'float above' the national political system, it conjoins with the national political system. If the EU and the Europeanisation process is illustrated like a tree, the root system embeds itself between the national political levels (subnational and the national) binding them together as well as being nourished by the member states. During the integration process, policy areas have been delegated to the supranational—EU—level from the national level through changes in the EU's various treaties. The Single European Act (1986), for example, focused on the single market and how it would be realised. This meant deeper integration in areas connecting to the free movement of goods, service, persons, and capital, as well as changing decision-making rules such as policy areas in which qualified majority voting was introduced. The Maastricht Treaty (Treaty on European Union, 1992) deepened the co-operation within the area of the Economic and Monetary Union and the common currency, the euro. With the Maastricht Treaty, Justice and Home Affairs was added to the EU level, although as intergovernmental co-operation between the member states; however, this changed to become more supranational with the Amsterdam Treaty (1997). Since the Amsterdam Treaty, the EU and the member states share competences within Justice and Home Affairs. The national polity has through the deepening of the integration process become (more) Europeanised and the dividing line between domestic and foreign policies has become blurred.

Through this loosening or blurring between what is domestic policy and what is foreign policy Warleigh-Lack and Stegmann McCallion (2012) have shown that EU membership has been used as a bargaining tool within the power relations between administrative levels within a member state and thus can shape the national policy, with Sweden as their case. Although the pattern is not identical in each member state, it is clear that each of them is now part of a continental system of ***multi-level governance*** (see, for example, Hooghe and Marks 2001; Marks and Hooghe 2004)—being part of the EU has changed the balance of power between centre and periphery in the member states. This trend of indirect Europeanisation and changes in the balance of power within the member states has been discussed under the heading of hollowing out the welfare—and/or the nation-state (Jessop 2013). The transference of decision-making authority to the EU level in combination with decentralisation processes within member states, where power has been devolved or delegated to regional, municipal, and/or local authorities, has led to a relative weakening of the national level's importance in domestic politics. What were once policy areas where the sole competence was with the national government of member states are now shared with other levels in society, and also with the EU. This can result in member states needing to implement political decisions that go against the national line in a policy issue or question, because the state cannot veto EU decisions if the Treaties apply qualified majority voting and equal legislative powers to the European Parliament unless it can generate a blocking minority in the Council of Ministers.

Warleigh (2006) explored the reasons why member states have chosen to participate in a political system where decision-making powers have been delegated to supranational political institutions (European Commission, European Parliament, and Council of Ministers[5]). He

[5] Although the Council of Ministers represents national governments it has become a supranational institution in three important ways. First, qualified majority voting means that

found seven reasons for this in the academic literature, which are as follows: (1) ideological conviction; (2) to strengthen the central/national level's power in international negotiations; (3) to strengthen the national level towards other domestic administrative levels, actors, and interest organisations; (4) to bind success or administrations to follow the political course laid out; (5) to use the EU as a scapegoat for unpopular decisions; (6) to meet political goals which could not otherwise be met; and (7) because they feel that they have no other option. In other words, member states can be Europeanised to *some* extent against their will: they can be outmanoeuvred in the legislative process at EU level, but this is a matter of policy content, not the power to legislate—as stated above, the EU can only make policy in areas of competence given to it by the member states. In relation to a member state being outmanoeuvred, EU membership has shifted the power balance of the national level to sub- and supranational levels of governance. The subnational level as in the regional level one can argue has become empowered in, for example, regional policy (Keating 1998; Keating and Hooghe 2001), and at the supranational level the ordinary legislative procedure has empowered the European Parliament, and one has to bear in mind that with qualified majority voting a member state can be outvoted when this is applied. Thus, the power a national government once held independently has become shared with a range of other actors through participation in a multi-level EU political system that requires, at times, new ways of doing politics as well as new policy approaches for representatives of the national level. This leads us to the third dimension that is shaped by Europeanisation processes, namely *politics*, which has been defined as actors' relative power and their [political] conflict strategies. What is of interest here is how the member states influence the EU, and how successful the member states are in uploading their preferences to the supranational EU level. This can be understood from a bottom-up perspective of Europeanisation.

national governments cannot use veto and must thus form alliances. Second, co-decision makes it into a co-legislator with the EP which, not least, the conciliation procedure bears witness to. Third, national governments in the Council do not work in a vacuum. They are lobbied by, and make alliances with, non-state actors just like officials in the Commissions or Members of the EP, even if this is less visible and often done within the member states themselves.

Europeanisation Through a Bottom-Up Perspective

Europeanisation processes from a bottom-up perspective can be understood as changes taking place at the EU level which can be traced back to member states. The EU is a political system in which different interests are represented, for example, in the institutions. The European Commission should work for the 'EU', that is, for what is the best possible political solution for the EU as a whole, and it is also the only institution that has the right in the treaties to put forward legislative proposals. In the ordinary legislative procedure, the member states are represented in the Council of Ministers. The Council of Ministers shares the legislative power with the European Parliament which in turn represents the EU citizens. The member states are also represented in the European Council through their Heads of State or Government; however, the European Council is an institution which does not participate in the ordinary legislative procedure. Rather, it is the body that can give powers to the EU by means of a new Treaty. It also agrees with the EU's strategic framework. To study Europeanisation processes from a bottom-up perspective is complicated as politics at the EU level is often the result of compromises between institutions, member states, and other actors. It can therefore be hard to differentiate how individual member states have influenced EU politics.

How successful a member state has been in uploading its political preferences and thus influencing the politics at EU level depends upon, among other aspects, how the member state has carried out its political 'actorness'. This includes how skilful the member state has been strategically, which conflict solving strategies it has used, and which power it has compared to other member states, institutions, and actors. These combined together can indicate the real capability and ability to influence and act at the EU level when it comes to influence over the European integration process. The member state's arguments, the ability for alliance building and co-operation, as well as its ability to find common interests and act upon these with the other member states become key if the member state is successful in uploading its preferences to the EU level.

Within the policy areas where the EU institutions have exclusive competence, or the policy areas where this is shared between the EU and the member states, a member state needs to find a common agenda with other member states in order to be able to influence the political and legislative decisions taken. How the EU membership has influenced the member states' polity and policy (the content of politics) becomes visible when one studies Europeanisation processes from a bottom-up perspective. This is because it shows not only what the member state in question has had to do to secure its objectives in policy terms, but also how the member state has had to adapt itself structurally to facilitate such influence.

When a member state, Sweden, for example, wishes to influence the politics and policies at EU level it needs to show a common agenda with other member states and be able to argue for its position. Even though it is the Swedish government which is representing (public/official) Sweden at the EU level in the ordinary legislative procedure, through its representation in the Council of Ministers, the Swedish government receives its mandate from the Swedish *Riksdag* (national parliament). Before meetings in the Council of Ministers, the Swedish government confers with the Riksdag's Committee on EU Affairs. Although the Swedish government is not legally obliged to follow the recommendations of the Committee on EU Affairs, the Rikdag's Committee on the Constitution has established that the government should do so. That the Swedish parliament has a Committee on EU Affairs is one example of both top-down and bottom-up Europeanisation processes. It is an example of indirect top-down Europeanisation as the Riksdag has changed its way of working as a result of EU membership by introducing a new committee—the Committee on EU Affairs—which deliberates with government with the objective of putting forward a *Swedish* position, that is, not just the wishes of a political party or institution, in negotiations at EU level. It is also an example of how bottom-up Europeanisation may take place, as Sweden sees it as important to have broad consensus and political support for the Swedish position in negotiations at the EU level, either in the Council of Ministers or the European Council. This can be achieved by the government as the Swedish (government's) position is based upon agreements reached in the Committee on EU Affairs where all political parties elected to the national parliament are represented. How a member state organises itself administratively in order to influence and upload its preferences to the EU level varies from member state to member state, but they have *all* had to adapt.

Other actors than the member states can of course also influence politics at EU level, for example, McCauley (2011) has shown in his research how the anti-genetically modified organisms (GMO) movement has influenced the EU's position in this issue. What is of interest for this chapter's discussion is, however, if the member states either support or reject the political and legislative decisions at the EU level as well as what explains differences in their action. The support or rejection of EU by national leaders, influential national politicians, and/or media can influence popular opinion and the dominant narrative around EU membership. Shenhav (2006: 246) argued that 'the dominant role of narratives in political discourse is … based on the centrality of narrative in the formulation and maintenance of worldviews', in this case, the formulation and maintenance of the view(s) regarding EU membership. What also plays a role in the bottom-up Europeanisation process is the national leaders' commentary upon EU co-operation in the national, domestic, and political debate. This connects to one of Warleigh's reasons why member states engage in a multi-level political system, that is, the need for a scapegoat. That the EU is often portrayed negatively by political leaders is something that the European Commission President Jean-Claude Junker (in the office between 2014 and 2019) has reacted to. In a speech in connection to the release of the White Paper on the EU's future, Junker expressed that it was time for the member states to stop using the EU as a scapegoat for unpopular decisions that the member states themselves have been part of making. This brings us back to the tension between intergovernmental and supranational collaboration and co-operation, and the member states' actions within politically sensitive policy areas that are closely connected to the states' sovereignty.

Pace-Setting, Fence-Sitting, or Foot-Dragging

Even though the concept of Europeanisation analytically can be spilt into top-down and bottom-up, these are actually two different sides of the same coin and should therefore be understood together. How well a member state has uploaded its preferences and influenced the policies at EU level is, according to Börzel (2002), a question of how successful the member states have been in using different strategies. Börzel identifies three different strategies: (1) that a member state takes the lead in the European integration process (which she calls 'pace-setting'), (2) that the member state positions itself on the side, that is to say, the member state may not have a (very) strong position on the issue and therefore does not actively engage in the discussion (Börzel calls this 'fence-sitting'), or (3) that the member state pulls the brake and through this action hinders or slows down co-operation at the supranational level ('foot-dragging' in Börzel's terminology).

One example of a group of member states that have chosen to influence EU environmental policy by adopting the first strategy and being in the vanguard is the *'greener'* member states that is, Austria, Denmark, Finland, Germany, the Netherlands, and Sweden. According to Börzel, these member states have taken the lead in different environmental issues and raised them onto the agenda of EU by building coalitions with each other. One reason why a member state or a group of member states chooses to put on the yellow jersey within a policy issue or problem is that it can minimise the cost of implementation when legislation has been enacted at the EU level. By transferring their national policy solutions to EU level, that is, the above-mentioned uploading, the member state, or member states not only achieve their political objectives but they may not need to adapt their existing policies to a great extent. What actually happens in such cases is that it is the EU that has to adapt to a member state's or a group of member states' national policy, in other words, member states can 'export' their policy to others.

Another example is how Denmark, Estonia, Finland, Ireland, Latvia, Lithuania, the Netherlands, and Sweden have come together in the Hanseatic Group to counterbalance the French President Emmanuel Macron's reform agenda of the Economic and Monetary Union (EMU). In Macron's speech at the Sorbonne in September 2017, he suggested deepened integration as a solution to the national debt crisis within the euro zone. Among other things, Macron suggested that the euro zone countries should have a common finance minister and budget. The Hanseatic Group counter-argued that if changes are to happen within EMU to solve the national debt crisis the changes within EMU should instead focus upon euro zone member states' adherence to current rules and regulations that is, the budgetary regulations. The Hanseatic Group's collaboration has according to Financial Times (19 July 2018) been somewhat influential as Macron's suggestion has been revised and is not as far-reaching in its deepening of the co-operation within EMU as it was when it was first presented.

The second strategy that member states have been using in the integration process is according to Börzel (2002) that they place themselves on the side, that is, they are neither proactive nor throwing spanners in the integration process by actively hindering further deepening. This strategy can be used when a policy area is discussed which is of lesser importance for the member state in question. The member state (let's say, state A) then uses the opportunity to be 'neutral' in order not to antagonise other member states (let's say, B and C), which could be beneficial in future alliance building with these member states in future political negotiations in which state A has high stakes and needs to avoid states B and C creating barriers unnecessarily.

Some member states have used the third strategy, which means that a member state or a group of member states try and slow down or hinder further deepening of the integration process through either blocking or delaying, decisions which are due to be taken in the Council of Ministers or the European Council. One reason for this could be that a member state would like a temporary exemption or opt-out from a new legislation or to receive financial compensation for the costs that implementation of the policy would entail. It could also be about attempting to resolve an issue that is of greater importance to the member state, that is, the use of power to secure a preference over an unrelated policy! One such example, according to Börzel (2002), is the negotiation strategy that Greece, Ireland, Portugal, and Spain used during the Intergovernmental Conference that resulted in the Maastricht Treaty. In order to agree to the treaty, these member states demanded a special fund was introduced that would finance environmental and infrastructure investments. The reason for this was so that these four member states could carry the extra costs imposed by the implementation of EMU. Another way in which member states can slow down the integration process is by deliberately not implementing already agreed legislation or other agreements reached. Hungary, Poland, and the Czech Republic used this strategy when they chose not to implement the emergency relocation of asylum seekers mechanism which resulted in the European Commission initiating an infringement procedure against Hungary, Poland, and the Czech Republic in June 2017.

There are instances in the European integration process when almost all member states have disagreed on how the collaboration and co-operation should be organised and if decision-making powers should be delegated to the EU institutions. Within the academic literature the solution often suggested to this type of stalemate is 'differentiated integration', as this allows for the member states, who wish to do so, to further deepen the integration in the policy areas in which they want to progress their collaborations while the more hesitant member states are allowed to choose to opt out of the deepening integration within specific policy areas (for possible consequences of this please see Brianson & Stegmann McCallion 2019).

Is the Solution a More Differentiated Integration Process?

Differentiated integration was formally introduced in the EU as *flexible integration* in the Amsterdam Treaty. Differentiated integration is an alternative to a widened collaboration and co-operation between the member states as a whole. Those member states that do not want a deepening of the integration process can position themselves outside of the initiatives and do not need to slow down or hinder other member states' attempt to develop new co-operation. This deepens the element of choice in Europeanisation. Within the academic literature several typologies of differentiated integration are explored (see, for example, Schimmelfennig, Leuffen and Rittberger 2015). Warleigh (2002) argues that there are many different ideal types of co-operation and that these have different meaning and importance within the European integration process. A *Europe à la Carte* would see that member states are allowed to choose which policy areas they want to co-operate and collaborate within and to what extent, allowing significant differentiation. An EU with *concentric circles* is supposed to work in a similar way but bundles policy areas together so that member states effectively choose which division of the EU they want to join. A *multi-speed* EU would entail that those member states that so wish are allowed by the other member states to continue deepening the co-operation or starting new co-operation within a policy area, and others commit to join later once they are ready. A multi-speed EU could handle such situations by allowing member states to participate fully once they meet all the formal criteria for participation, as is the case with the single currency; although Denmark and Sweden[6] have opt-outs, the other member states must adopt the euro when they meet the entry criteria. However, one has to ask the question in the light of formal opt-outs by member states in, for example, the EMU, Brexit, and the difficulties in finding common solutions in the migration and asylum policies are collaboration at EU level now saturated? Would differentiated integration be the solution for member states to minimise further transformation of their domestic polities by their participation in (trans)forming the EU polity?

[6] For a discussion on Sweden's (non-formal) opt-out of the EMU please see Brianson and Stegmann McCallion (2019).

Leruth and Lord (2015) have argued for a changed way of viewing differentiated integration, namely as a normal procedure in the European integration process, not as an exception. This is an interesting suggestion and one advantage of it is that it opens up possibilities for deepening policy areas that have so far been resistant. Differentiated integration would then not be seen as something diverging from or as a failure of the 'European Project' but rather as a part of its core being. The member states that choose not to participate in the deepening process would not then be seen as awkward or reluctant, nor would they be accused of slowing or hindering the European integration process.

There are however risks with a normalisation of differentiated integrations that could influence the integration process negatively. One such risk would be from a citizen perspective and especially in relation to transparency in the decision-making processes (Dyson and Sepos 2010: 13). A reoccurring criticism of the European integration process is that it is elite driven, that citizens currently experience the EU's political system as complex, and that it is hard to hold politicians accountable for decisions taken at the EU level, and a normalisation of different types of differentiated integration could make this worse. If the member states can choose within which policy areas they are to participate in *and* to what extent it may become (even) harder to distinguish between the influence specific member states have at EU level and who is responsible for what decisions. Even though, at first thought, one could assume that this would make it clearer—member states that opt in have influence whereas member states that have opted out have none—the EU's already complex shared competences and decision-making processes would become more opaque. This could deepen the democratic gap between the EU and its citizens. This should be contrasted to past instances when the EU has faced crises and the solution has been to deepen the integration process,[7] for example, the economic crisis in the 1970s and 1980s was solved by starting a deepened collaboration between the then member states and which was institutionalised in the Single European Act. Another example is how the EU reacted

[7] Although this has not always been the case, De Gaulle 'solved' the crisis of opposing qualified majority voting and deeper integration by simply refusing to turn up to the Council of Minister meetings thus creating the 'Empty Chair crisis' of the EU illustrating how all member states have to agree in an intergovernmental institutional set-up, which raises the question if it is better or worse to wait for a time in the integration process when all member states agree to further the integration?

to the collapse of the communism, the break-up of the Soviet Union, and the fall of the Berlin Wall which influenced the Maastricht Treaty and the 1995, 2004, and 2007 enlargements. Even though parts of these solutions of contained, at the core, some extent of differentiation, that is, the freedom of movement initially allowed only to nationals from Central and Eastern European states by Ireland, Sweden, and the UK, as well as the multi-speed approach to EMU and its final stage of introducing the single currency, the differentiation solution was *temporary* as opposed to *permanent*.

In the early 2010s, the EU experienced financial and national debt crises within the euro zone of which it is now undergoing the aftermath. The EU also is treading delicately in its relations with Hungary and Poland which are currently challenging the rule of law (for the delicate balancing act needed in relation to Article 7 TFEU see the chapter by Moberg in this volume). Other types of challenges that EU is currently experiencing include the increase in political extremism, the wave of right-wing populism both in a number of member states and also within the European Parliament, as well as how the member states cannot reach an agreement in deepening their co-operation in refugee and asylum policies. If differentiated integration were to be a solution to these crises of the EU what effect would this have for the future of EU? Would a differentiated deepening of co-operation within these areas threaten the co-operation and the Union long-term? One possible risk could be that the member states that choose to not participate experience that they become members of a 'B team' compared to the member states which advance in the integration process. Such divisions could lead member states to develop more diverse interests which in turn would make it harder to co-operate within the overarching integration process. If the member states to a larger extent can choose when and in which policy areas they will co-operate and to what degree, this could lessen the cohesion within the Union (see, for example, Brianson and Stegmann McCallion 2019 on the specific case on Sweden, EMU, and Banking Union).

A decline in the feeling of belonging to the EU, as in popular support the member state's EU membership, could mean that the member states start de-Europeanisation or re-nationalisation of already Europeanised policy areas. That the member states are transformed and deeply Europeanised has become very explicit through Brexit, which has ironically shown just how difficult it is for even a 'large' member state to disentangle itself from EU membership.[8] One then has to ask what were the reasons for the member states initially to become members of a supranational political entity like the European Economic Community, European Community or the European Union?[9] And do those reasons still hold? Alan Milward (2000) answered the question in the title of his book *The European Rescue of the Nation-State*, explaining that Schuman, Adenauer, and de Gasperi had 'a strong conviction that the nation-state could be rescued and made to serve as the foundation of a successful post-war European order' (Milward 2000: 337). In other words, the process of European integration was an essential part of the remaking of the European state system after the destruction of 1939–1945. As this chapter has shown, participation in the integration process has both facilitated the re-establishment of nation-states as a viable form of government and fundamentally altered participating states as a *quid pro quo*. As the EU enters its seventh decade, is this fundamental bargain still considered worthwhile? And has the EU reached the point beyond which it cannot integrate further as a whole group?

To Fix and Mend the European Integration Process?

We now return to the question that was asked at the beginning of the chapter, that is, *how can Europeanisation processes be understood in a time when the pendulum is moving towards more intergovernmental features of EU integration?* At the end of the 2010s, the EU is standing at a crossroads; solutions have to be found to current issues, but also to how (and which) long-term reforms should be agreed upon. Is there more reluctance in some, or many, member states in relation to the European integration process? Is this reluctance for the same reason in each member state? Has the UK's decision to leave the EU resulted in a view across member states that deepened integration is not as obvious a solution to crises as in the past? The French President Emmanuel Macron has suggested deepened co-operation within the euro zone as a solution to the

[8] For an analysis of the process of Brexit, see Armstrong (2017) and Forslid and Nyberg (this volume). For updates on the daily politics of Brexit, see www.politics.co.uk.

[9] Depending on when member states joined, they entered an organisation whose name and nature has changed over time, meaning that those which joined from the first enlargement in 1973 onwards had to make calculations that differed from those of the original Six. And in the case of these founding states, the question is *why did they embark upon forming the supranational collaboration process that is today the EU?*

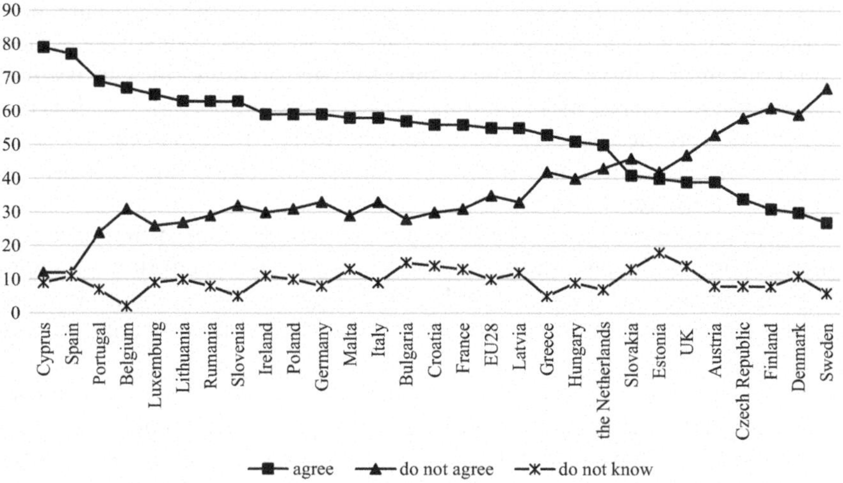

Fig. 9.1 More decisions should be taken at the EU level % (Source: European Commission 2018)

national debt crisis. If and how Macron will be successful in getting this through depends upon how successful he is in getting other member states' Head of States and Government to agree to it as well as which concessions he is prepared to make. One concession that can already be noted is the one made towards the Hanseatic Group (as discussed earlier).

This raises the issue of how far national leaders are prepared to further deepen the integration process when it comes to supranational co-operation but also *if* such reforms have support among the citizens of the EU, because what national leaders agree at EU level will depend in part upon the calculations they make about their domestic reception. In a Eurobarometer opinion poll (March 2018), citizens answered a question if more decisions should be taken at the supranational level (see Fig. 9.1).

In 20 of the member states, 50 per cent or more of the citizens agree that further decisions should be taken at the EU level. One possible interpretation of this is that these member states, there is (tentative) support for deepening of the European integration process.[10] If focus is shifted to

[10] The question asked in the Eurobarometer is general and does not ask about a particular policy area or areas. 'QA18a6 Please tell me to what extent you agree or disagree with the each of the following statements. More decisions should be taken at EU level (Eurobarometer 89: 169).

what citizens within the member states that do not use the single currency want, as an example of a policy area where member states have either opted out or do not yet fulfil the criteria for participation, one can assume that President Macron may find it harder to secure support for his ideas on how to deepen the co-operation within the EMU. Less than 50 per cent of the citizens in these member states would like to see more decisions taken at the EU level (see Fig. 9.2).

As previously discussed, the EU has experienced many different kinds of crises; one could even think that the EU has been in a continuous stage of crisis throughout the last decade. This began with the financial crisis, continued with the national debt crisis within the euro zone, and in the mid-2010s Europe experienced a wave of refugees and asylum seekers without precedent in modern time, which led Rhinard (2019) to explore if this has led to a 'crisisification of EU policy-making'. The previously mentioned crises have tested the solidarity between the member states also in an unprecedented way. Domestically within some member states, it can also be noted that the rule of law has been, and is, threatened, and that a wave of right-wing populist parties receives increased electoral support. As the EU has either exclusive or shared competences in these policy areas

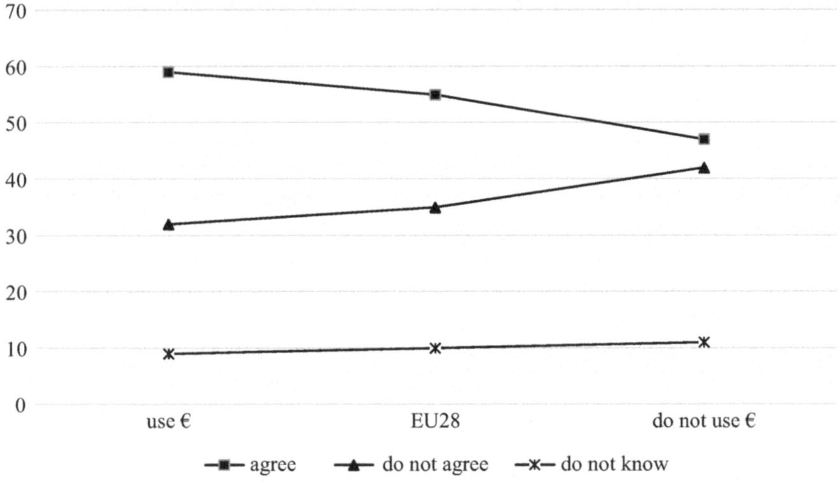

Fig. 9.2 More decisions should be taken at the EU level %, part of the euro zone or non-euro zone (Source: European Commission 2018)

can citizens of the EU not expect that the EU should find solutions to them, or that they are resolved at the EU level?

This chapter has argued that member states have transformed as a result of EU membership—that is, they have been Europeanised—and that they have been so to a significant degree. It has also argued that member states are capable of blocking further Europeanisation, and with a current swing towards more intergovernmental co-operation and the increased right-wing populism on the European continent provide both pressure and incentives to national leaders, like the French President Emmanuel Macron and German Chancellor Angela Merkel to provide the population of the EU with an alternative worldview to the right-wing populist one. Differentiated integration may be one way forward for those member states that would like to further the integration process. Thus, the political cost that the member states that choose not to participate initially would likely be to end up in a 'B team', with the attendant loss of not being able to upload their preferences in a number of policy areas into the supranational collaboration that the EU is. The Europeanisation processes are ongoing; at times the member states' preferences rise to the surface and what becomes visible then is tension between supranational and intergovernmental solutions, that is, whether the member states' governments or the EU institutions should have the final say in the decision-making process. As discussed, these Europeanisation processes take place within the polity, politics, and policies of the EU member states, and how interwoven the process is between a member state and the EU has probably not been really visible or understood until now with the UK set to leave the EU on the last day of October 2019.[11] These weavings-together of the member states and the EU already vary, through the operation of differentiated integration, meaning that some states are more Europeanised than others, and this may be a pattern that increases in the coming years if the crises of climate change, migration, and economic prosperity are not sufficient to generate an EU-wide response. The member states of the EU are still nation-states, and they still have national sovereignty; but their membership of the EU has transformed them into nation-states unlike elsewhere in the globe, woven into a fused continental polity that requires them to use their sovereignty collectively. This is the paradox of European integration, and although the way in which it is expressed institutionally

[11] At the time of writing, August 2019, unless something unforeseen happens Brexit is set to be in place by 1 November 2019.

and in policy terms will likely change again over time, its fundamental nature remains: states choose to be Europeanised because by so doing they enhance their own longevity and gain influence over how their partners are governed.

References

Alter, K. (2003). *Establishing the Supremacy of European Law. The Making of an International Rule in Europe*. Oxford: Oxford University Press.

Armstrong, K. (2017). *Brexit Time: Leaving the EU – Why, How and When?* Cambridge: Cambridge University Press.

Blomberg, M., & Bergman, T. (2005). *EU och Sverige – ett sammanlänkat statsskick*. Stockholm: Liber.

Börzel, T. A. (2002). Pace-Setting, Foot-Dragging, and Fence-Setting: Member State Responses to Europeanization. *Journal of Common Market Studies, 40*(2), 193–214.

Brianson, A., & Stegmann McCallion, M. (2019). Bang-a-Boomerang? Sweden, Differentiated Integration and EMU After Brexit. In S. Gänzle, B. Leruth, & J. Trondal (Eds.), *Differentiated Integration and Disintegration in a Post-Brexit Era*. London: Routledge.

Dyson, K., & Sepos, A. (2010). Differentiation as Design Principle and as a Tool in the Political Management of European Integration. In K. Dyson & A. Sepos (Eds.), *Which Europe? The Politics of Differentiated Integration* (pp. 3–23). Basingstoke: Palgrave Macmillan.

European Commission. (2018). Spring 2018 Standard Eurobarometer 89. Retrieved September 30, 2018, from https://ec.europa.eu/commfrontoffice/publicopinion/index.cfm/Survey/getSurveyDetail/instruments/STANDARD/surveyKy/2180.

Financial Times. (2018, July 19). EU's New Hanseatic League Picks Its Next Battle. Retrieved September 30, 2018, from https://www.ft.com/content/aedbe32a-8af7-11e8-bf9e-8771d5404543.

Hooghe, L., & Marks, G. (2001). *Multi-Level Governance and European Integration*. Lanham: Rowan & Littlefield Publishers.

Jacobsson, B., & Sundström, G. (2006). *Från hemvävd till invävd – Europeiseringen av svensk förvaltning och politik*. Stockholm: Liber.

Jessop, B. (2013). Hollowing Out the 'Nation-State' and Multi-Level Governance. In P. Kennett (Ed.), *A Handbook of Comparative Social Policy* (2nd ed., pp. 11–25). Cheltenham: Edward Elgar.

Johansson, K. M. (2010). Varför är det nödvändigt att forska om Europeiska unionen?. In M. Jerneck & B. Badersten (Eds.), Kontraster och nyanser svensk statsvetenskap i brytningstid. *Statsvetenskaplig tidskrift, 112*(5), 633–645.

Keating, M. (1998). Is There a Regional Level of Government in Europe? In P. Le Galès & C. Lequesne (Eds.), *Regions in Europe* (pp. 11–29). London: Routledge.

Keating, M., & Hooghe, L. (2001). By-passing the Nation State? Regions and the EU Policy Process. In J. Richardson (Ed.), *European Union Power and Policy-Making* (pp. 239–256). London: Routledge.

Leruth, B., & Lord, C. (2015). Differentiated Integration in the European Union: A Concept, a Process, a System or a Theory? *Journal of European Public Policy, 22*(6), 754–763.

Macron, E. (2017) *A Sovereign, United Democratic Europe*, Speech held 26 September 2017. Retrieved September 30, 2018, from https://www.diplomatie.gouv.fr/en/french-foreign-policy/european-union/events/article/president-macron-s-initiative-for-europe-a-sovereign-united-democratic-europe.

Marks, G., & Hooghe, L. (2004). Contrasting Visions of Multi-Level Governance. In I. Bache & M. Flinders (Eds.), *Multi-Level Governance* (pp. 15–30). Oxford: Oxford University Press.

McCauley, D. (2011). Bottom-Up Europeanization Exposed: Social Movement Theory and Non-state Actors in France. *Journal of Common Market Studies, 49*(5), 1019–1042.

Milward, A. S. (2000). *The European Rescue of the Nation State* (2nd ed.). London: Routledge.

Nugent, N. (1999). *The Government and Politics of the European Union* (4th ed.). Houndmills: Macmillan Press Ltd..

Rhinard, M. (2019). The Crisisification of Policy-Making in the European Union. *Journal of Common Market Studies, 57*(3), 616–633.

Schimmelfennig, F., Leuffen, D., & Rittberger, B. (2015). The European Union as a System of Differentiated Integration: Interdependence, Politicization and Differentiation. *Journal of European Public Policy, 22*(6), 764–782.

Shenhav, S. R. (2006). Political Narratives and Political Reality. *International Political Science Review, 27*(3), 245–262.

Snyder, F. (Ed.). (2000). *The Europeanisation of Law. The Legal Effects of European Integration*. Oxford: Hart Publishing.

Warleigh, A. (2002). *Flexible Integration Which Model for the European Union?* Sheffield: Sheffield Academic Press.

Warleigh, A. (2006). Multi-Level Governance and Policy Networks: Conceptual Combinations and the Study of the Euro-Policy. In M. Cini & A. Bourne (Eds.), *Palgrave Advances to European Union Studies* (pp. 77–95). Houndmills: Palgrave Macmillan UK.

Warleigh-Lack, A., & Stegmann McCallion, M. (2012). Europeanisation and the Uses of Discourse: Evidence from the Regionalization of Sweden. *Journal of European Integration, 34*(4), 379–396.

Wessels, W. (1997). An Ever Closer Fusion? A Dynamic Macropolitical View on Integration Processes. *Journal of Common Market Studies, 35*(3), 267–299.

CHAPTER 10

The Dream of the Nation-State: Is Regional Secessionism a Threat to European Integration?

Niklas Bremberg

Introduction

The United Kingdom's planned withdrawal from the European Union (EU), or 'Brexit', Hungary's refusal to abide by commonly agreed decisions on EU migration and asylum policy, as well as the rise of Eurosceptic political parties in almost every EU member state are all examples that seem to suggest that claims to defend national independence against supranational decision making are re-emerging in European politics to an extent and with an intensity not seen since the end of the Cold War (see e.g. Abts et al. 2009; Kriesi 2014; Hobolt and Tilley 2016). Populist parties, often with a right-wing and nationalist slant, such as Marine Le Pen's *Rassemblement National* (previously *Front National)* in France and Matteo Salvini's *Lega* in Italy, typically present the EU as undemocratic since 'bureaucrats' or officials instead of elected politicians are said to

N. Bremberg (✉)
Stockholm University, Stockholm, Sweden

The Swedish Institute for International Affairs, Stockholm, Sweden
e-mail: niklas.bremberg@statsvet.su.se

A. Bakardjieva Engelbrekt et al. (eds.), *The European Union and the Return of the Nation State*,
https://doi.org/10.1007/978-3-030-35005-5_10

control the policymaking process and marginalise the interests of 'ordinary people' in favour of 'the elite' in Brussels (cf. Müller 2016; Norman 2017). According to this strand of populist discourse, the only way to restore popular sovereignty and national democracy is to drastically reduce the scope of EU competences and decision-making power, if not to leave the EU entirely. This obviously challenges how the EU functions and threatens to undo more than 60 years of European integration.

However, there are also claims that advance national independence and challenge the current status quo in the EU but not necessarily the principles on which the EU was built. These claims are often formulated by political parties and movements promoting independence for non-sovereign regions of EU member states, such as Scotland and Catalonia, which are currently the two most salient examples (see e.g. Duerr 2015). These parties and movements often combine demands for national independence with support for European integration, which might seem paradoxical. Why struggle for independence if you are prepared to have your country's sovereignty circumscribed by the EU? This constitutes a research puzzle for EU scholars since only a few decades ago there was a reason to believe that independence for non-sovereign regions in the EU would become politically less appealing as a consequence of European integration (cf. Linz and Stephan 1996).

Scotland and Catalonia are part of the UK and Spain, respectively. Both have distinctive cultural and linguistic features as well as a comparatively high degree of regional autonomy (Hooghe et al. 2016). To many citizens who support Scottish or Catalan independence, Scotland and Catalonia are nations in the same way as Denmark and Sweden. The difference is that, for various historical reasons, they do not have a state of their own. In their eyes, however, Scottish and Catalan independence claims are just as legitimate as Danish and Swedish ones. The questions that this chapter addresses relate to the overall theme of the book and revolve around the extent to which the dream of political elites and citizens in some regions of creating new nation-states presents a challenge to the EU. It has recently been suggested that in the context of European integration, if a region were to secede from an EU member state it should be understood as an instance of 'territorial rescaling' and 'as a move to change the status or affiliation of a territory within a wider constellation of polities' (Bauböck 2019: 3). This raises a number of questions. Are claims to Scottish or Catalan independence compatible with the idea of an increasingly integrated Europe? Or are such claims in reality a threat to European integration? What role should the EU play in relation to the question of independence for non-sovereign regions in its member states? What normative and democratic problems are brought to the forefront by regional secessionism in the EU? What might the potential solutions be?

This chapter first provides a summary of the research, first and foremost in political science, on regional secessionism and European integration since the 1990s. Next, two perspectives on the relationship between regional secessionism and European integration are discussed, as well as different interpretations of EU law and EU enlargement of relevance to the question of a region becoming an independent state. Fourth, the chapter describes current developments in Scotland and Catalonia, where the question of independence and EU membership has been addressed, with an emphasis on the importance of the EU to the actors who support and promote independence claims. A comparison of these two cases is highly relevant since an independent Catalan state would have to reapply for EU membership even though a majority of Catalans would like to remain in the EU, whereas Scotland is about to lose its EU membership as a result of Brexit even though a majority of Scots voted against leaving in the 2016 referendum. Finally, following up on this comparative analysis, the chapter sheds light on the democratic and normative challenges that regional secessionism poses to the Union and presents a set of proposals on how to enhance the role of the regions in the EU.

Regional Secessionism and European Integration: An Overview

Sovereignty (*de jure* and *de facto* control over a territory by a state) and secession (the act of part of a sovereign state establishing a new state) are often portrayed as two sides of the same coin in processes of state-building in Europe and in the classical works of historical sociology (see e.g. Rokkan and Urwin 1983; Tilly 1992). State sovereignty and national self-determination are today considered cornerstones of international law, albeit that these principles are not always easily reconciled in practice. Many European states have more than one economic centre, multiple national identities and more than one national language. Several also have constitutions that seek to recognise such political and social realities by, for instance, protecting the rights of ethnic and linguistic minorities and upholding regional autonomy. Managing the tensions between centre and periphery arising from competing demands on resource allocation and political representation is a fundamental aspect of the modern state in Europe and the trend towards increased decentralisation in several European states is often referred to as a response to such enduring tensions (Keating 1998). However, there is a difference in decentralisation in states where state boundaries are not challenged (e.g. Sweden and Denmark) and in states where competing visions of nationhood exist (e.g. Spain and the UK). In the second case, decentralisation is often pursued to fend off independence claims by offering greater subnational autonomy (cf. Moreno 2001).[1] Nonetheless, independence claims are still being voiced in several European states, such as in Scotland (the UK), the Basque Country and Catalonia (Spain), Flanders (Belgium) and Corsica (France), to name just a few.

It is worth noting that regional separatism as a political project need not always entail secession since it might also mean self-determination in terms of aspiring to higher degrees of regional autonomy for a group of people or a territory within an established state. In this chapter, it is regional separatism that involves secession claims by non-sovereign regions within the EU that is of interest. Regional secessionism in the EU here refers to any political project that seeks to turn part of an existing EU member state into an independent state. 'Region' can refer to a fairly diverse set of entities. For example, the EU's Committee of the Regions (CoR) represents a highly diverse set of local and regional authorities from EU member states,[2] ranging from purely administrative constructs such as

[1] For example, as part of the democratization of Spain in the 1970s Catalan home rule was re-established under *Generalitat de Catalunya*. The statutes that regulate Catalan regional autonomy were adopted after a popular referendum in 1979 in which 90 per cent of the participants supported it on a turnout of 59 per cent. Catalonia currently has a high degree of autonomy on issues related to education, health care and police. After a referendum in Scotland in 1997 (supported by 74 per cent on a turnout of 60 per cent), the British Parliament passed the *Scotland Act* in 1998 through which various 'devolved competencies' were transferred to the Scottish Parliament. These devolved competencies were later expanded in 2012 and 2016 and currently cover education, health care, agriculture and the judiciary, albeit the British Parliament embodies parliamentary sovereignty across the whole of the UK.

[2] The Committee of the Regions (CoR) was created in 1994. It represents local and regional authorities across the EU. It is a political assembly composed of 350 members from all EU member states, elected at local or regional level, although the Council of the European Union officially appoints the CoR members on the recommendation of the member states. The European Commission and the Council must consult the CoR whenever new proposals

Upper Norrland in Sweden to subnational entities with a high level of political autonomy and a sense of collective identity linked to historical, linguistic or cultural traditions, as in Catalonia and Scotland. In this chapter, it is this latter category of regions that is referred to by the term 'non-sovereign regions' of the EU.

In the post-Cold War period, and in the wake of the break-up of the Soviet Union and Yugoslavia, secessionist movements gained increased attention as a global political phenomenon among social scientists, not least in political science and international relations (IR) (see e.g. Buchanan 2007; Roeder 2007). The evidence from 1945 onwards, however, suggests that actual secession is a rare phenomenon among Western democracies, although secessionist movements and parties are in principle tolerated in all democratic states in Europe. Nonetheless, the right to secede for non-sovereign regions and territories is typically not granted in national constitutions (Sorens 2012). For example, the German Constitutional Court ruled in 2016 that a referendum on independence for Bavaria could not be held since the Constitution of the Federal Republic of Germany does not allow it (Bundesverfassungsgericht 2016). In other words, in most European states, it is possible to campaign for secession but not to put such claims into practice, unless constitutional changes are made first (cf. Reinikainen 2019).[3] The sensitive nature of independence claims by non-sovereign regions of the EU is of course related both to the principle of the rule of law in liberal democracies and to the norm that the national borders that emerged in Europe after the devastating experience of World War II should not be violated, unless it is done in a peaceful and negotiated way (cf. Kornprobst 2008).

Importantly, in the context of European integration secessionism has taken on a somewhat different meaning compared to other parts of the world (Keating 2019; Bauböck 2019). Since the 1950s, the process of

are made in areas that have repercussions for the regional or local level (e.g. economic, social and territorial cohesion, Structural Funds, the European Regional Development Fund, the European Social Fund, employment and social affairs). The CoR makes recommendations on draft EU laws and proposals for new policies on the basis of its local and regional experience and expertise. It can also propose new laws and put new issues on the EU agenda.

[3] The Canadian Clarity Act is often referred to as an example of how democratic states can address secessionist claims. The Act makes clear that no Canadian province has the right to secede by unilaterally declaring independence but if a clear majority of the population expresses support for independence then the Federal government should seek a negotiated solution (see e.g. Dion 2012).

European integration has reshaped relations between the supranational, national and regional levels of governance in Europe (Bartolini 2005). Questions about the effect of EU membership on democratic governance in member states and the nature of the EU's democratic deficit, more generally, gained increased scholarly attention with the entry into force of the Maastricht Treaty in 1993. In addition, debates on the role of non-sovereign regions in EU governance also intensified in the 1990s under the slogan 'Europe of the regions', which was championed by the former President of the European Commission, Jacques Delors.

The EU's democratic deficit is predominantly described in terms of an increasingly asymmetrical relationship between citizens and political representatives, as EU decision-making procedures are not accountable to the same extent as those in national political systems (Bellamy and Castiglione 2000; Follesdal and Hix 2006). Other scholars question whether there is a democratic deficit at all, since the authority of the EU is delegated from its member states in the first place (Brexit suggests that it can be revoked) and decision making rests on the legal principles enshrined in the EU treaties (Majone 1998; Moravcsik 2002).

The Treaty of Maastricht introduced the concept of EU citizenship, which stipulates that any person who holds the nationality of an EU member state is automatically also an EU citizen, and grants that person certain rights such as freedom of movement and residence within the EU, to vote and stand as a candidate in elections for the European Parliament and municipal elections, and the protection of the diplomatic and consular authorities of any EU member state. Even though these rights are dependent on national citizenship, they suggest that individuals are recognised as subject to EU law beyond the rights and duties conferred on them by regulations governing the functioning of the EU's internal market (Eriksen and Fossum 2000).[4]

When it comes to the role of non-sovereign regions in EU governance, some scholars go as far as to describe the EU as a 'post-sovereign' political system (Keating 2001), whereas others stress the less dramatic but still profound shift from European *nation-states* to *member states* of the EU (Bickerton 2012). Still, others suggest that the EU undermines the sovereignty of its member states as an increasing number of 'core state functions'

[4] There are nonetheless scholars who argue that the way the EU has evolved has increased de-politicization of its member states and the 'hollowing out' of national democracy (Mair 2013).

have gradually been integrated into the EU's political system, even though this has not turned the EU itself into a state (Genschel and Jachtenfuchs 2016). More importantly in this context, European integration is said not only to foster peaceful relations among EU member states and to consolidate the European 'security community', but also to reduce territorial tensions between the centre and the periphery within member states (Linz and Stephan 1996; cf. Adler and Barnett 1998; Bremberg 2015, 2018).

However, the most visionary interpretations of the EU's post-sovereign order in the post-Cold War era have not yet come to fruition, not least because member states have successfully guarded their powers within the EU's decision-making system. The enduring political attractiveness and mobilising potential that appeals for national independence still enjoy in many parts of Europe, such as Scotland and Catalonia, suggest that the questions of European integration and regional secession are not settled. Instead, the process of European integration seems to have opened up new avenues for fragmentation and contestation within EU member states, especially when European political arrangements are subjected to the strains and stresses emanating from global developments. The question of what would happen to a non-sovereign region of an EU member state if it were to become independent in terms of EU membership and protection of the rights of EU citizens was perhaps considered rather academic not too long ago, but that is no longer the case.

Two Perspectives on Regional Secessionism and European Integration

In the 1990s, decentralisation within European states combined with European integration suggested to several political scientists that the role of the regions would increase at the same time as the appeal and mobilising potential of secessionist claims in regions such as Scotland and Catalonia would decrease. From this perspective, it was thought that European integration would lead to less demand for regional secessionism among political elites and citizens in the EU. This was hypothesised for a number of interrelated reasons. First, changes to the rules on EU structural funding, together with the legal and institutional innovations of the Maastricht Treaty, such as Committee of the Regions, created new opportunities for regional political elites to gain access to new material resources and participate in EU policy processes (Elias 2008). Second, the strengthening of region-level political institutions in many western European states (e.g. Catalan regional autonomy and Scotland's devolved competencies) empowered regional elites to develop new strategies for securing funds and access to political arenas beyond the state (Marks et al. 1996). Third, the successes of political parties with a more or less outspoken pro-secessionist agenda in obtaining representation at the regional level in a number of EU member states meant that many were forced to transform themselves from single-issue parties to 'normal' parties in order to situate themselves on the left-right ideological spectrum and to respond to multiple policy issues. This meant that radical demands for independence were gradually transformed into more moderate calls for greater regional autonomy (Hepburn 2011). Over time, these trends were thought likely to diminish calls for independence for Scotland, Catalonia and other non-sovereign regions across the EU.

It therefore appeared that there were a number of good reasons to expect that European integration would lead to reduced demand for regional secessionism. However, these theoretical expectations did not correspond with the empirical evidence. Previous research on European integration and regional secessionism does not seem to be able to explain why support for Scottish and Catalan independence has not decreased in recent years but instead increased. It is true that Scottish voters voted against independence in the referendum of 2014 (55 per cent voted 'no' on a turnout of 84 per cent) but the support for independence in Scotland

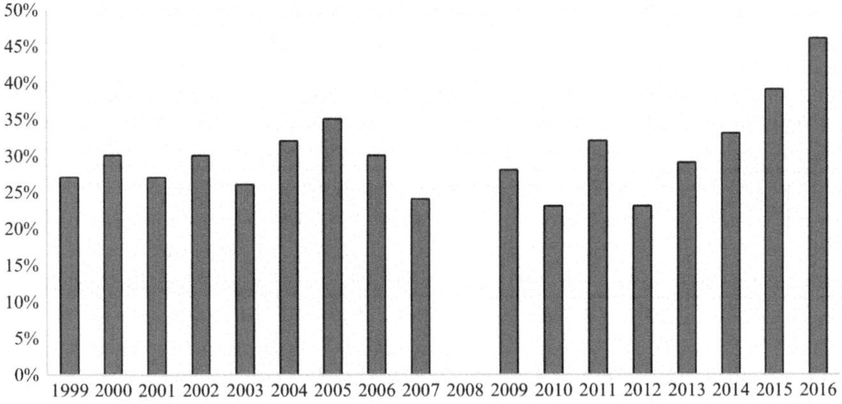

Fig. 10.1 Support for Scottish independence, 1999–2016 (Source: Scottish Social Attitudes. Data for 2008 is missing)

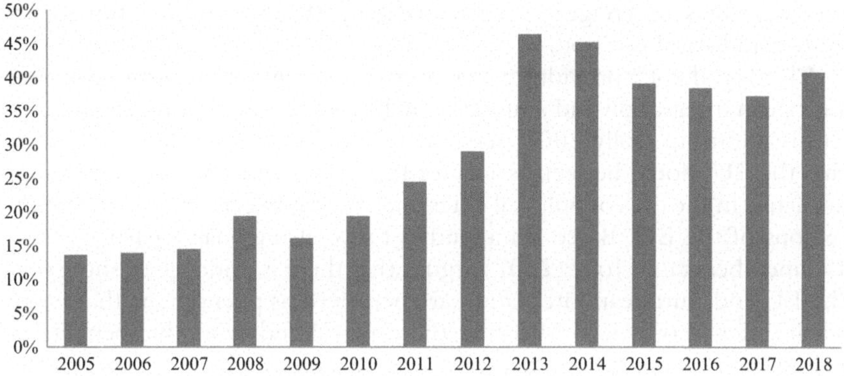

Fig. 10.2 Support for Catalan independence, 2005–2018 (Source: *Centre d'Estudis d'Opinió* (CEO))

is still historically high at above 40 per cent (see Fig. 10.1) and the same applies for Catalonia (see Fig. 10.2).

In Catalonia in 2017, some 42 per cent of eligible voters participated in an unconstitutional 'referendum' organised by the Catalan regional government.[5] An overwhelmingly majority of those who participated voted in favour of independence. It should be said that there is still no clear majority in either Scotland or Catalonia in favour of independence. Nonetheless, the comparatively high levels of support for independence raise a number of questions, not least since the costs of independence, at first sight, seem to be significantly higher than the benefits. For example, Catalonia would probably have to reapply for EU membership under uncertain circumstances, and thus risk not having access to the internal market at least for an unknown period of time. The question is even more complicated in the Scottish case since Brexit implies that Scotland is about to leave the EU even though a majority of Scottish voters (62 per cent) supported remaining in the 2016 referendum. In both Scotland and Catalonia, the majority position among the pro-secessionist political elites is to strive for independence and full membership of the EU at the same time. Why support independence if you are willing to be part of a union that circumscribes its

[5] The Spanish Constitutional Court had previously ruled that the Catalan government did not have the authority to organise a referendum on independence.

member states' sovereignty to such an extent? What can explain this apparently paradoxical position?

Viability theory provides a perspective on regional secessionism and European integration and a fundamentally different way of understanding this relationship (Jolly 2007; see also Laible 2008). The theory suggests that the EU should be seen as a factor that makes secessionist claims more attractive in the eyes of political elites and citizens in certain non-sovereign regions of the EU. Based on a study of several regionalist parties across EU member states, Jolly (2007) argues that there is evidence to show that the EU and European integration are perceived as phenomena that make small states 'more viable' because the political and economic benefits of belonging to a larger state decrease when a state can be a member of the EU. The argument is that over time the process of European integration has made it possible for political elites at the regional level to more credibly portray regional secessionism as a viable political strategy, since the EU provides a large market and a common currency as well as enhanced cooperation on foreign and security policy. This is basically also what Cram noted when she suggests that 'the EU can play an instrumental role, for example in Catalonia and Scotland, making nationalist demands more palatable in the context of a stabilising framework' (Cram 2009: 105). The fact that the UK and Spain provided national markets, currencies and military defence to Scotland and Catalonia in the past does not mean that these states will always have to continue to do so in the future. It can rather be seen as a historical condition that no longer applies in modern-day Europe. At least, this is what certain political leaders are arguing, and a not insignificant proportion of citizens seems to be willing to support them. If Malta and Luxembourg can thrive as EU member states, why should Scotland and Catalonia not? From this perspective, regional secessionism and European integration are not contradictory but rather mutually reinforcing.

Thus, in this view, combining demands for Scottish and Catalan independence with a positive attitude to the EU is perfectly logical. However, the fact that certain political leaders and citizens embrace this idea does not mean that EU membership would automatically follow at independence. To judge from what officials at the European Commission say on this matter, it is rather the case that any new state that wishes to become an EU member state would need to wait in line with the rest of the candidate countries.

Can Regions of the EU Become Independent States and Still Be Members of the EU?

Viability theory appears to clash with statements from leading EU officials on the subject of what would happen if a region of an EU member state were to become an independent state. For example, the European Commission's official position is that both Catalan and Scottish claims to independence should be regarded as 'internal matters' of EU member states, and thus not something that the Commission should be involved in. The former President of the European Commission, Romano Prodi, formulated a sort of doctrine with regard to this question that basically stipulates that any part of an EU member state that becomes an independent state would need to reapply for EU membership according to Article 49 of the Treaty on European Union (TEU) and follow all of the procedures by which membership applications are dealt with.[6] This means that the Commission would first need to assess whether the new state meet all the requirements for EU membership and that the existing EU member states would have to unanimously agree to accept the new state as a new member. Obviously, such a process could take a considerable amount of time.[7] In addition, it is not impossible that certain EU member states would object to admitting the new state for a variety of political reasons. During their time as Presidents of the European Commission, José Manuel Barroso and Jean-Claude Juncker have stated on numerous occasions that the 'Prodi doctrine' still applies. Given that Spain has still not recognised Kosovo, which in practice makes it impossible for the country to initiate membership negotiations with the EU, it is not hard to imagine that an independent Catalonia would be forced to leave the EU for an indeterminate period of time.

[6] In March 2004, Prodi stated that 'When a part of a territory of a Member State ceases to be part of that state, i.e. because that territory becomes an independent state, the Treaties no longer apply to that territory. In other words, a newly independent region would, by the fact of its independence, become a third country with respect to the Union and the Treaties would, from the day of its independence, not apply anymore on its territory' (Prodi, quoted in Piris 2017a: 82). For an overview of the legal reasoning that underpins the 'Prodi doctrine', see Piris (2017a, b).

[7] Turkey, for example, became an official EU candidate country in 1999. Accession negotiations began in 2005 but there cannot be too many who believe that Turkey will be joining the EU any time soon.

However, there are scholars who argue that the Prodi doctrine is neither the only nor necessarily the most obvious way of interpreting EU treaties and EU law, and that it can be challenged on both legal and normative grounds (Kenealy 2014). When Barroso was asked by the British Broadcasting Corporation, ahead of the Scottish referendum in 2014, about what would happen to Scotland if it became an independent country, he stated that Scotland would need to reapply for EU membership but that the UK would not. (This was before Brexit.) At the time, Scotland's loss of EU membership was a major factor in the campaign of those arguing against independence. This way of interpreting the case is well in line with how state secession is seen in international law. From this viewpoint, the sovereign rights of new states (e.g. Scotland) need to be formally recognised, while the rights of old states (e.g. the remaining parts of the UK) are retained. A historical example from international politics is Russia, which was recognised as a 'successor state' of the Soviet Union after the end of the Cold War and as such retained a seat on the United Nations Security Council, whereas the former-Soviet Republics such as Armenia, Ukraine and Uzbekistan had to receive international recognition as new sovereign states. The problem here, however, is that when this kind of reasoning is applied to the question of regional secession in the EU, it implies that 'standard' international law would be applied instead of EU law. This is problematic since the EU often portrays itself as something more than a 'standard' international organisation, and the legal order that has been carefully crafted over several decades to manage and regulate relations between EU institutions, member states, regions, business and citizens is often understood as being something much more far-reaching than the 'thin' legal order underpinned by international law. It is worth pointing out that the Court of Justice of the European Union (CJEU) has ruled in favour of EU law when it has not been in congruence with international law, and scholars such as Joseph Weiler (1991) and Neil MacCormick (1997) have emphasised that the EU is not to be understood as a 'standard' league of states but as a *sui generis* political-legal community.[8]

There are thus different interpretations of the proper relationship between EU law and international law with regard to the question of regional secession, and intimately linked to this issue is the question of

[8] However, Weiler has harshly criticised the 'siren claims of secession' in some EU member states (Weiler 2017).

what would happen to EU citizens of a non-sovereign region if a region were to become an independent state but be forced to leave the Union. EU citizenship rights as defined by Article 20 TEU, Article 20(1) of the Treaty on the Functioning of the European Union (TFEU) and chapter V of the Charter of Fundamental Rights (e.g. the right to free movement, the right to vote in European elections as well as the right to receive consular protection) could be violated in a such case. It is true that the EU treaties make clear that EU citizenship is additional to citizenship of EU member states, but 'a series of judicially activist rulings by the [CJEU] […] has caused a sort of schizophrenia at the heart of the concept of EU citizenship. It exists in the Treaties as one thing, and it exists in the jurisprudence of the [CJEU] as something considerably more far-reaching' (Kenealy 2014: 591).

It is also worth noting that siding with the EU member states, as the European Commission seems to be doing in relation to the question of regional secession, is perhaps not hard to understand for more or less obvious political reasons, but it nonetheless risks increasing the tensions between the notions of a 'Europe of the states' and a 'Europe of the citizens' in ways that do not necessarily strengthen support for European integration. Moreover, there are reasons to believe that the CJEU need not automatically support the 'Prodi doctrine' in the case of a region of an EU member state becoming an independent state, albeit that the Court would be likely to pay close attention to how the secession process unfolds in practice. For example, illegal or unconstitutional acts of secession would probably not be recognised.

Furthermore, Article 4(3) TEU stipulates that the EU and its member states shall 'Pursuant to the principle of sincere cooperation […] in full mutual respect, assist each other in carrying out the tasks which flow from the Treaties'. It would not be too much of a stretch to argue that one of the main tasks of the Commission and the EU as a whole is to maintain the functioning of the internal market. Forcing Scotland or Catalonia to leave the EU in order for them to reapply for membership risks creating a sharp dislocation within the internal market since it would probably entail regional authorities, transport networks, companies and consumers that were once fully integrated into the market being removed from it, at least temporarily. It is curious that the Commission seems to have made such a narrow interpretation of the EU treaties, and one that seems to assume an exclusion mechanism that does not really exist. On the contrary, the withdrawal mechanism that does exist in the treaties is Article 50 TEU, which was invoked by the British government in March 2017 to commence the Brexit negotiations. This assumes that it is impossible to throw out an EU member overnight, since the integration of economic activities, harmonisation of rules and regulations, and deepening of cooperation in various policy fields have reached such an advanced stage. Article 50 TEU stipulates that withdrawal needs to be accomplished through a negotiated transition, and that the negotiations need to take account of the future relationship between the EU and the withdrawing state.

In this light, it appears impractical and not entirely in compliance with the spirit of the EU treaties to argue that a region of the EU that has become an independent state would need to leave the EU more or less on the day of its independence, reapply for membership, place itself at the back of the queue of EU candidate countries and negotiate for membership from the outside. Instead, it does not seem far-fetched that a region would be able to negotiate the terms for state secession and EU membership in parallel, and at the same time retain its status as an EU member state, and thereby secure access to the internal market and uphold the EU citizenship rights for its citizens during the transition period. For example, it took Greenland several years to get an agreement in place through which it left the European Community (EC) in 1985 and it now enjoys the status of one of 25 Overseas Countries and Territories (OCT) in relation to the EU, although it is still under Danish sovereignty.[9] In addition, after German unification in 1990, the expanded Federal Republic of Germany did not have to reapply for EC membership and the Commission acted to ensure that the internal market was not disrupted. It also helped the Council and the European Parliament to find solutions to adapt the EC to the 'internal enlargement' that German unification entailed in practice (Kenealy 2014: 595; see also Spence 1992). Hence, there are historical examples that suggest that the 'Prodi doctrine' does not make full use of the possibilities for negotiation and compromise that the EU treaties, CJEU jurisprudence and the Commission's past praxis provide.

However, Bauböck suggests a different interpretation by saying that the above arguments are only plausible if the EU is understood as a federation in the making, rather than a voluntary association of independent

[9] The OCT-EU Association is based on articles 198–204 of the TFEU and the OCTs are located in the Atlantic, Antarctic, Arctic, Caribbean, Indian Ocean and Pacific. OCTs are not sovereign countries but depend to varying degrees on four EU member states (Denmark, France, the Netherlands and the UK).

states. Seen from this perspective, 'Brexit as well as potential decisions for Scottish or Catalan independence put these territories outside the Union. The fact that EU law had been deeply entrenched in all these polities while they were inside should facilitate negotiations about terms of separation in the former case and of accession in the latter, but it does not affect the question of membership status itself' (Bauböck 2019: 15). Thus, the fact that the 'Prodi doctrine' can be criticised for making the European Commission less constructive than it might ideally be is not the same as saying that it is an easy task to determine what would happen if a non-sovereign region of the EU were to become an independent state.

If there is anything that is clear, it is that the question is highly complex and multifaceted. This uncertainty might be a cause for caution, in the sense that when political leaders and citizens are forced to consider the likelihood of different outcomes of a hypothetical secession process it might be assumed that not knowing exactly what would happen with the relationship with the EU would act as a deterrent. In politics, however, this is not always the case. Uncertainty might in some cases encourage risk-taking behaviour among citizens, especially if political leaders are implying that you can have independence and EU membership at the same time. This would mean that what really matters is how credible citizens believe the 'Prodi doctrine' to be, and what they think the EU would do if a region really did become an independent state through secession from an EU member state. Judging from recent developments in Scotland and Catalonia, it appears that a not insignificant proportion of the citizens in those regions do not think the doctrine that credible, or at least that they are prepared to take a chance. However, it could also be that they do not care that much about EU membership at all, and that those citizens that support independence for Scotland and Catalonia have other priorities.

Scotland and Catalonia: Postmodern and Pro-European Nationalism?

The political parties in Scotland and Catalonia that support independence, such as the Scottish National Party (SNP), *Esquerra Republicana de Catalunya* (ERC) and *Partit Demòcrata Europeu Catala* (PDeCAT), differ in terms of their position on the left-right political spectrum. The SNP and the ERC are left-of-centre parties, whereas PDeCAT is right-of-centre. All the parties embrace a pro-EU position and express support for

European integration, although the left wing *Candidatura d'Unitat Popular* (CUP) supports Catalan independence but not the EU or NATO. The main pro-independence parties in Scotland and Catalonia can be said to adhere to a kind of 'postmodern nationalism' in the sense that the battle for national independence is not based on armed struggle, violent nationalism or exclusive national identities, but rather portrayed as an expression of a new kind of political community (King 2012). It is of course open to debate whether Scottish or Catalan nationalism really is more tolerant and progressive than British or Spanish nationalism, but most of the political leaders who support Scottish and Catalan independence claim that they do so because they argue that the creation of an independent state is necessary to implement political and economic reforms that are said to be more modern, inclusive and just than the kind of policies that Scotland and Catalonia are, allegedly, forced to pursue as parts of the UK and Spain.

For instance, the SNP, which has been in power in Scotland since 2011, often portrays Scotland and Scottish society as more attuned to social democratic values, and claims that it has more in common with the Scandinavian countries than with the rest of the UK. Catalonia has been governed by pro-independence parties in different constellations since 2012 but even though the ERC favours left-leaning redistributive policies and PDeCAT favours right-leaning market-friendly policies, they both coalesce around the position that independence would make it possible for Catalonia to pursue radically different policies. A leading Catalan politician, Artur Mas (PDeCAT), has said that an independent Catalonia would become like a Mediterranean version of Denmark, that is, a small, well-governed and prosperous country. Economic aspects also play a role. For the SNP, control over the revenues from North Sea oil has been a key issue, at least in the past, and for the ERC and PDeCAT it is clear that Catalonia does not profit as much as it could from the fiscal arrangements it has as part of Spain. In addition, in the wake of the euro crisis of 2010 and the austerity policies of many states in southern Europe, it is quite frequent to see slogans such as '*Espanya ens roba*' ('Spain steals from us') at pro-independence demonstrations across Catalonia, which might perhaps prompt some less credulous observers to think that Catalan nationalism is not that different from 'normal' nationalisms after all.

Importantly, for these political parties and their representatives, an independent Scotland or Catalonia in an integrated Europe is not a contradiction but a political objective that to a large extent is congruent with viability theory discussed above. In the case of the SNP, this is quite remarkable since the party was opposed to British membership of the EEC in the 1970s as a matter of principle, which it saw as an 'assault on sovereignty' (Keating 2001: 58). However 'by the 1975 referendum [which confirmed the UK's EEC membership] the official position had softened to one of waiting until independence so that the Scottish could take the decision on EC membership themselves' (ibid.). In the 2016 referendum on leaving the EU, the tables were turned and a majority of Scottish voters endorsed remaining in (62 per cent) whereas across the whole of the UK a majority voted to leave (52 per cent). The SNP leader, Nicola Sturgeon, said after the referendum that Scots had voted to remain and were now being forced out of the EU against their will. This has led to speculation about a second referendum on Scottish independence in the not too distant future, although for that to happen, the governments in London and Edinburgh would need to agree on procedures. This does not seem very likely before the UK withdraws from the EU. Nonetheless, Brexit has completely shifted the debate in Scotland in the sense that ahead of the 2014 Scottish referendum the discussion centred on the question of whether Scotland could remain in the EU. Now it is rather about the extent to which Scotland could have a different relationship with the EU than the rest of the UK after the UK has left.

However, it is worth asking at this point how large support for EU membership really is in Scotland, especially among citizens who support

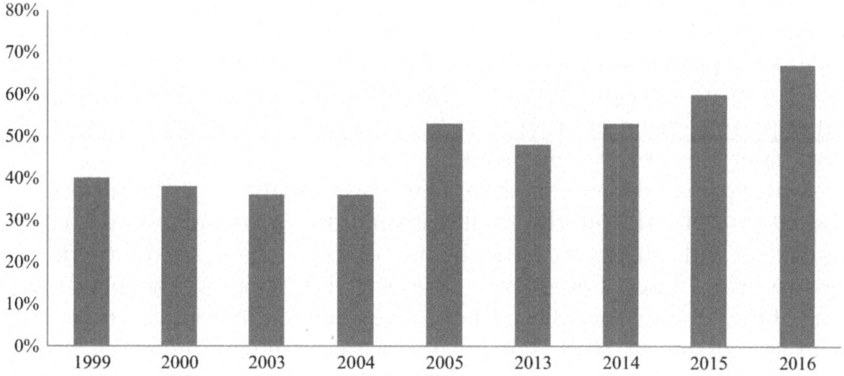

Fig. 10.3 Euroscepticism in Scotland, 1999–2016 (Source: Scottish Social Attitudes. Data for 2001–2002, 2006–2012 is missing)

independence. The SNP has long defended the position that an independent Scotland should be a full member of the EU, but opinion polling seems to suggest that Eurosceptic attitudes are on the rise (see Fig. 10.3). If the groups of citizens who either want to leave the EU or to reduce its powers are combined, Eurosceptic attitudes have increased from around 40 per cent in 1999 to about 67 per cent in 2016. According to opinion data from 2016 gathered by *NatCen Social Research*, about one-third of the citizens who support Scottish independence want Scotland to leave the EU. Given that the SNP would need to convince a larger proportion of Scottish voters to support independence in a second referendum, it is not certain that the party will continue to see a pro-EU stance as a successful political strategy. This could indicate that even though political elites think that the EU makes small countries more 'viable', it is not certain that voters agree, and that might lead to a shift in political strategies in order to increase electoral support.

It is also possible that something similar is happening in Catalonia. The pro-independence parties, the ERC and PDeCAT, are traditionally pro-EU and European integration, and Catalonia is even more deeply integrated into the EU as part of both the euro and the Schengen area (Gillespie 2015a, b). It is hard to imagine that the Catalan economy, which represents about 20 per cent of Spain's gross domestic product, would thrive without access to the internal market. The Catalan business sector reacted strongly to the turmoil that struck the region after the unconstitutional referendum on independence held in October 2017, the unilateral declaration of independence by the Catalan government under Carles Puigdemont enacted a few weeks later and the Spanish government's temporary suspension of Catalan regional autonomy. Several banks and companies decided to move their headquarters out of Catalonia to other parts of Spain in order to reduce the negative consequences of the uncertainties over the region's future status.

Both Spain and Catalonia have new governments since the turmoil of the autumn of 2017 but the conflict is still unresolved and several Catalan politicians and activists are either in exile or in jail condemned for sedition against the state. For many citizens who support independence, part of the solution would be to hold a legal referendum similar to the one held in Scotland in 2014. For the Spanish government, however, that is out of the question since it is not deemed to be in line with the Spanish Constitution, which stipulates that Spain's territory is inviolable. The Spanish Socialist Party (PSOE) has been in government since June

2018 and it says that it is open to constitutional reforms, albeit not Catalan independence. For many supporters of Catalan independence, however, this is not enough. With the Catalan government still controlled by pro-independence parties and an increasingly complex political landscape in Spain, there are few signs that the conflict will be resolved any time soon.

During the unconstitutional referendum of 2017, there were dramatic scenes in Barcelona and the rest of Catalonia as Spanish police sought to prevent people from entering the polling stations set up by the Catalan government. Several Catalan politicians and civil society representatives appealed for international intervention to counter what was seen as state repression by Spain, and such appeals were directed at the EU in particular. However, EU officials said that this was an 'internal matter' for Spain and thus that there was nothing that the EU could do. The governments of other EU member states predominantly expressed concern about police brutality but voiced no support for Catalan independence. This might have come as a shock to citizens in Catalonia who had expected more support from the EU and other member states, and this may have contributed to an increase in Euroscepticism among pro-independence supporters. According to opinion data, there has been a shift in the level of trust in the EU among Catalans. The level of trust has decreased among those who support Catalan independence and increased among those who support Catalonia remaining a region of Spain (see Fig. 10.4).[10]

It does not seem unreasonable to presume that pro-independence supporters were disappointed by the, in their view, feeble response of the EU, although it is of course debatable whether it was ever realistic to expect anything else. Nonetheless, if this trend persists, it seems reasonable that we might observe a similar situation in Catalonia as in Scotland, that support for independence remains at a relatively high level but support for the EU declines. If that proves to be the case, then the Catalan pro-independence parties might be expected to tone down their pro-EU positions. For instance, Carles Puigdemont tweeted in November 2017: 'Is this the Europe you want to build? How long can Europe ignore what is happening in Catalonia?' In addition, on several occasions from his exile in

[10] Trust in the EU is measured on a scale of 0 (low) to 10 (high). 'Region' signifies that the respondent would like to reduce Catalonia's autonomy; 'autonomy' signifies a preference for the status quo; 'federation' signifies a preference for constitutional reforms in Spain in order to make it a federal state; and 'state' signifies a preference for Catalan independence.

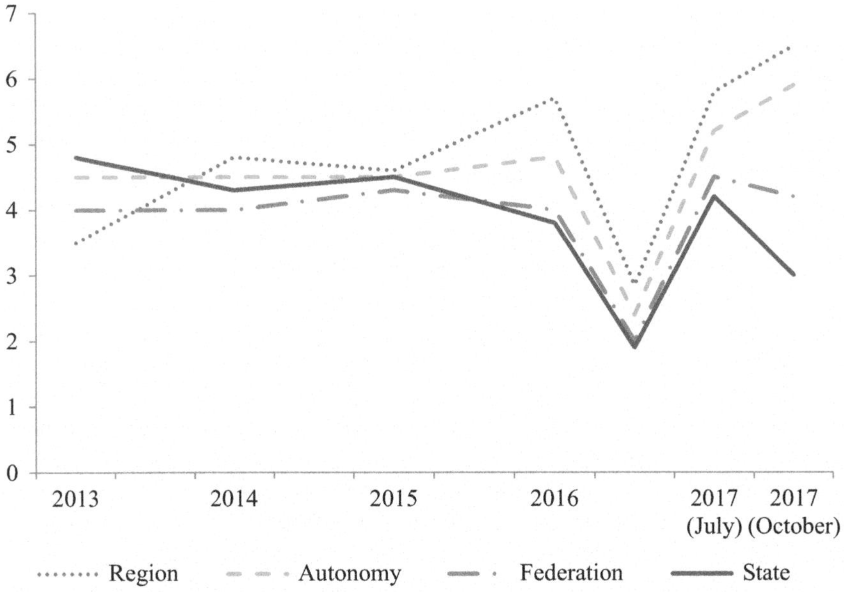

Fig. 10.4 Trust in the EU by political preference in Catalonia, 2013–2017 (Source: Aumaitre (2017))

Brussels, he has criticised the EU for not standing up for the elected Catalan politicians who are were put on trial and sentenced in Madrid in 2019.

In an interesting study based on survey data, Muro and Vlaskamp (2016) point out that the risk of losing EU membership does not seem to have much of an effect on opinion for or against independence in either Scotland or Catalonia. In both cases, they find support for the notion that it depends on how strongly individuals feel they belong to their region (or 'state-less nation' in their terminology), and how much they trust the EU to begin with. It is really only individuals who feel that they are as much Scottish as British or as much Catalan as Spanish, and also have a high level of trust in the EU who seem to reduce their support for independence if it comes at the cost of losing their EU membership. For those individuals who only feel Scottish or Catalan, and have low levels of trust in the EU, loss of EU membership does not seem to matter very much. Support for independence would actually increase if it entailed Scotland or Catalonia leaving the EU. However, according to Muro and Vlaskamp, this combination of pro-independence and Eurosceptic attitudes was more prevalent in Scotland than in Catalonia, at least prior to October 2017.

Regional Secessionism and European Integration: Democratic and Normative Challenges in a Multi-Level Setting

The EU and its member states face a host of challenges, a wide number of which are addressed in the other chapters of this book. It is therefore perhaps tempting to disregard the problem of regional secession and European integration as something that primarily affects affluent but unhappy citizens in comparatively well-functioning European states. In my opinion, this would be a mistake. There is no need to support Scottish or Catalan independence in order to understand that such claims pose a set of political and normative challenges to the EU that risk undermining the possibilities of fostering 'an ever closer union among the peoples of Europe, in which decisions are taken as closely as possible to the citizen in accordance with the principle of subsidiarity', as is stated in the preamble of the Treaty on European Union. It is probably a prudent course of action for the European Commission to maintain its position that the territorial set-up of EU member states is not something that the Commission should address, but that should not prevent it from seeking to formulate policies and suggestions, based on EU competencies and resources, that contribute political solutions to the problems that Spain and Catalonia and the UK and Scotland are currently grappling with.

From a normative perspective, this question can be said to ultimately reflect the kind of political and legal community that the EU is seeking to foster in Europe, and the ways in which the EU is seeking to address the problems that EU citizens perceive. At the time of writing, in mid-2019, it is impossible to say when or how Brexit will take place, and it is of course wise not to pre-empt the outcome by suggesting, for example, that Scotland (or Northern Ireland) should be given a special status vis-à-vis the EU and the internal market post-Brexit. Nor should the Commission offer to 'mediate' between Catalonia and Spain, since that might imply that Catalonia is considered a subject of international law on a par with the sovereign Spanish state, which it obviously is not.

Nonetheless, the question of independence for non-sovereign regions in EU member states is essentially a question about the norms and practices of contemporary democracies. In many European countries, there are many citizens who feel a sense of belonging to the nation that in many instances provides the basis for the state at the same time as they feel a sense of belonging to other nations or national identities. In Catalonia, some citizens say that they feel that they are only Catalan, whereas others feel that they are as Catalan as they are Spanish and still others feel that they are only Spanish. To allow historically contingent nationalities and state borders determine in which state a person exercises her civic and democratic rights is undoubtedly well in line with established conventions, but that does not mean that it has to be seen as natural or even desirable. That democratic states recognise that they might rest on distinct yet intertwined political communities and that it is always the people who must ultimately decide how they wish to be represented does not have to lead to a situation in which the states of Europe disintegrate or where some citizens' rights are recognised at the expense of others.

This is because the burden of proof lies with anyone who seeks to break away part of a comparatively well-functioning and democratic state to show how the new state would promote and protect the civic and democratic rights of all the citizens of that state—not only those who supported independence in the pre-secession phase. In short, any instance of regional secession in today's integrated Europe should be able to show with a reasonable degree of plausibility that the problems that the region faces could somehow be better dealt with if it became an independent state rather than remaining part of an existing EU member state. It could be argued that such reasoning has a conservative bias, and that it unduly favours the status quo. However, the argument goes both ways since anyone arguing against regional secession in the EU needs to show how the current member state can promote and protect the civic and democratic rights of the citizens who somehow do not feel a strong sense of belonging to that particular state.

Nonetheless, the role of the regions could become more pronounced in order to strengthen democratic governance in a multi-level system such as the EU. The EU's Committee of the Regions currently acts as an advisory body representing local and regional authorities. Importantly, it is not an organ in which more or less autonomous regions, such as Catalonia and Scotland, are exclusively represented in EU decision-making processes. There is thus no doubt room for further discussions regarding the question of whether regions with a comparatively high degree of political autonomy and distinct democratic institutions such as regional parliaments should be allowed greater influence over issues and policies within the EU that directly concern them, such as for instance regional funds, public investment, infrastructure and transport networks.

One proposal that might seem feasible could be to create something akin to a 'Council of the European Regions', with proper decision-making powers that would partly replace today's Committee of the Region. However, this would almost certainly require treaty changes, which are of course very difficult to achieve. Something that might seem more realistic would be for the European Commission to initiate a proposal to investigate the role of regions in the EU with the explicit purpose of studying the extent to which and how democratic governance in the EU would be enhanced if autonomous regions were given a more pronounced role in EU decision making. Such an exercise might possibly lead to a detailed debate among citizens, politicians and experts in which those who support independence for non-sovereign regions would need to explain why independence is preferable to enhanced regional autonomy in a more integrated Europe. In line with Keating's recent remarks, strengthening the role of the regions in the EU should ideally be based on the notion that 'self-determination […] is a matter of political practice and accommodation of competing claims' (Keating 2019: 7), that is, not necessarily of pursuing national independence at any cost.

Another, admittedly quite radical, proposal—which in any case reaches well beyond the EU's competencies—would be to 'constitutionalise' the right to secession in EU member states (cf. Sorens 2012). This would in principle entail that, in those cases where it is needed, EU member states would make constitutional changes to allow for the principle of territorial integrity to be circumvented if a clear majority of the citizens in a region expressed a will to secede and create a new state. What counts as a 'clear majority' can of course be debated at length, but it should at least be well above half of the citizens—and it is not certain that referendums always provide the best way to capture what people think about complex and multifaceted questions such as these. While this proposal should primarily be seen as a thought experiment, constitutionalising the right to secession might possibly reduce the attractiveness and mobilising appeal of independence claims if citizens felt that they were being granted the right to create a new state, even if the requirements for doing so would be demanding (cf. Bauböck 2019). Such an institutional reform might perhaps also increase the willingness among elites at the national and regional levels to negotiate and seek compromise on the form and content of regional autonomy, since secession would be both legal and legitimate.

Maintaining the position that secession is illegal because the constitution does not allow it might make perfect sense from a legalistic point of view but it is a circular argument in political terms that obviously cannot resolve the problem, but instead seems to exacerbate it. Instead of seeing regional secessionism only as a threat to European integration, the EU and its member states should try to see it as an opportunity to strengthen democracy in Europe and the sense of community among European nations and citizens by way of furthering the debate on what kind of political community Europe should strive for in the twenty-first century.

References

Abts, K., Heerwegh, D., & Swyngedouw, M. (2009). Sources of Euroscepticism: Utilitarian Interest, Social Distrust, National Identity and Institutional Distrust. *World Political Science Review, 5*(1), 1–26.

Adler, E., & Barnett, M. (1998). *Security Communities*. Cambridge: Cambridge University Press.

Aumaitre, A. (2017, November). Four Graphs About Catalonia and Citizens' Attitudes Towards the EU. *LSE Eurocrisis: The Politics of Public Discourse in Europe*. https://blogs.lse.ac.uk/eurocrisispress/2017/11/17/four-graphs-about-catalonia-and-citizens-attitudes-towards-the-eu/

Bartolini, S. (2005). *Restructuring Europe: Centre Formation, System Building, and Political Structuring Between the Nation State and the European Union*. Oxford: Oxford University Press.

Bauböck, R. (2019). A Multilevel Theory of Democratic Secession. *Ethnopolitics, 18*(3), 227–246.

Bellamy, R., & Castiglione, D. (2000). Reflections on the European Democratic Deficit. In E. Eriksen & J. Fossum (Eds.), *Democracy in the European Union: Integration Through Deliberation?* (pp. 65–84). London: Routledge.

Bickerton, C. (2012). *European Integration: From Nation-States to Member States*. Oxford: Oxford University Press.

Bremberg, N. (2015). The EU as Security Community-Building Institution: Venues, Networks and Cooperative Security Practices. *Journal of Common Market Studies, 53*(3), 674–694.

Bremberg, N. (2018). The European Security Community: History and Current Challenges. In A. Bakardjieva Engelbrekt, A. Michalski, N. Nilsson, & L. Oxelheim (Eds.), *Security Issues in the European Union: Threats and Opportunities* (pp. 18–41). Cheltenham: Edward Elgar Publishers.

Buchanan, A. (2007). *Justice, Legitimacy, and Self-Determination: Moral Foundations for International Law*. Oxford: Oxford University Press.

Bundesverfassungsgericht. (2016, December 16). Beschluss der 2. Kammer des Zweiten Senats – 2 BvR 349/16. https://www.bundesverfassungsgericht.de/SharedDocs/Entscheidungen/DE/2016/12/rk20161216_2bvr034916.html

Cram, L. (2009). Introduction: Banal Europeanism: European Union Identity and National Identities in Synergy. *Nations and Nationalism, 15*(1), 101–108.

Dion, S. (2012). Secession and the Virtues of Clarity. *Ottawa Law Review, 44*(2), 403–418.

Duerr, G. (2015). *Secessionism and the European Union: The Future of Flanders, Scotland, and Catalonia*. Lanham, MD: Lexington Books.

Elias, A. (2008). Whatever Happened to the Europe of the Regions? Revisiting the Regional Dimension of European Politics. *Regional & Federal Studies, 18*(5), 483–492.

Eriksen, E. O., & Fossum, J. E. (Eds.). (2000). *Democracy in the European Union: Integration Through Deliberation?* London: Routledge.

Follesdal, A., & Hix, S. (2006). Why There Is a Democratic Deficit in the EU: A Response to Majone and Moravcsik. *Journal of Common Market Studies, 44*(3), 533–562.

Genschel, P., & Jachtenfuchs, M. (2016). More Integration, Less Federation: The European Integration of Core State Powers. *Journal of European Public Policy, 23*(1), 42–59.

Gillespie, R. (2015a). Between Accommodation and Contestation: The Political Evolution of Basque and Catalan Nationalism. *Nationalism and Ethnic Politics, 21*(1), 3–23.

Gillespie, R. (2015b, June). *Pro-European Nationalist Parties and EU Negativity: The Place of Europe in Basque and Catalan Sovereignty Politics*. EvoNat Research Brief, No. 1. http://nationalismsinspain.com/researchbriefs/.

Hepburn, E. (Ed.). (2011). *New Challenges for Stateless Nationalist and Regionalist Parties*. London: Routledge.

Hobolt, S., & Tilley, J. (2016). Fleeing the Centre: The Rise of Challenger Parties in the Aftermath of the Euro Crisis. *West European Politics, 39*(5), 971–991.

Hooghe, L., Marks, G., Schakel, A. H., Osterkatz, S. C., Niedzwiecki, S., & Shair-Rosenfield, S. (2016). *Measuring Regional Authority: A Postfunctionalist Theory of Governance* (Vol. 1). Oxford: Oxford University Press.

Jolly, S. (2007). The Europhile Fringe? Regionalist Party Support for European Integration. *European Union Politics, 8*(1), 109–130.

Keating, M. (1998). *The New Regionalism in Western Europe: Territorial Restructuring and Political Change*. Cheltenham: E. Elgar.

Keating, M. (2001). *Plurinational Democracy*. Oxford: Oxford University Press.

Keating, M. (2019). Is a Theory of Self-Determination Possible? *Ethnopolitics, 18*(3), 315–323.

Kenealy, D. (2014). How Do You Solve a Problem Like Scotland? A Proposal Regarding "Internal Enlargement". *Journal of European Integration, 36*(6), 585–600.

King, C. (2012). The Scottish Play: Edinburgh's Quest for Independence and the Future of Separatism. *Foreign Affairs, 91*(5), 113–124.

Kornprobst, M. (2008). *Irredentism in European Politics: Argumentation, Compromise and Norms.* Cambridge: Cambridge University Press.

Kriesi, H. (2014). The Populist Challenge. *West European Politics, 37*(2), 361–378.

Laible, J. (2008). *Separatism and Sovereignty in the New Europe: Party Politics and the Meaning of Statehood in a Supranational Context.* Basingstoke: Palgrave Macmillan.

Linz, J., & Stephan, A. (1996). *Problems of Democratic Transition and Consolidation.* Baltimore, MA: Johns Hopkins University Press.

MacCormick, N. (1997). Democracy, Subsidiarity, and Citizenship in the "European Commonwealth". *Law and Philosophy, 16*(4), 331–356.

Mair, P. (2013). *Ruling the Void: The Hollowing of Western Democracy.* London: Verso Books.

Majone, G. (1998). Europe's "Democratic Deficit": The Question of Standards. *European Law Journal, 4*(1), 5–28.

Marks, G., Hooghe, L., & Blank, K. (1996). European Integration from the 1980s: State-Centric v. Multi-Level Governance. *Journal of Common Market Studies, 34*(3), 341–378.

Moravcsik, A. (2002). Reassessing Legitimacy in the European Union. *Journal of Common Market Studies, 40*(4), 603–624.

Moreno, M. F. (2001). *The Federalization of Spain.* London: Frank Cass.

Müller, J.-W. (2016). *What Is Populism?* Philadelphia, PA: University of Pennsylvania Press.

Muro, D., & Vlaskamp, M. (2016). How Do Prospects of EU Membership Influence Support for Secession? A Survey Experiment in Catalonia and Scotland. *West European Politics, 39*(6), 1115–1138.

Norman, L. (2017). Defending the European Political Order: Visions of Politics in Response to the Radical Right. *European Journal of Social Theory, 20*(4), 531–549.

Piris, J.-C. (2017a). Political and Legal Aspects of Recent Regional Secessionist Trends in Some EU Member States (I). In C. Closa (Ed.), *Secession from a Member State and Withdrawal from the European Union: Troubled Membership* (pp. 69–87). Cambridge: Cambridge University Press.

Piris, J.-C. (2017b). Political and Legal Aspects of Recent Regional Secessionist Trends in some EU Member States (I). In C. Closa (Ed.), *Secession from a Member State and Withdrawal from the European Union: Troubled Membership* (pp. 88–105). Cambridge: Cambridge University Press.

Reinikainen, J. (2019). What Is the Democratic Approach to Plebiscitary Secessionism? *Ethnopolitics, 18*(4), 362–378.

Roeder, P. (2007). *Where Nation-States Come From: Institutional Change in the Age of Nationalism*. Princeton, NJ: Princeton University Press.

Rokkan, S., & Urwin, D. (1983). *Economy, Territory, Identity: Politics of West European Peripheries*. London: Sage Publications.

Sorens, J. (2012). *Secessionism: Identity, Interest, and Strategy*. Montreal and Kingston: McGill-Queen's University Press.

Spence, D. (1992). The European Community and German Unification. *German Politics, 1*(3), 136–163.

Tilly, C. (1992). *Coercion, Capital, and European States, AD 990–1992*. Oxford: Blackwell.

Weiler, J. (1991). The Transformation of Europe. *Yale Law Journal, 100*(8), 2403–2483.

Weiler, J. (2017). Secessionism and Its Discontents. In C. Closa (Ed.), *Secession from a Member State and Withdrawal from the European Union: Troubled Membership* (pp. 12–31). Cambridge: Cambridge University Press.

Index[1]

[1] Note: Page numbers followed by 'n' refer to notes.

A. Bakardjieva Engelbrekt et al. (eds.), *The European Union and the Return of the Nation State*,
https://doi.org/10.1007/978-3-030-35005-5

The manufacturer's authorised representative in the EU is Springer Nature Customer Service Centre GmbH, Europaplatz 3, 69115 Heidelberg, Germany. If you have any concerns regarding our products, please contact ProductSafety@springernature.com

Printed and bound by CPI Group (UK) Ltd, Croydon, CR0 4YY
30/09/2026
02225644-0006